Politics in Pakistan

Westview Replica Editions

The concept of Westview Replica Editions is a response to the continuing crisis in academic and informational publishing. Library budgets for books have been severely curtailed. Ever larger portions of general library budgets are being diverted from the purchase of books and used for data banks, computers, micromedia, and other methods of information retrieval. Interlibrary loan structures further reduce the edition sizes required to satisfy the needs of the scholarly community. Economic pressures on the university presses and the few private scholarly publishing companies have severely limited the capacity of the industry to properly serve the academic and research communities. As a result, many manuscripts dealing with important subjects, often representing the highest level of scholarship, are no longer economically viable publishing projects--or, if accepted for publication, are typically subject to lead times ranging from one to three years.

Westview Replica Editions are our practical solution to the problem. We accept a manuscript in camera-ready form, typed according to our specifications, and move it immediately into the production process. As always, the selection criteria include the importance of the subject, the work's contribution to scholarship, and its insight, originality of thought, and excellence of exposition. The responsibility for editing and proofreading lies with the author or sponsoring institution. We prepare chapter headings and display pages, file for copyright, and obtain Library of Congress Cataloging in Publication Data. A detailed manual contains simple instructions for preparing the final typescript, and our editorial staff is always available to answer questions.

The end result is a book printed on acid-free paper and bound in sturdy library-quality soft covers. We manufacture these books ourselves using equipment that does not require a lengthy make-ready process and that allows us to publish first editions of 300 to 600 copies and to reprint even smaller quantities as needed. Thus, we can produce Replica Editions quickly and can keep even very specialized books in print as long as there is a demand for them.

About the Book and Author

Politics in Pakistan:
The Struggle for Legitimacy
Louis D. Hayes

Focusing on the problems associated with Pakistan's political development, this book identifies and evaluates the factors that have determined the effectiveness of the country's political institutions. Professor Hayes examines the relationship of Islamic values to political organization and public policy and discusses the basic features of the country's three constitutions. He also shows how effective government has been hindered by social and geographical divisions and a lack of consensus on the rules of political conduct. He concludes by discussing the ways in which international pressures and the requirements of foreign policy have shaped Pakistan's domestic politics.

Dr. Hayes is professor of political science at the University of Montana and the author of *The Impact of U.S. Policy on the Kashmir Conflict*.

Politics in Pakistan
The Struggle for Legitimacy

Louis D. Hayes

Westview Press / Boulder and London

A Westview Replica Edition

Copyright © 1984 by Westview Press, Inc.

Published in 1984 in the United States of America by
  Westview Press, Inc.
  5500 Central Avenue
  Boulder, Colorado 80301
  Frederick A. Praeger, Publisher

Library of Congress Cataloging in Publication Data
Hayes, Louis D.
  Politics in Pakistan
  (A Westview replica edition)
  1. Pakistan--Politics and government. I. Title.
DS384.H37   1984   320.9549   84-7418
ISBN 0-86531-841-7

Printed and bound in the United States of America
10 9 8 7 6 5 4 3 2 1

Contents

1
Theories and Concepts

Introduction

Pakistan has attracted more scholarly attention than have most other third world countries, many of which are also underdeveloped, Islamic, or have colonial backgrounds. The level of interest in Pakistan is due to the considerable variety of factors that have determined its destiny. Unlike most "newly emerging" countries, it did not exist prior to independence in discrete form but rather was always part of larger systems such as the Persian, Afghan, Indian, or British empires. More than 2500 years ago a great civilization grew up along the banks of the Indus River where Pakistan now stands, but since then the area and its people have been subject to the political authority of others. Religion has played an unusually important role; indeed, the country's existence is predicated upon it. At the same time there has been considerable experience with secular and modern institutions and practices. Pakistan is thus a new state built on a complicated historical legacy consisting of modern, traditional, secular and religious components.

The political experience of this unusual country affords an opportunity to observe and to assess many of the problems, opportunities, and frustrations of modernization. Unfortunately, the experience has not been altogether satisfactory. Politically, Pakistan must be considered a failure. But in that failure there are lessons which hopefully can be learned and their benefits derived. The purpose of this inquiry is to determine the reasons why the political system has not functioned properly. It is the central thesis of this study that Pakistan's political system has failed because the foundations of the state and the requirements of modernization have not yet been bridgeable by any institutional arrangement yet employed. As a result, there have been repeated political crises since the creation of the country in 1947, including several constitutional fail-

1

ures, three military coups, and the secession of the East wing. For its part, Bangladesh, as East Pakistan has been called since achieving its independence, had had little more success in developing a workable political system than did united Pakistan.

Explanations for the failure of Pakistan to develop an effective and durable political/constitutional arrangement are to be found in the following factors. First, there is incompatibility among the concepts of authority which compete for dominance within the system. Second, there is incongruity between the more traditional of these concepts and the demands of the modern state. Third, the political process has been more accessible and responsive to certain political interests, especially regional and economic, than it has to others, resulting in frustration and hostility. Fourth, there has been a failure to evolve a political culture defining the limits of political behavior and prescribing ways in which political institutions are supposed to work. "Rules of the game" have been absent or ill-defined. Finally, international events have conspired to frustrate developmental efforts.

Several terms require definition at the outset. The 'political system' consists of the totality of the political universe, i.e., everything pertinent to the political life of the country. This includes formal and informal relationships, procedural aspects (how these relationships work), and philosophical or ideological aspects (rules of the game). 'Regime' refers to the particular configuration of institutions that exist at a given time. The focus here is upon political institutions, but economic, social, and cultural institutions are also pertinent and, of course, interrelated. In Pakistan the regime has at various times been parliamentary, "basic democracy," military dictatorship, and presidential. 'Government' refers to the specific individuals who occupy positions in the regime. Thus the government of a certain political party might be replaced by another while the regime remains the same. It is important to note that in Pakistan regimes tend not to survive longer than governments. The reasons for this are a central issue of this study. The 'political process' includes both the regime and its operation, that is, actual events and the context in which they occur.

While this is not intended to be an historical survey, it will be necessary to consider various issues from the origins of Pakistan to the present. This will mean reaching far back into the past, since the genesis of Pakistan includes both the history of Islam and of British India. Although some reference will be made to the later period, the inquiry essentially ends with Bhutto. There are several reasons for this. Political developments, especially in Pakistan, have a frustrat-

ing tendency to change dramatically, making descriptions
and discussions of contemporary events instantly obsolete. Moreover, developments since Bhutto are not
essential to the analysis, although the conclusions
continue to be pertinent. In a sense, the fall of
Bhutto marks the culmination of an historical period.
There was a continuity that was broken with the advent
of General Zia ul-Haq. Bhutto was both an important
figure during the Ayub period and a product of its
frustrations. Under Bhutto, Pakistan did not include
East Pakistan and can, as a result, be considered a
more "realistic" polity, one with a greater chance of
political success. With the fall of Bhutto, just about
everything had been tried and had failed. Under Zia,
Pakistan is in many respects starting at the beginning.
Moreover, developments since 1977 have been transitional; even Zia portrays himself as an interlude preparing the country for a return to civilian rule.

The departure of the British, the rise of communal
identities and antagonisms, nationalism and self-determination, and world opinion converged in 1947 to produce
a political redefinition of the Indian subcontinent.
Part of this redefinition was the creation of the state
of Pakistan, a curious entity composed of two wings
with 1,000 miles of Indian territory in between. In
general, political systems are synthesized out of
smaller units either from the push of outside threats
or from the pull of shared interests.[1] These unifying
tendencies must exceed the pressures which tend to drive
the units apart. In Pakistan's case there were some
pressures for unity, such as Islam expressing a common
interest and India expressing a common threat. But in
the long run Islam was not a sufficiently durable common
interest to hold the two wings together in the face of
physical, economic, social, and political differences.
The threat of India was an insufficient force promoting
common anxiety, given the diverging interpretations of
the nature of that threat. This meant that the East
and the West wings lacked the necessary ingredients for
a successful political synthesis. The divergence of
interest between the two was at once a cause and a consequence of the country's failure to evolve a political
system that "worked." Indeed, the problems of constitutional development involve questions concerning the
nature of the polity itself.

For Pakistan, the idea of an Islamic community is
the essence of its being. But Islam has not been able
to narrow parochial interests nor serve as an effective
vehicle for building a sense of political community.
"The trappings of modern statehood have been a sort of
borrowed finery, fitting awkwardly upon the remains of
the Islamic body politic."[2] The emphasis upon Islam in
the partition recognized a basic cultural division of
the subcontinent. But Islam did not provide durable

linkage among the component parts of the country and especially between East and West Pakistan.
Thus, Pakistan set itself a very difficult task. The definition of the political system is somehow to be derived from Islam, and this in turn must be synthesized with the requirements of a modern state. This is a demanding task, but in addition Pakistan has been plagued with more than its share of misfortunes. Assassinations destroyed leadership and created problems of continuity. Disorder undermined the integrity of the political process. Economic disparities created discontent, while military adventures brought on unbearable financial burdens. In addition, Pakistan's history has been littered with the wreckage of unsuccessful attempts at institution-building, including three constitutions.

Authority and Legitimacy

Two concepts that are essential in the consideration of any political system are authority and legitimacy. While the two are closely related, they deal with different issues. Authority is a philosophical matter, a value consideration regarding the nature of rule and claims to exercise it.[3] Legitimacy involves acts of governance and is determined by the response to such acts by the governed.
In all political systems there exist authoritative relationships. The capacity to make rules and issue instructions must exist somewhere. Such action works because it is based on something other than force, although force may be involved. The act of governance occurs because of an implicit or explicit acceptance of an argument justifying its existence.[4] Rule does not just happen; it occurs as a result of conscious acts. Such arguments may be simple or complex, and several competing ones may exist at the same time. If authority is to be effective, however, it must be accepted by most members of the community.[5] Authority exists in practice when in the minds of the governed it is justified or appropriate. It is not possible to rule, at least not for long or very effectively, relying solely on force. Populations can be cowed by violence or the threat of it, but they are not really being governed. If people have to be coerced at the point of a bayonet to do what they should do as good citizens, then authority does not exist. Authority can be enhanced by punishment for disobedience, but this is not without limit. The use of force may be necessary where there is a significant absence of voluntary consent or where a society is so large and diverse that some subgroups seek to opt out of it.[6]
It is not appropriate here to attempt a detailed exegesis of the various sources and methods of deriva-

tion of political authority. Two essential questions in considering any political system are: Where is authority located and what is its justification; or in even simpler terms, who governs and why? If governance is to work, authority must be located somewhere - in a king, in a council, in a certain group, or even in the entire population. It does not really matter, as long as the assignation is accepted by the governed. The king is sovereign only so long as the people accept his sovereignty. Once they deny it, his authority ceases to exist.

The essence of any political system is the rationalization of authority. Where is it located and why? While opinion is never unanimous, to the extent that there is a consensus, the political system will have at least the potential of being orderly and effective. But strong differences over the nature of authority and its location will mean that the political process, which is based necessarily on some kind of authority consensus, will be unable to function or will have difficulty doing so.

Upon the rationalization of authority must be built a political regime. That this configuration of institutions must be compatible with the structure of authority should be obvious. When rationalization of authority and political institutions are fused, the regime will perform much more effectively than if they are not. The capacity to govern will be restricted if institutions do not fit into the scheme of authority. For example, if the accepted rationalization of authority is, say, the doctrine of the divine right of kings, then those who seize the instruments of power by force have no legitimate claim to rule. When such events have occurred historically, the usurpers have immediately declared themselves king to legitimize their rule. In modern times with fewer opportunities to be king, they have made themselves president.[7]

Traditional authority refers to concepts of authority that are of long-standing duration and are part of the social value system. In contrast, "innovative" authority involves concepts that are new and are not part of or derived from one value system, although they may be compatible with it.

Another useful approach to traditional authority refers to leader-follower relationships. A sense of moral obligation to do the leader's bidding induces obedience.[8] This obligation is perceived as long-standing and mutually binding.[9] While this authority is not articulated in detail, it is rationalized in that, if asked, leaders and followers would have no problem explaining their actions. However, political and ideological issues outside this personal context would have little significance for the individual. Political mobilization entails the diffuse involvement of leaders, and thereby their followers, with no direct connection to larger institutional authority questions.[10] Thus it is difficult to develop a broad base of popular support for regime legitimacy. Traditional authority, which encompasses a much smaller constituency, does not need a broad base of support and in fact may be threatened by greater involvement.

A second important concept is legitimacy, which is the acceptance of the operation of the political process and a willingness to live with and abide by the decisions made within it.[11] This does not mean that all government decisions are necessarily liked by everyone, but it does mean that there is an inclination to abide by the commands of the government because they are considered rightful, and obedience is regarded as morally and legally obligatory.[12] It also means there is a correspondence between the political ideals and expectations of the rulers.[13] When a significant number of citizens reject government decisions and refuse to obey on the grounds that the government has failed to meet their valid expectations, then the legitimacy of the political process is undermined.[14] Legitimacy crises occur frequently and at all levels of political development. These crises are not absolutes or discreet states of affairs but must be regarded in all instances as matters of degree.[15] The critical consideration is whether or not the political process is able to reestablish its claim to obedience by adapting to or removing the threat to its integrity. A political process can be based on accepted rationalization of authority and still encounter challenges to its legitimacy as a result of inept governance. On the other hand, legitimacy can be enhanced by effective governance.[16]

In the course of Pakistan's history, there have been several competing arguments on the issue of authority. Unfortunately, no consensus has emerged on its nature, location, or limits. The political process has not been predicated on a broadly accepted rationalization of authority, resulting in no institutionalized mechanisms for determining and promoting legitimacy. Controversies over authority, particularly in the constitutional experience, have precluded the emergence of a workable and effective political process. The chronic legitimacy crises that have plagued the country are due in large measure to the existence of a perpetual authority crisis.

Political Values and Political Behavior

An ingredient of political consensus is a sharing of values and beliefs among members of the community. In fact, it is this sharing that defines the community. No political community in the world has an absolute uniformity of values and beliefs. But the extent to

which values and beliefs are harmonious or compatible
is an important factor in determining political via-
bility. In an expanded sense, this idea encompasses
the concept "political culture."[17] Pakistan, like all
societies, has a political culture, but it is charac-
terized by deep divisions and a poorly defined sense of
self. Above all, it has lacked a body of propositions,
a philosophy, an ideology that would serve its citizens
as a point of reference and a guide for action. As
Wheeler notes: "the basic weakness of Pakistan has
been a lack of a firm set of shared values in the
society."[18]

It has already been noted that authority and legitimacy are essential elements of any political system.
These, in whatever configuration they might exist, are
dimensions of the political culture. But beyond that,
political culture determines the nature of institutions,
delimits behavior, and defines the rules of the game;
in short, it sets the parameters and provides the
methodologies for social and political intercourse.
Political systems are not born with fully developed
political cultures; they evolve over time and are
synthesized out of experience. Moreover, the conflicts
and inconsistencies, which are present in varying com-
binations and intensities in all societies, determine
the character of political life.

Political values can be changed in specific ways,
especially in modern times, given communication tech-
niques and understanding of opinion and attitude formation. The Chinese Communists have gone to great
lengths to develop a particular kind of value system.
Such an approach requires a strong commitment to the
use of communications and social controls. In Pakistan,
consideration of the ends of social and political life,
except in the context of Islam, has been truncated.
Unfortunately, the political dialogue has not provided
guidelines around which social, economic, and political
attitudes, values, and structures can grow and mature.

A political culture equal to the task of sustaining
the political process has not been nurtured by a rich
and vigorous discussion of the essence of the political
community. A sense of identity with one's fellow
countrymen through the sharing of culture, language,
symbols, and historical heroes, real or mythical, has
been limited. This sharing, which is a conventional
definition of nationalism, has very shallow historical
roots. There has been for a long time a strong sense
of Muslim identity, but this is not a sufficient condition for nationalism.[19] Rather, it is a common ingredient among competing nationalisms which are defined on
the basis of other criteria. Alternatively, one might
regard nationalism in Pakistan as a "heterogeneous"
variety, that is, composed of several "small" nationalisms.[20] Instead of a Pakistani nationalism, there de-

veloped, especially in the late 1960's, a vigorous
Bengali nationalism which was an identity that owed
little to Islam.[21] Upon achieving independence,
Bangladesh declared itself a secular state. Bengali
nationalism did not become a dominating and integrating
force in united Pakistan because of the East wing's
political weakness, but instead became a force for
separation.

Pakistan's political culture has not provided
accepted standards for appraising and evaluating political conduct.[22] For those who exercise political
power, there has been little security in the thought
that conformity with the written and unwritten rules of
society will enhance the probability of political
effectiveness or survival. The result has been a tendency to dissipate time and energy, preserving and expanding political power rather than using it to achieve
substantive ends. For the citizenry, there has been
little against which to measure the performance of
political leaders except personal satisfaction.

Pakistan's political culture, composed of diverse
elements such as provincial or group loyalties, has
lacked a unifying cement apart from Islam. Islam is an
important political factor as far as it goes, but it
has not proved sufficient to sustain the institutions
of the state. To say Pakistan is Pakistan because it
is Muslim is like saying Ireland is Ireland because it
is Catholic. There is more to it than that. As a
system of moral principles, Islam provides a basis for
social intercourse among the citizenry. It has not,
however, proved sufficient to chart the country's political course.

Political Recruitment and Political Participation

In all political systems it is necessary that individuals be recruited into political roles and that
these roles be acted out in the political process.
Such political recruitment can follow one of two very
general patterns. Political roles can be distributed
among those who, according to some ascriptive criteria,[23] are entitled to them. Family or caste are
such criteria. Alternatively, political roles can be
filled by persons with achievable qualifications, such
as talent or the ability to win an election. The
recruitment pattern used in any given society will be a
function of its value system. Actual participation can
occur in any number of ways, but the critical determination is the extent to which such participation
includes those who feel they are entitled to participate. Failure to include politically significant elements of society in the process of social decision-
making is likely to result in antagonism and opposition.
Even when opposition exists, its effects can be dimin-

ished by drawing it into the political process. "Where potentially subversive groups are under identifiable leadership, co-option of these leaders is most likely to increase support and compliance for the regime."[24]

Not only must the political process be accessible to the political elites, but they in turn must accept its existence and not devote themselves to altering or destroying it. In Pakistan there has been little inclination to accept the legitimacy of political institutions. Governments have been more inclined to restrict access to the political process by placing limitations on public meetings, party activities, and communication. They have been preoccupied with their own survival and in doing so have contributed to the decay of political institutions.[25] Nor have competing groups been willing to support the political process. An important reason for the failure to develop a workable political process has been the tendency to reject regimes rather than to reform governments, as in the case of Ayub and Bhutto. This has meant that the processes for satisfying demands and resolving conflicts have periodically ceased to exist. Political recruitment and political participation have been episodic and erratic, and as a result the political process has worked at a very low level of effectiveness.

Effective political recruitment results from the active participation of significant groups in decision-making and the development of ways to include newly emergent groups. Groups are significant to the extent that their exclusion from the political process weakens its operation and long-term integrity. The exclusion of such groups is likely to lead to frustration, which in turn can lead to rebellion. Satisfaction may be obtained by simply removing individuals from power and replacing them with others. This presumably is the virtue of elections. But if the removal of these persons does not have the desired salutary effect, then antagonisms may shift toward institutions themselves. As support for institutions weakens, their effectiveness deteriorates in proportion. If opposition to political institutions, such as the opposition to Basic Democracies under Ayub, fails to produce changes or responses which satisfy demands, then legitimacy of the regime is compromised. The use of violence as the only recourse to bring about change becomes more attractive when working within the system is perceived as unrewarding. It is not necessary that these developments occur in sequence. Especially where institutions possess little support, telescoping of the process is virtually assured. Nor for that matter is it necessary that such conditions exist in fact as long as enough people think they do.[26]

The problems of recruitment and the workings of a viable political process are exacerbated by the gulf between the modern and the traditional elements of society. In Pakistan this gulf has widened over time as the two have had less and less in common. Pakistan's political leaders have tried to build a political process based on or at least to include traditional values. However, these leaders have come mainly from the more modern sector of society and have sought to shape political and constitutional practice according to their own preferences. The direction of politics and public policy has been away from the traditional view. Hence, the political process has not served the long term interests of either modern or traditional interests but has consistently fallen ineffectively between the two.

Modernization

Modernization is a ·very frustrating business. Social, economic and political changes frequently result in disequilibrium. Improving economic conditions stimulate expectations which rise at an accelerating rate, sometimes resulting in more demands than the system can deliver. Social and economic changes create new conditions and groups which conflict with vested interests, biases, and traditional beliefs. As the modern sector (industrial workers, college students, and the intelligentsia) grows in size and importance, it becomes an increasingly powerful engine accelerating the pace of change. The traditional sector--peasants, religious groups, and village political leaders, for example-- faces growing insecurity. Peasants find the value of their labor diminished by the modernization of agriculture. Secularization erodes the importance of religion. The power of village leaders declines in the face of centralization of governance. In general, the traditional sector is in various ways inclined to resist change. Thus, the political system is faced with a dilemma. It needs to modernize in order to accommodate social and economic change while at the same time observing those traditional values which it needs to retain broad social support.[27] This involves the delicate balancing of accommodation and repression, a burden of statesmanship of the highest order. Those forces and conditions leading to growth and stability need to be nurtured, while those contributing to decay and conflict must be controlled. This is not an easy task.

Tension between the old and the new is present in all countries, but especially in less developed ones. It can be and often is a creative tension where the excesses of the new and different are moderated by the old and familiar. The appropriateness of established ideas and practices are continually tested in the context of innovation and change. But where 14th century habits of mind exist side by side with 20th century requirements, the tension can be perilous. This is especially true in the political arena, where the need to create more effective institutions and practices is often at odds with the interests of established elites and traditional authority. Nevertheless, the growing complexity of contemporary life places great burdens on social and political institutions. New problems, new conditions, and new forces which subject institutions to considerable stress are continually emerging. Significant developments are occurring in communications, in economics and technology, in information and knowledge, and in social consciousness. The adjustments that are required by the changing social environment brought on by these revolutions require institutional development.

While change is universal, it does not occur everywhere in the same way or at the same rate. Some countries are economically and technologically advanced, while others are primitive. Even in the same society, nuclear technology may exist side by side with a primitive agricultural system. A country may be technologically sophisticated and politically backward. Conflicts exist to the extent of variance in the development of different social sectors. Internally this might take the form of conflict between rural agricultural interests and urban industrial interests. Externally, there is the conflict between rich and poor nations.

In the West during the 17th century, tightly structured political arrangements based upon the territorial state became the norm. Fundamentally the nation-state is predicated upon the idea of a population living within precise geographical boundaries who possess the right to control their own affairs. The means whereby this right of self-determination was translated into actual practice is not as important as acceptance of the concept. Over the ensuing centuries, Western countries have grown materially and sometimes expanded physically, all the while exporting their philosophies and practices to other parts of the world.

For many countries, however, the nation-state experience has been retarded. Some did not even exist until recently but instead were parts of larger empires, governed mostly by Europeans. The processes of institution-building, industrialization, urbanization, and the other dimensions of modernization have only recently begun. In most emerging countries the state is in its infancy. Experience with national loyalties and the forms of modern government is limited. Identities and loyalties tend to be parochial: family, tribe, or region. In Europe, China, and Japan, for the most part, the state grew up from the bottom, while in many emerging countries there is an effort to impose it from the top.

While modernization brings about changes in the composition of societies, traditionalizing forces resist what are considered "excesses" of new developments. People are generally reluctant to abandon ingrained habits and may look upon change and innovation as a threat to their existence or way of life. In countries like Pakistan where most members of society have a traditional outlook, the conflict between the new and the old is particularly acute. Landed elites resist the demands of urban industrial groups for a larger share of political power. Groups which control wealth are unwilling to share their riches with industrial workers and professional people. Modernity produces growth, expansion, interaction, and interdependence. Tradition tends to be introspective and parochial with limited and restricted social processes. Modernization expands the social, political and economic context and heightens self-awareness. Tradition is conservative and favors the status quo. Very few societies have been able to chart a middle course between these two extremes without serious conflict and upheaval.[28]

Problems of Democracy

One way of measuring the development of a political system is the extent to which the political process works in managing, adjusting, and accommodating the various demands made of it. Another way of assessing political performance is the degree of popular control over the instruments of political power. To be both effective and democratic is a goal which seems to be generally accepted, although there is considerable disagreement over exactly what "democracy" means. While Pakistan, particularly after 1969, expanded popular participation, as measured by free elections, the result was not more effective government. This might suggest that conditions at that time made democracy an impractical alternative. Similar conditions in many countries today make the appropriateness of democracy for them a hotly debated issue.

Before proceeding further, a working definition of democracy is in order. Unfortunately, democracy is not something that can be "set up" by the introduction of institutions and procedure. Democracy is not an absolute but a variable. It is a relative condition of more or less popular control over policies and decision-makers rather than a state described by the existence of certain institutions or procedures. In these terms, a system is democratic to the extent there is meaningful participation in decision-making. That such participation must be meaningful excludes such symbolic exercises as voting when there is only one candidate or ratifying an already-agreed-upon policy.

The degree of democracy that exists at a given

time in a given place is defined by two fundamental
variables. First, there is the extent to which control over political office and public officials is
shared throughout the community.[29] The greater the
actual potential involvement in decision-making the
greater the degree of democracy. This does not mean
that democracy is incomplete unless 100% of the eli-
gible voters actually cast ballots. Participation may
not be necessary if there is satisfaction with the
workings of the political process. In this situation,
political institutions function in a "representative"
manner, fulfilling expectations without direct public
involvement. The key factors are the opportunity to
participate and satisfaction with the operation of the
political process.

The other measure of democracy is the extent of
social control, or the degree to which the government
uses its monopoly of force to regulate behavior.[30] A
system in which behavior is restricted is that much
less democratic. Democracy means behavior is guided by
individual and collective self-interest and conscience
and not by those who exercise political power. But the
full realization of this idea is limited by the constraints of the political universe. Conflicts inevi-
tably exist, depending on the degree of social dishar-
mony. It is the primary task of the political process
to manage and regulate conflict so that the maximum
degree of order and tranquility may be achieved. Since
there are always a few people willing to take unfair
advantage, some measure of coercion is always necessary.
Unfortunately, this is often used as an excuse for
oppression.

Pakistan's experience is a clear illustration of
the dilemmas of developing and maintaining a democratic
political process. Repeated efforts to introduce
institutions that possessed the potential for meeting
both the tests of effectiveness and democracy were unsuccessful. Governments increasingly used their power
to protect their own existence. Ultimately the country
could not remain intact even with extensive controls
and coercion. Democratization furthered the process of
disintegration because it allowed the release of pent-
up frustrations produced by the tremendous divisions
within the country. The proposition that Pakistan was
not ready for democracy begs the question of the via-
bility of the system in any form.

Problems of International Relations

An especially important source of change is transnational interests and relationships. No society can
protect itself from outside influences. The existence
of Pakistan is the result of such influence when Islam
expanded into the Indian subcontinent from Arabia. The

legacy of the British Raj is another example of external
penetration. Today modern communications and travel
allow all nations to encroach on one another. In a
larger sense, transnational activities necessitate
agreements, processes and agencies for their control
and effective operation, all of which are beyond individual states. There is increased economic interdependence among nations as shown by the international
monetary system, trade relations and transportation
systems. Economic growth and the uneven distribution
of resources and industrial capacity put the nations of
the world increasingly at the mercy of one another.

As new states, India and Pakistan had little
experience in the conduct of foreign relations. Until
they became independent in 1947, foreign relations were
in the hands of the British. As a result of expanding
communications, education, and participation in the two
world wars, a growing number of Indians developed awareness and understanding of the larger international context. The abilities of this first generation of leadership would be sorely tested in the years after 1947.
Neither India nor Pakistan fully appreciated the impact
foreign relations would have on their own development.
Under Nehru's guidance, India became one of the leading
advocates of non-alignment. India sought to avoid the
machinations of power politics. By using this strategy
it was thought the non-aligned and mainly underdeveloped
nations could play an important role in international
relations. The significance of non-alignment was diminished when Western nations began to take it less
seriously and when conflicts developed within the movement which weakened its unity. Pakistan, less certain
of itself and much weaker than India, sought friends
and benefactors and found a most willing one in the
United States.

American policy toward South Asia has been consistent in goal and erratic in execution. The goal has
been to contain communism, deter Soviet involvement and
promote the stability and development of all the countries of the area. While these would seem to be
compatible, in practice they are frustratingly inconsistent. Many Americans, especially some in Congress,
have a genuine fondness for India, while official
relations have often been abrasive. There is less
warmth for Pakistan, although there would appear to be
more agreement on strategic issues. This agreement is
more apparent than real, however. While the conflict
with India is central to Pakistan's existence, it is no
more than an inconvenience to the United States. In
fact, the United States has shown little sympathy and
less understanding for Indo-Pakistan relations.

Pakistan has been unfortunate in its foreign
relations. Kashmir has not been acquired. India played
a key role in the secession of East Pakistan, which

would become the independent state of Bangladesh. There is now a threat posed by the Soviet presence in Afghanistan. It remains to be seen if the shift to stronger ties with the Islamic world initiated by Bhutto will produce significant dividends in the long run. But most important, foreign relations have added to and worsened internal problems. The main issue is the continuing quarrel with India, mainly over Kashmir. The United States has been a powerful but unreliable supporter; China has been a reliable but essentially powerless friend; the Soviet Union, which has played a lesser role in the subcontinent, may now be in a position to influence the course of events.

The chapters that follow deal in various ways with the four issues discussed above. Chapter two considers the historical background of Pakistan and particularly the flow of events that led up to partition in 1947. The controversies over authority and legitimacy are discussed here. Islam as the basis of the state and the definition of authority is considered in the next chapter. The fourth chapter details the similarities and differences of the three constitutions. Chapter five is concerned with the operation of the political process and focuses upon the difficulties encountered in making the constitutional apparatus function. This theme is continued in the next chapter, which explores the ill-fated efforts to establish democracy after the end of the Ayub regime. The secession of East Pakistan and international reactions to it are detailed in the next chapter. The contribution of foreign relations to Pakistan's political experiences are considered in chapter eight. In chapter nine the significant innovations of the Bhutto period are considered as well as the consequences of Bhutto's preoccupation with protecting and extending his power. In the final chapter an attempt is made to draw lessons from Pakistan's experience, not only for that country but for political development in general.

NOTES

1. On this subject see, for example: Philip E. Jacob and James V. Toscano, (eds.), The Integration of Political Communities, Philadelphia: J. B. Lippincott, Co., 1964; Amitai Etzioni, Political Integration: A Comparative Study of Leaders and Forces, New York: Holt, Rinehart, and Winston, Inc., 1965; and Claude Ake, A Theory of Political Integration, Homewood: Dorsey Press, 1967.

2. Abdul A. Said and Daniel M. Collier, Revolutionism, Boston: Allyn and Bacon, 1971, p. 38.

3. "It is suggested here that the right or capacity to command is a dimension conceptually distinct from the dimension of acceptance." Young C. Kim, "Authority: Some Conceptual and Empirical Notes," The Western Political Quarterly, XIX (June, 1966) p. 228. I use authority in the sense of the right of command and legitimacy as acceptance.

4. According to Friedrich, the communications of persons who have authority "possess the potentiality of reasoned elaboration--they are 'worthy of acceptance.'" Carl Friedrich, "Authority, Reason, and Discretion," in Carl Friedrich (ed.), Authority, Cambridge: Harvard University Press, 1958, p. 35. De Jouvenel defines authority to "mean the faculty of gaining another man's assent. Or again it may be called, though it comes to the same thing, the efficient cause of voluntary associations." Bertrand de Jouvenel, Sovereignty: An Inquiry Into the Public Good, Cambridge: Cambridge University Press, 1957, p. 29.

5. John Day, "Authority," Political Studies, XI (October, 1963) p. 270; Peter M. Blau, "Critical Remarks on Weber's Theory of Authority," The American Political Science Review, LVII (June, 1963) p. 307.

6. Ronald Glassman, "Legitimacy and Manufactured Charisma," Social Research, (Winter, 1975) p. 623.

7. Richard Lowenthal, "Political Legitimacy and Cultural Change in West and East," Social Research, (Autumn, 1979) p. 403.

8. Karl D. Jackson, Traditional Authority, Islam, and Rebellion: A Study of Indonesian Political Behavior, Berkeley: University of California Press, 1980, p. xix.

9. Ibid., p. 186.

10. Ibid., p. 185.

11. Legitimacy means the acceptance of and obedience to the orders and rules issued by authority. "Effective authority thus depends upon cumulative, individual acts of compliance or confidence. Those in authority proceed on the assumption that the requisite compliance or confidence will be forthcoming; it is only on this basis that the policeman can hope to order a crowd or the bank can invest its funds for long periods of time. Public good will in these cases consists in the willingness to let the policeman or the bank proceed; and these authorities do so on the assumption that they possess an implicit mandate (or credit) which will become manifest through the public's willingness to let them proceed." Reinhard Bendix, Nation-Building and Citizenship: Studies of Our Changing Social Order, Garden City: Doubleday and Co., 1969, p. 24. Also see, Seymour Martin Lipset, Political Man: The Social Bases of Politics, Garden City: Doubleday and Company, Inc., 1963, p. 64

12. Herman Melville's Billy Budd is an example of such an acceptance of authority. The Captain sentences

Billy to death for committing murder. Billy accepts
this sentence although his crime resulted from serious
provocations. A modern court would probably reduce the
sentence. But the severity of the punishment and the
circumstances of the crime are not at issue; Billy
accepts the authority of the Captain to impose the
penalty.

13. "We may therefore say that the legitimacy of a
political order requires, in addition to the clarity,
consistency, and effective functioning of the legally
established procedures, two things: a value consensus
between the governing (meaning the kind of persons who
become charged with decisions under the given procedure)
and the governed, and a confidence of the governed,
rooted in their experience, that this procedure will
normally promote successful action in the direction of
those common values." Lowenthal, "Political Legitimacy
and Cultural Change in West and East," p. 406.

14. David O. Friedrichs, "The Legitimacy Crisis in
the United States: A Conceptual Analysis," Social Problems, 27 (January, 1980) p. 541.

15. Ibid., p. 546.

16. Lipset, Political Man: The Social Bases of
Politics, p. 70.

17. Political culture means "that the traditions of
a society, the spirit of its public institutions, the
passions and the collective reasoning of its citizenry,
and the style and operating codes of its leaders are
not just random products of historical experience but
fit together as a part of a meaningful whole and constitute an intelligible web of relations. For the
individual the political culture provides controlling
guidelines for effective political behavior, and for
the collectivity it gives a systematic structure of
values and rational considerations which ensures co-
herence in the performance of institutions and organizations." Lucien W. Pye and Sidney Verba, eds.,
Political Development, Princeton: Princeton University
Press, 1965, p. 7.

18. Richard S. Wheeler, The Politics of Pakistan: A
Constitutional Quest, Ithaca: Cornell University Press,
1970, p. 310.

19. A detailed case for Pakistan nationalism is
Hafeez Malik, Moslem Nationalism in India and Pakistan,
Lahore: People's Publishing House, 1980. See also
Anthony D. Smith, Theories of Nationalism, New York:
Harper and Row, Publishers, 1971, p. 221, for a con-
sideration of the relationship between nationalism and
colonialism.

20. Edward Mortimer, Faith and Power; The Politics
of Islam, New York: Vintage Books, 1982, pp. 186-229.

21. This development was lamented by many Islamic
theoreticians such as Maulana Maududi as a corruption
of the Islamic basis of Pakistan. Interestingly,

Maududi had opposed the creation of Pakistan in the first place, worrying that it would prove to be a conventional secular creation rather than truly Islamic.

22. On this aspect of political culture, see Lucian Pye, Politics, Personality, and Nation-Building: Burma's Search for Identity, New Haven: Yale University Press, 1962, p. 123-4.

23. Talcott Parsons and Edward A. Shils, eds., Toward a General Theory of Action, New York: Harper and Row, Publishers, 1951, pp. 82-3.

24. Richard Rose, "Dynamic Tendencies in the Authority of Regimes," World Politics, XXI (July, 1969) p. 618.

25. Samuel P. Huntington, Political Order in Changing Societies, New Haven: Yale University Press, 1968, pp. 192ff.

26. For a summary of the "frustration-aggression syndrome" see Mark N. Hagopian, The Phenomenon of Revolution, New York: Dodd, Mead & Co., 1974, pp. 168-77.

27. Huntington, Political Order in Changing Societies, p. 140-3.

28. I do not mean to suggest that there is a clear and precise dichotomy between modernity and tradition, but rather to focus attention upon its existence and importance. The relationship can be viewed from several different perspectives. For example, see Lloyd I. and Susanne Hoeber Rudolph, The Modernity of Tradition: Political Development in India, Chicago: University of Chicago Press, 1967.

29. Robert A. Dahl, A Preface to Democratic Theory, Chicago: University of Chicago Press, 1956, p. 3.

30. David E. Apter, The Politics of Modernization, Chicago: University of Chicago Press, 1965, pp. 453-58.

2
The Creation of Pakistan: Background

Origins

The creation of the independent state of Bangladesh
ended a political marriage that was destined to fail in
large measure because the two partners were so far from
each other in both physical and cultural terms. Only
one other country has existed in recent times composed
of two parts separated by an intervening land mass:
the United States with Alaska separated from the conti-
nental states by a portion of Canada. While more than
1,000 miles separated East from West Pakistan, the
physical distance was not the only thing dividing them,
since the two wings had little more than religion in
common.

Religion accounts for the existence of Pakistan,
and it was the main reason the two wings stayed together
as one nation for 24 years. Events leading up to the
political union of the two areas are complex. To dis-
cover the origins, one must look back at least as far as
the Muslim conquest of the Indian subcontinent. Muslim
penetration of the subcontinent began as early as the
8th century when Arab traders reached the northwest
coast of India. Moving outward from Arabia, Islam over-
whelmed almost everything in its path. Syria, Iraq, and
Egypt were conquered within a century of Mohammed's
death. The center of power of the Islamic world shifted
to Persia by 750. The Seljuk Turks dominated Islam
politically but accepted it as a religion. The Turks
spread Islam into Central Asia and Afghanistan. A
series of raids by Afghan rulers beginning in the late
10th century carried the banner of Islam to the northwest corner of the subcontinent.

Except for Punjab and Sind, the Muslim conquest of
India did not begin until the end of the 12th century.
The depradations of the Mongols, from which many civi-
lizations in Central Asia and elsewhere never fully
recovered, put an end to the "classical" phase of
Islamic history.[1] The center of Muslim power shifted

19

eastward marked especially by the growth of Moghul power in India. By the end of the 16th century, the authority of Islam extended to almost all of the subcontinent. Muslim political power was finally contained and gradually overcome by the British, although the religion continued to thrive.

Like Christianity and Judaism, Islam is a religion revealed by God directly to man. The receiver of this divine message was Mohammed ibn Abd-allah born in Arabia sometime around 570 A.D. The Judeo-Christian prophets are accepted as genuine by Muslims, but they consider Mohammed's prophecy to be the last and most complete. Religion for Muslims is not strictly a spiritual matter. Belief in the message of Allah does not mean life is dominated by it. Indeed, it is life.

Five duties are required of all Muslims--the five pillars of Islam. First is a strict monotheism called the creed: "There is no God but Allah, and Mohammed is his prophet." The second pillar is the requirement of prayer five times a day. The third is alms or the payment of a tax for the needy. Fourth, all Muslims are expected to fast during the month of Ramadan from dawn to dusk. Only travelers and the ill are allowed exception. Fifth, all able-bodied Muslims are expected to take a devotional pilgrimage to the holy shrine in Mecca.

Over the centuries Islam came to be the dominant cultural force in many areas and a significant factor in others. Ultimately, the banner of Islam would be found from Spain to Indonesia. In South Asia, Muslim political influence expanded until it reached its zenith with the establishment of the Moghul dynasty that held sway over an area encompassing Afghanistan, Pakistan and most of India by the 16th century. The Moghuls brought not only political unification but introduced a considerable measure of administrative and financial sophistication. The Muslims also had a tremendous cultural and social impact. Hinduism and Buddhism, the religions of South and Central Asia, were completely different from Islam. Since Islam is considered by Muslims as the only true faith, accommodation with Hinduism and Buddhism was difficult and, at times, impossible. As a result, these indigenous religions were reduced or eliminated from Muslim-dominated areas. For example, a Buddhist culture flourished in the region of Afghanistan and Pakistan under the Kushan Empire from the first to the third centuries A.D. After the arrival of Islam, this culture disappeared. Only a few relics of this culture remain today; the Buddhist community itself is gone.

In many areas non-Muslim communities endured, especially Hindu and later Sikh. Friction between these groups and the Islamic community has been an essential feature of political history for centuries. This conflict took on a different and ultimately a more politically significant aspect with the arrival of the British. Muslim political dominance was challenged and overcome by the British, which was a favorable development for the Hindu community. During the course of the British Raj, the Hindus were more amenable to cooperation with the British than were the Muslims, who felt themselves more aggrieved at the hands of British imperialism.

With the end of British rule in 1947, the latent rivalry between the two communities became a critical factor in determining the course of political development. While Indian and Pakistani nationalists often blamed the British for Hindu-Muslim hostilities, the problem originates with the establishment of Islamic rule. Nevertheless, through their presence and their methods of governance, the British furthered the politicization of communal rivalries. In South Asia, as in other colonial areas, the combination of cultural forces, historical conditions and the essentially foreign institutions grafted on by the Europeans produced a potent political brew. Although India was beginning to move toward self rule as early as 1857, when the time came to take the actual step, it was traumatic. Under the British, India was an amorphous collection of hundreds of political units enjoying various degrees of autonomy. This arrangement served the colonial interests of the government fairly well. But an independent, self-governing country was faced with a different set of priorities. One such priority was the need to give expression to the social and cultural composition of the subcontinent, especially the Muslim/non-Muslim division. This was done in a dramatic way when British India was divided into two countries--India and Pakistan. Pakistan's existence was predicated on its being Islamic. India has always claimed to be secular and, ironically, contains more Muslims than does Pakistan, i.e., since the secession of Bangladesh.

A commitment to the brotherhood of all the followers of Mohammed is one of the essential features of Islam. While this idea of brotherhood does not transcend or overcome political differences, it does provide the basis for a sense of community among Muslims, a sense most strongly defined among Arab peoples. The concept of a Muslim community is the basis of Pakistan as a state, but as experience has shown this has not proved sufficient to produce a modern polity. The matter is exacerbated by the fact that in the 20th century the nation-state itself is becoming less capable of dealing with the problems and issues of modern life. Political systems based essentially on religion were effective and survived for long periods of time in the past when no great demands were made of them, at least by contemporary standards. But a fundamental question facing Pakistan throughout its history has been whether a state which is tied closely to religion is sufficiently broad and flexible to survive.

A serious complication was the fact that apart from religion, East and West Pakistan shared few common traits. In the West, Middle Eastern cultural characteristics predominated, while the East had much in common with South and Southeast Asia. The British divided the population of India into two groups: martial and non-martial races. In the former category they placed the Pathans and Punjabis--the people of what later became West Pakistan--and recruited them in large numbers for the army. The Bengalis were considered unsuited for military life, and relatively few actually found service. This underrepresentation of Bengalis in the military was a pattern which continued after the creation of Pakistan. There were ethnic and linguistic differences as well. The two wings did not experience parallel or even complementary economic development. Little effort was made to keep the distance between the two wings from permanently dividing the two peoples. Because of the great distance involved, it was prohibitively expensive for most Pakistanis to travel between the two wings. The people had little opportunity to gain understanding of their countrymen because the exchange of newspapers, literature and cultural material was minimal.

A divided country with few common characteristics is fertile ground for secessionist movements. Fragmentation and disintegration have confronted societies in many parts of the world. In many cases secession and civil war have occurred in countries with longer histories and more compelling forces for national integrity than existed in Pakistan. A successful secession occurred when Ireland obtained its independence from Britain in 1922. In Canada there continues to be a secessionist movement among French-Canadians calling for an independent Quebec. The attempted Biafran secession in Nigeria resulted in a bloody civil war that lasted from 1966 to 1970. If there is little argument in favor of a unified state and so much for separation, then how did Pakistan come into existence in the first place? This question is best answered by considering the circumstances leading up to the end of British rule in India.

British Policy Since 1857

The traumatic experiences of 1857 permanently altered the relationship between the British and the peoples of India and set in motion developments that would culminate in the end of the Raj some ninety years later. While the British refer to these momentous events as the Mutiny, Indians regard them as a war of independence during which Indian national self-awareness was born. There would be no more pretense of gentlemanly cooperation and understanding between ruler and ruled. The British were foreigners who were only able to maintain their control by the use of force. The fragile legitimacy of British rule had survived only because there were no significant challenges to it. The Mutiny ended that, and Indians began demanding a greater voice in their own affairs, a demand for which the British themselves were partly responsible. By introducing Western political thought and methods into the subcontinent and educating Indians along Western lines, it would only be a matter of time before they began to ask why principles of democracy and self-government seemed to be inapplicable to colonial peoples. As the Westernized Indian intelligentsia grew in numbers and political sophistication, the British were confronted with a rising chorus of demands for reform. The response of the government to these demands increasingly acknowledged the existence of two political cal communities in the subcontinent. Also contributing to the momentum for reform was a shift in British public opinion, first made evident in the elections of 1906, away from the idea "of an endless wardship for a permanently adolescent India."[2]

The British had always recognized that social and cultural differences existed among the Indian population and often took political advantage of them. British rule probably affected Muslims more significantly than it did other communities in that the Muslims were displaced as the dominant ruling group. The economic well-being of the elite minority of Muslims was not so much affected as was their way of life. The Muslim aristocracy fared no worse under the British than they had under the Marathas who had extended their control over most of India by the middle of the 18th century. But British dominance was more offensive because they placed little value on the Moghul past and the cultivated culture of the Moghul court. Muslim officeholders were reduced from positions of importance to mere functionaries in a society dominated by foreigners. As such they had little hope of becoming members of the top elite. Muslim soldiers probably suffered most of all, since there were fewer opportunities to employ their martial skills and acquire glory and furtune than there had been during the days of Moghul rule. Muslim civil servants working within the British system could achieve personal enrichment by exploiting British regulations and governing processes to their own advantage. Muslim farmers suffered no more than others except to the extent that in some areas there were more Muslim farmers.[3]

British actions were guided by the basic recognition that they were in India to make money, not to

spend it. Hence, an inexpensive administrative structure relying on local notables and landowners was used
to collect revenue. Over time these people became
politically and economically powerful at the expense of
the poorer classes. Even the Land Alienation Act of
1900 which was supposed to relieve the peasants' burdens
at the hands of the money lenders allowed the big landowners to become even bigger. Thus, the British encouraged the perpetuation of a system in which landowners and spiritual leaders, often themselves landowners, dominated.[4]

In the frontier areas, the forward policy relied on
the tribes to maintain order in return for subsidies
from the British government. As a result, the political significance of tribal organization was enhanced at
a time when tribalism was declining. The British
desire to mak money, keep costs down, and maintain
order and tranquility frequently led to the perpetuation
and/or creation of conditions which had the effect of
retarding the development of the Indian population.
This was particularly true for Muslims and would have
considerable bearing on the political development of
Pakistan.

The British were effective in isolating Muslim dis-
contents within their own community by playing one group
off against the other. Upperclass Muslims who looked
nostalgically back at the cultural accomplishments of
the Moghul period were especially amenable to British
inducements. They felt their culture, at least, could
be perpetuated by the financial rewards and recognition
received from the new rulers. Within the Muslim community it was difficult to mobilize opposition to
British rule, since many Muslims, especially those with
something to lose, were willing to cooperate with the
British.[5]

Self-government in the subcontinent would have
come about eventually as the result of slow processes
of evolution. But a series of major international
developments accelerated the process. World War I
brought about the end of a European-centered, European-
managed world system. Several dynastic empires came to
an end--the Romanov, the Hapsburg, the Hohenzollern and
the Ottoman. Revolutionary communism became an important force. Colonialism itself found fewer apologists
and more critics, including the United States and the
Soviet Union. World War I also marked the beginning of
total war, the costs of which very nearly bankrupt
the belligerents. The war thus made it militarily and
economically less practical for colonial powers to
maintain far-flung empires. World War II would make
this even more evident. To aid in the cause, Britain
and other colonial powers expected their colonial subjects to assist in the war effort. Indian troops not
only came home with different perspectives about Europe

but also increasingly asked why they should fight and die in wars that seemed to be of little significance to them.

Indian historians place a great deal of the blame for Muslim separatism on the British. While this is no doubt an exaggeration, British policies did contribute to the growing frustration and political consciousness of Muslims. Through the practice of "divide and rule," colonial administrators exploited cultural divisions within the native population in order to prevent unified resistance. For example, in 1846 they permitted a Hindu prince to assume the rulership of the largely Muslim state of Kashmir. By such actions the British reduced the chances of cooperation between native rulers and the people. Moreover, the British were quick to accept the concept of reserved seats for Muslims in the legislative assemblies. As early as 1906 a Muslim petition to the viceroy, Lord Minto, raising the issue of separate electorates drew this response: "any electoral representation in India would be doomed to mischievous failure which aimed at granting a personal enfranchisement regardless of the beliefs and traditions of the communities composing the population of this continent."[6]

Complicating British governing efforts was the appearance of Indian political organizations. The first of these, the Indian National Congress founded by an Englishman Allan Octavian Hume in 1885, initially cooperated with the British but gradually became more of a spokesman for self-rule. The Muslim League appeared in 1906 and concerned itself exclusively with Muslim interests. While the Congress and the League shared common interests, their ultimate goals diverged, with the Congress advocating a unified, independent India and the League calling for a separate Islamic state. During the years before independence it was unusual for British policy not to be faced with the opposition of at least one of these two political groups.

In the Morley-Minto reforms of 1909 and the Montagu-Chelmsford reforms of 1919, significant steps toward ultimate self-government were taken as well as acceptance of the separate political status for Muslims. The 1909 reforms worked toward bettering Indian representation, broadening powers of the legislative councils and adding Indian representation to the executive branch. The Imperial Legislative Council was expanded to 60 from 25. The size of the official majority was reduced at the national level, while at the provincial level non-official majorities were introduced. Direct election and communal representation for Muslims were also provided. The Montagu-Chelmsford or Montford reforms of 1919 made the gradual establishment of self-government the goal of British policy. Self-government was extended from the local to the provincial levels, and more power was shifted from the national to the provincial governments. The retention and expansion of communal representation for Muslims were also provided. The Montagu-Chelmsford or Montford reforms of 1919 made the gradual establishment of self-government the goal of British policy. Self-government was extended from the local to the provincial levels, and more power was shifted from the national to the provincial governments. The retention and expansion of communal representation made this practice a permanent feature of the political landscape. The official majority in the national legislature was abolished and the number of members increased to 106. The second chamber, the Council of State, had 61 members.[7]

By the Government of India Act of 1935 the British made a major step toward granting independence to India. The Act provided for a federal constitutional system and a government of ministers responsible to provincial legislatures. The central government was the link between the provinces and the various princely states. The entire arrangement was ultimately responsible to the Secretary of State for India in London. The reaction of political groups in India toward the Act was generally negative. The Congress opposed it on the grounds that the central government was responsible to Britain rather than India. Moreover, the Act did not recognize the movement for dominion status which the Congress advocated. The Muslim League was dissatisfied with restrictions upon provincial autonomy, which the League desired so as to increase the political strength of the Muslim community in areas where Muslims constituted a majority of the population. While the Act envisaged a unified state, the Muslim League was beginning to espouse the idea of partition. The British accepted the possiblity of partition in 1942 but did not adopt it as official policy until after World War II. Although Congress continued to oppose partition, the issue was no longer whether it would happen, but how. The eagerness of the British to depart the subcontinent in effect forced a decision on the matter.

Congress and the League

The Indian National Congress was founded in 1885 with the support of a number of Englishmen such as Allan Octavian Hume. Hume called upon graduates of Indian universities to gather and debate issues of social and political reform. The founding of the Congress marks the dramatic rise of Indian national self-awareness. Before 1900 the activities of the Congress consisted of relatively moderate efforts to get the British to permit Indians an increased involvement in governmental service. At first the Congress gave little thought to the implications of the Hindu-Muslim issue. But the Muslims soon became anxious over their minority status, fearing that the Hindu majority would take actions contrary to their interests. Responding to their concerns, Hume wrote on January 5, 1888, to the Secretary of the Standing Congress Committee about the fears of Muslims that the numerically stronger Hindus "at some time press and carry in Congress some resolution directly hostile to Mohammedan interests."[8] He drafted a rule, later adopted by Congress, which would prevent such resolutions from even being debated.

By the turn of the century, the Congress had become a vigorous organization. Increasingly nationalistic, it also became a part of a revival of Hindu orthodoxy. The emphasis upon religious fundamentalism among Hindus spelled trouble for other religions. Incidents of Muslim persecution increased considerably, although not at the hands of the Congress itself. Confronted with the growing power of the Congress and the assertiveness of Hindus, Muslims founded their own organization in 1906, the All-India Muslim League. Although the Congress claimed to represent both Hindus and Muslims, the League was concerned only with the Muslim community. The Congress attempted to maintain the fiction of representing both religious communities, but soon after the turn of the century it had become primarily a Hindu organization.

Events during the latter part of the 19th century and the early part of the 20th reflected a growing estrangement between Hindus and Muslims. For their part, the Muslims had remained aloof from political collaboration with other groups, preferring instead to promote their interests by remaining loyal to the British. But Hindu protests over fragmentation of the Muslim-dominated province of East Bengal and Assam by Lord Curzon and apprehension over the possibility that the new liberal government in Britain would yield to Hindu demands led Muslims to seek an expanded voice in the legislative bodies. Such demands went to the extent of requesting representation in excess of the Muslim proportion of the population. The British government acceded to these demands in the reforms of 1909.

Since communal rivalry is part of traditional South Asian civilization, the possibilities of developing common interests and integrating activities among communities have never been great. Communalism was a particularly important aspect of the social landscape in the northwestern part of India where, by the 1890's, several different religions were practiced. Commenting on the situation in the Punjab, Jones noted that "there was an impressive array of societies, sects, and organizations--Hindu, Muslim, and Sikh--orthodox, heterodox, and reform, each with its own ideology and program, each caught up in a struggle with one or more opponents."[9]

Among the Muslims, the Ahmadiya movement aggressively pursued the interests of Islam. Important Hindu revivalist groups included the Arya Samaj and cow protection societies. These groups discouraged Hindu participation in Muslim festivals and sought to prevent cow slaughter, especially as sacrifice at the Baqr Id. The Arya Samaj sought to convert Muslims and Christians to Hinduism and denounced Islam. The emerging sense of national identity for both Hindu and Muslim groups involved symbols and historical references that were mostly communal. For Muslims, this involved Moghul greatness which had come at the expense of Hindus, while the Hindus pointed with pride to Shivaji who had fought against Aurangzeb. Communal frictions intensified between 1885 and 1895 and again between 1907 and 1914.[10] In response to this, and at the same time contributing to it, the British established separate electorates based on communal factors. This contributed to further politicization of the communal issue.

Despite the growing difficulties between the two communities, the Congress and the Muslim League were at least able to agree on the desirability of ending the British Raj. Of the two, the Congress was the more cosmopolitan and the only element of the national movement even to claim an all-India representation. The Muslim League consistently claimed to be a representative of the Muslim community only. With diminishing success, the Congress attempted to downplay the communal issue in order to present a broader political appeal. Especially in Punjab where communal differences were clearly defined, Congress' efforts to include all groups under its banner were frustrated. In opposing the Communal Award of 1932, which determined the proportion of communal representation in the provinces, Congress opted to lose support among Muslims in return for new Hindu adherents attracted by its nationalist position.[11]

During World War I, the Congress and the League cooperated in an effort to win concessions from the British. The high point of such cooperation was the Lucknow pact of 1916 in which, among other things, the Congress agreed to the size of separate Muslim electorates in the various provinces. The principles of the Lucknow Pact were accepted by the British in the Government of India Act of 1919.

Prospects for success of the Lucknow Pact were undermined by various developments during this period. Extremists in both Hindu and Muslim communities made accommodations difficult. The association of Hindu revivalism with the Congress movement was never far from the minds of the Muslims. The Congress had consistently opposed separate electorates for Muslims, while this was an essential point for the Muslim League. Thus, by moderating its stand on the issue in the Lucknow Pact,

Congress was only creating the appearance of cooperation. The British contributed to polarization by
actions such as the annulment of the partition of
Bengal which had created a Muslim majority province.
This decision pleased the Hindus and angered the
Muslims. The British also upset Indian Muslims by campaigning against the Ottoman Empire and by supporting
the Empire's dismemberment at the hands of Christian
states in World War I.[12] Finally, the Lucknow Pact was
frustrated by the fact that the Muslim League was coming
increasingly under the influence of people of nationalistic persuasion, many of whom would tolerate no compromise with Congress. The League was emerging from its
rather narrow and defensive posture and beginning to
think in terms of broader political perspectives, ultimately including the idea of a separate state.

The advocates of an autonomous Pakistan drew upon
every argument available at hand. Jinnah combined
ideas of race, culture, national origin, tradition,
manner of life, civilization and religion. He argued
that Hindus and Muslims are different on almost all
counts. The assertion that these differences justify
the demand for an independent country led Jinnah to
point to Europe as a precedent. Since Europe is not
united but consists of several states each with distinctive social characteristics, it follows that a
similar arrangement is appropriate for the subcontinent.
Following another line of reasoning, Jinnah argued that
the social majority ultimately dictates to the minority.
"Such majority tyranny is the result of both the natural
desire and efforts on the part of one to dominate the
social order and establish political supremacy over the
other."[13]

In 1937 the Congress did well in elections in
areas where Hindus were in the majority. The Muslim
League did less well even in Muslim-dominated areas.
Although the two cooperated during the election, the
Congress refused to form coalitions with the League,
arguing that only a unified government could deal
effectively with the British.[14] Several proposals for
Muslim autonomy or independence surfaced in the late
1930's. It was clear at that time that the Muslims did
not have a precise idea of their political objectives.
Finally, meeting in 1940, the Muslim League issued the
Lahore Declaration which brought the matter into focus
by advocating political independence. While the language of the Declaration suggested the possibility of
several Muslim states, it is clear from the comments of
Muslim leaders that they had one state in mind.[15]

After independence the Muslim League and the
Congress were the basis of political organization by
means of which the two countries attempted to govern
themselves. The Indian Congress has proved to be one
of the few national movements in the underdeveloped

world which has endured successfully as a political
party long after attaining independence. During the
1960's the Congress Party showed many signs of disintegration and atrophy, and by the end of the decade it
had not only lost its parliamentary majority but had
split into two rival factions. In March 1971, however,
the branch of the Congress Party under Mrs. Gandhi
scored an impressive victory and remained the primary
political force in Indian politics thereafter.

Such was not the case with the Muslim League.
Prior to independence, the League was based on a much
narrower social and philosophical foundation than was
its Congress counterpart. The state of Pakistan rests
upon the assertion that the Muslims of India constituted
a nation and as such must have their own state. The
Muslim League was considered to be the organization,
and indeed the only organization, entitled to speak for
this nation. Consequently, the political apparatus of
the Pakistani state in earlier years overlapped directly
with the Muslim League structure. The League might
have been more effective as a political vehicle had it
been able to benefit from the personal strength and popularity of leading political figures. Mohammed Ali
Jinnah, regarded as the father of the country, enjoyed
great personal popularity. Unfortunately he died within
a year of the founding of Pakistan. Moreover, the
first Prime Minister, Liaquat Ali Khan, was assassinated
in 1951. What ensued was a bewildering succession of
prime ministers and governors general and considerable
governmental instability. The relationships among the
Muslim League, the government of Pakistan and the
various provincial governments became confused and
strained.

Partition

To many Britishers, the independence of the Indian
Empire was an accepted inevitability, a perception that
was reinforced by World War II. Britain's preoccupation
with its own survival during the war meant that full
attention could not be given to governing an increasingly unruly colony. In 1939 and 1940 the British put
forward somewhat vague proposals for independence. In
March 1942, a mission headed by Sir Stafford Cripps
offered a more specific mechanism for self-determination. It was proposed that after the war the pro-
visional legislatures would together function as an
electoral college to select a constitution-making body,
the size of which would be 10% of the electoral college
itself. The princely states would be invited to send
representatives in proportion to their populations.
The possibility of an independent state for Muslims was
acknowledged in a statement by Sir Stafford Cripps:
"With such non-acceding provinces, should they so

desire, His Majesty's Government will be prepared to agree upon a new Constitution, giving them the same full status as the Indian Union, and arrived at by a procedure analogous to that here laid down."[16] The Cripps proposals were rejected by the Congress because they accepted the principle of an independent Pakistan. They were rejected by the League because the principle was stated in language that was too vague.

The Congress then pursued the idea of a federation whereby the Muslims would have a degree of autonomy but would remain within an Indian union. This possibility was the subject of discussions between Gandhi and Jinnah, but the two leaders failed to reach an agreement.

The next British initiative did not come until after the war. In May 1946, a Cabinet Mission brought proposals for eventual transfer of power. These proposals sought to accommodate the inevitable Hindu-Muslim differences while at the same time retaining an overall union. Under this scheme, the subcontinent would be divided into three sections consisting of the primarily Muslim areas in the Northwest, the area of Bengal and Assam which had a Muslim majority, and the remainder of India with a predominately Hindu population. Separate representation in the constitution-drafting process would come from each of these three areas. Key elements of the proposal included a requirement that any major communal issue must be acceptable to a majority of total representation. This was a concession to the Muslims designed to prevent decisions which would be obnoxious to them. Another provision allowed for the possibility that these provincial groupings might establish their own constitution in addition to that of the union constitution.[17]

The Cabinet Mission proposals were initially accepted by both the Congress and the League. But they ultimately failed because the Congress refused to accept equal representation with the League in an interim cabinet. Nehru, who was elected President of the Congress in July, asserted that while the proposals were acceptable in principle, the option should be retained for altering them in specific detail. This was unacceptable to the Muslim League, which regarded the suggestion as an indication of Congress's intention to weaken guarantees to Muslims.[18]

The League's response to these developments was to reject the Cabinet Mission proposals and call for a day of direct action, which was scheduled for August 16 by Jinnah. The result was widespread violence, especially in Calcutta, lasting for three days.

The last British Viceroy, Lord Louis Mountbatten, was appointed in February 1947 with instructions to engineer a transfer of power by no later than June 1948. Mountbatten kept the feuding parties together at the

conference table long enough to reach agreement on a
plan for the transfer. Working to Mountbatten's advantage was a rapidly deteriorating political situation
throughout India. Communal rioting was spreading, and
there was a general breakdown of law and order in many
areas. Army and police forces were reluctant to act
because the structure of authority was undefined. Since
they were leaving, the authority of the British was
vitiated, while that of independent India and Pakistan
had not yet been established. Thus all parties were
encouraged to reach an agreement as soon as possible
before the situation deteriorated completely. On June
3, 1947, tentative agreement was given by both Congress
and League leaders to a plan for partition.[19]

In the Mountbatten Award of June 3, 1947, the
British government accepted the inevitability of partition. The predominantly Muslim areas of the Empire
were given the opportunity through their provincial
legislatures to decide in favor of partition or union.
In those areas where the ratio between the Hindus and
Muslims was more equal, the problem of joining either
India or Pakistan presented an administrative problem.
In an attempt to solve this problem, a procedure for
boundary demarcation was established which, as might be
expected, did not leave everyone happy.[20]

On August 14, 1947, British rule in India ended.
On the following day India and Pakistan joined the community of sovereign, independent nations. But the
transfer of power and partition did not end all the
problems; in fact, some were just beginning. First,
there was the problem of allocating the resources of
the government of undivided India. Somehow the military
and financial resources had to be partitioned equitably.
Moreover, the boundaries between the two countries had
to be defined. The states of Punjab and Bengal were
partitioned, the new boundaries had to be drawn. There
was the overwhelming problem of refugees streaming by
the thousands into both countries--Hindus and Sikhs to
India and Muslims to Pakistan. Communal rioting and
slaughter did not abate with partition and independence
but instead worsened. Both governments were faced with
the need to re-establish law and order. To add to the
difficulties, disagreements and mutual recriminations
between the two governments occurred almost immediately.
Pakistan charged India with negligence in failing to
live up to agreements concerning the partition of resources. India charged that Pakistan was making excessive and unrealistic demands.

Unfortunately, a tone of suspicion and hostility
was set. Even after the immediate issues had been resolved, there remained several vexing matters that
would sour Indo-Pakistan relations for some time and
would, in the long run, contribute to the undermining of
the political structure of Pakistan.

Controversies

Pakistan was born out of communal identity, and it is not surprising that one of the main problems confronting the new government concerned communal matters. After the violence had subsided, there remained the large population of refugees and their claims for lost property. Another important issue that would have long lasting consequences was the control and allocation of the waters forming the Indus river system. As it ultimately turned out, India would be in a position to control the waters that flowed into Pakistan. Diversion of the waters of this system, which for the most part had its headwaters in Kashmir, for Indian use meant that there would be that much less available for Pakistani downstream use. Enduring quarrels over the division of British assets frustrated the continuation of existing commerce and inhibited the development of new trade relations. Trade that had been internal now became international, and procedures for mutually beneficial trade relationships were not forthcoming. A particularly thorny issue was the division of military resources. The British commander, Auchenleck, opposed the idea of dividing the army, arguing that to do so would result in bloodshed. He favored keeping the army intact and under British command for at least a year. Pakistan wanted all the accoutrements of statehood, especially the army. Military units were accordingly apportioned.[21] It is interesting to note that both the Pakistani and Indian armies have continued to the present day to display their British military heritage.

But the biggest and most intractable problem would prove to be Kashmir. This issue in particular struck at the very heart of Pakistan's existence, and failure to resolve it in a satisfactory manner comprised the very reason for the country's existence. Moreover, futile efforts to settle the matter by force contributed to the secession of the East wing.

An immediate problem of the transfer of power and partition concerned the princely states. When the British left India, it was not simply a matter of transferring political control from one government to another. Transferring power involved the very complicated business of changing the patchwork quilt of British India to more simplified political structures in independent India and Pakistan.

British India had consisted of two kinds of political entities. Slightly more than half of the total surface area was administered by the British government through Parliament, the Secretary of State for India, and the Viceroy. The remaining portions of the country were divided into more than 500 separate princely states.[22] Most of these states were exceedingly small and relatively insignificant, but some were large and important. The internal affairs of the states were administered by an hereditary prince with a government subordinate to him. The princes were subordinate to the British government under the doctrine of paramountcy, which meant that the British controlled the diplomatic and military affairs of the various states. The states could not conduct international relations, nor were they completely free to conduct relations with each other. The British retained the right to interfere in the internal affairs of any state if it were in their interest to do so. The bridge between British-administered India and princely India was the Viceroy, who functioned as Governor General and Crown representative.

The transfer of power of British-administered India was a relatively simple process of handing it over either to India or to Pakistan. But for the Indian states to be transferred from the system of paramountcy to the new political system was a more complicated matter. The transfer of power involving the states followed the principle of accession.

> The basic principle of Accession was that it was vested in the personal discretion of the Ruler, since he was an autocrat. But it was recognized that this discretion should be qualified by the geographical contiguity of the State to the Successor Dominion, the communal composition of the State, and a plebicite if necessary to ascertain the will of the people.[23]

For the most part, the accession of the princely states went smoothly.[24] This was largely due to the fact that most of these states were ruled by Hindu princes; only about six were ruled by Muslims. A principality ruled by a Hindu which was located within India naturally acceded to India. In only three states did problems of accession occur. One was Hyderabad, a state about the size of Germany with a population of roughly 17 million located in central India. The Muslim leader of Hyderabad, the Nizam, delayed the accession decision but eventually chose Pakistan. However, the issue was forced by the Indian army, and in September 1948 Hyderabad was incorporated into India. A second holdout was the west Indian state of Jungagadh, whose ruler acceded to Pakistan in September 1947. But the Indian army entered the state and forced a plebiscite, whereupon the people, a majority of whom were Hindus, decided in favor of India. The third state was Kashmir, a situation not so easily resolved.

The question of Kashmir involves the very _raison d'etre_ of Pakistan and has been at the center of the country's national and international life. Kashmiris are mostly Muslims; Pakistan is a Muslim state. The logic is simple--Kashmir should be part of Pakistan.

The single-minded pursuit of this goal contributed to the estrangement of East Pakistan, where there was considerably less interest in the Kashmir issue.

Internationally, Kashmir has been the primary point of contention between India and Pakistan and the vortex of political and military relations in South Asia. The Kashmir problem has been particularly vexing for the United States. American foreign policy toward South Asia since World War II failed to appreciate the significance of the conflict over Kashmir. The foreign policy of the Soviet Union toward the subcontinent has been influenced by Kashmir, simultaneously creating problems and opportunities. China's activities along the Himalayas in courting Pakistan and harassing India are related to the Kashmir situation. These matters will be discussed in greater detail in later chapters.

India's position on Kashmir has been dictated in part by concerns over the integrity of the Indian union. Over the years India was unwilling to live up to its commitments regarding Kashmir, because to do so might have encouraged movements for local autonomy elsewhere in the country. India agreed to hold a plebiscite in Kashmir, and then put forth one reason or another for never holding it. Therefore, even though for many years Kashmir's status in the Indian union was unclear, should it have become independent or part of Pakistan by whatever means, encouragement would have been given to separatist movements in South India and West Bengal.[25]

The unresolved Kashmir issue more than anything else set the tone of Indo-Pakistan relations. Beyond defining the relationship with its neighbor, the issue of Kashmir has had great significance for Pakistan's political integrity. There have been continuing problems of territorial integration, with the division between the East and West wings eventually becoming the most critical aspect. To some degree, Pakistan has always had difficulty keeping its West wing fully integrated. There has been frequent agitation for additional provincial autonomy from the central government. This is due mainly to the fact that there are serious disparities in population and political and economic power among the provinces. Punjab, as the largest province, controls the central government.

Even within provinces there have been demands for autonomy. While one of the provinces in West Pakistan was Sind, in the city of Karachi which lies within Sind, there were demands in the early 1970's that the city itself be made a separate province.[26]

West Pakistan's frontier along the northwestern border has always been a loosely defined and poorly integrated area. The tribal people there have enjoyed considerable independence from the control of the central government. In March 1971, some of the tribesmen suggested that a new province be established within, but independent of, the Northwest Frontier Province. This new province, to be named Qabalistan, would be composed of the tribal agencies of Chitral, Dir, and Swat.[27] All are units of local government carried over from pre-independence days.

Pakistan and India have each blamed the other for the continuing hostility between them. Noted one Pakistani leader: "The root-cause of the Indo-Pakistan trouble is that India never really accepted the establishment of Pakistan."[28] Indian leaders continually see Pakistan as meddling in internal Indian affairs.

NOTES

1. Vincent A. Smith, The Oxford History of India, 3rd ed., edited by Percival Spear, London: Oxford University Press, 1958, p. 40.

2. Ibid., p. 320.

3. Peter Hardy, The Muslims of British India, London: Cambridge University Press, 1972, pp. 49-50.

4. Khalid B. Sayeed, Politics in Pakistan: The Nature and Direction of Change, New York: Praeger Publishers, 1980, pp. 4-7.

5. Hardy, The Muslims of British India, p. 60.

6. G. Allana, Pakistan Movement: Historic Documents, Lahore: Islamic Book Service, 1977, p. 20.

7. Smith, The Oxford History of India, pp. 330-1, 342-5.

8. Hardy, The Muslims of British India, p. 128.

9. Kenneth W. Jones, "Communalism in the Punjab: The Arya Samaj Contribution," The Journal of Asian Studies, XXVIII (November, 1968) p. 53.

10. Hugh F. Owen, "Negotiating the Lucknow Pact," "The Journal of Asian Studies, (May, 1972) p. 563-4.

11. Gerald A. Heeger, "The Growth of the Congress Movement in Punjab, 1920-40," The Journal of Asian Studies, XXXII (November, 1972) pp. 40, 50-1.

12. Owen, "Negotiating the Lucknow Pact," p. 568.

13. Aziz Ahmad, Islamic Modernism in India and Pakistan: 1857-1964, London: Royal Institute of International Affairs, 1967, p. 167.

14. Ibid., p. 170.

15. Ibid., p. 171.

16. Allana, Pakistan Movement: Historic Documents, p. 202; Smith, The Oxford History of India, pp. 825-7.

17. Ibid., pp. 416ff.

18. Aziz Ahmad, Islamic Modernism, p. 173; Chaudhri Muhammad Ali, The Emergence of Pakistan, New York: Columbia University Press, 1967, pp. 61-2.

19. For more details on the partition, see, for example: Kingsley Davis, "India and Pakistan: The Demo-

graphy of Partition," Pacific Affairs 22 (September, 1949) 254-64; Penderel Moon, Divide and Quit, Berkeley: University of California Press, 1962; V. P. Menon, The Transfer of Power in India, Princeton: Princeton University Press, 1957, O. K. H. Spate, "Partition of India and the Prospects of Pakistan," Geographical Review 38 (January, 1948) 5-29; Alan Campbell-Johnson, Mission with Mountbatten, London: Robert Hale, Ltd., 1952.

20. Hugh Tinker, "Pressure, Persuasion, Decision: Factors in the Partition of the Punjab, August 1947," The Journal of Asian Studies, XXXVI (August, 1977), pp. 695-704.

21. Being the larger of the two countries, India received the greater share of the resources. The military, for instance, was divided in the following manner:

	INDIA	PAKISTAN
ARMY		
Armored regiments	12	6
Artillery		
Regiments	15	8
Transport units	34	17
Hospitals	82	34
NAVY		
Sloops	4	2
Frigates	2	2
Minesweepers	12	4
Trawlers	4	2
AIR FORCE		
Fighter squadrons	7	2
Transport squadrons	1	1
MILITARY STORES*	3	2

*India gave Pakistan 60 million rupees in lieu of ordinance factories that could not be moved. Source: D. Som Dutt, "Foreign Military Aid and the Defense Strength of India and Pakistan: A Comparative Study," International Studies 8 (July, 1966-April, 1967) pp. 67-68.

22. There is no agreement of the exact number of these princely states. For instance, Alan Campbell-Johnson says there were 565 (Mission With Mountbatten, p. 357.) Josef Korbel says there were 584 (Danger in Kashmir, p. 46.) Alistair Lamb says there were 562, (The Kashmir Problem: A Historical Survey, p. 3.

23. Campbell-Johnson, Mission With Mountbatten, pp. 357-8. The instrument of accession itself recognizes the sovereignty of the prince. This legal aspect is an important element of the controversy. See A.G. Noorani, The Kashmir Question (Bombay: P. C. Manaktala

38

and Sons Private Ltd., 1964) pp. 89-91.

24. In 1971 the Indian government was still wrestling with the problem of the princely states. As compensation for their loss of political and economic status, the princes were given privy purses or annual stipends from the public treasury. Prime Minister Gandhi attempted to end this practice by executive order but the action was nullified by the Supreme Court. Elimination of this last vestige of the princely states required a constitutional amendment.

25. On the problems of Indian unity see Selig Harrison, India's Most Dangerous Decade (Princeton: Princeton University Press, 1960.)

26. Daily News (Karachi) March 1, 1971. For further background see Khalid B. Sayeed, The Political System of Pakistan (Boston: Houghton Mifflin Co., 1967) pp. 65-68.

27. Khyber Mail (Peshawar) March 17, 1971.

28. Summary of the White Paper on the Crisis in East Pakistan (Washington: Embassy of Pakistan, 1971.)

3
Islamic Politics
in Theory and Practice

Islam and Politics in South Asia

Many countries choose a different name for themselves especially to help eradicate the memory of a colonial experience. But in Pakistan's case, this was no simple name change. It was an entirely new country created out of diverse parts. There had been no previous existence or identity prior to achieving independence from Great Britain in 1947. There never was a country, empire, or Kingdom called "Pakistan" nor, for that matter, has there ever been a political entity centered in this area, although it was an important part of many. Moreover, East and West Pakistan did not constitute a discrete socio-cultural unit possessing a strong sense of common identity bred within a multinational political system. Bengal has historically been a unit, but the parts of West Pakistan have experienced little political integration.

The self-consciousness among part of the population of South Asia which would ultimately result in the creation of Pakistan did not come about as a result of oppression or persecution (real or imagined). Islam became politically dominant upon its arrival in the subcontinent. Even after Moghul authority was replaced by the British, Muslims were not a persecuted minority. The demand for Pakistan was not based upon grievances of the past, but upon those of the future. The leaders of the Pakistan movement argued that oppression would come about as a result of the Muslim's minority status vis a vis the Hindu majority after independence from Britain. If Pakistan had never existed before and was not the product of conventional nationalist forces, then what brought it into being?

Several arguments have been advanced purporting to explain the "cause" of the creation of Pakistan. One is the "pull" exerted by the distinctive Muslim social order which could not flourish in the non-Muslim Hindu environment of India. A similar idea is that Pakistan

39

was "pushed" into existence precisely by that non-Muslim environment. Another argument is that the essentially secular, economic interests of the Muslim bourgeoisie led them to seek institutional protection. The British themselves have been credited/blamed for the partition of India and the establishment of Pakistan by their practice of "divide and rule." This argument has it that the British pitted the communal sectors of India against one another in order to neutralize their political effectiveness. While it was in the interest of the British to prevent all-India political movements, it would not have served their purpose to provoke inter-community conflict and resulting disorder. In their attempts to impose rational, Western modes of governance on their subjects, they stimulated self-awareness. Moreover, as they moved toward self-government and es-tablished electorates based on religion, they contrib-uted to Muslim political consciousness. Another hypoth-esis concerns the competition for power among various groups and aspiring leaders. As is the case almost everywhere, there is insufficient room at the top for all the people who think they should be there. One solution to this is to carve out one's own political system, an approach that appeals especially to groups that are likely to be confined to permanent minority status.[1]

In the final analysis, the explanation for the creation of Pakistan no doubt lies in some combination of these arguments. But one thing is clear, all of them have one ingredient in common--Islam. The political and social essence of Pakistan is Islam. Attempts to separate Pakistan, its conception and history, from Islam, either in theory or in the real world of poli-tics, calls into question the country's very identity. In a very real sense, Pakistan has its roots in the teachings of Mohammed, the founder of Islam, who died in 632 A.D.

It is not within the scope of this discussion to detail the history and theology of Islam. A very general introduction will have to suffice. Islam comes out of the theological tradition that is also common to Christianity and Judaism. All are revealed religions and share a number of beliefs. There is certainly a greater affinity among Islam, Christianity, and Judaism than there is between any one of them and Hinduism or other Eastern religions. Muslims regard the prophets of the Old Testament as true prophets, but hold that Mohammed's prophecy was the last and most complete. (Some minor sects of Islam hold that there are more prophets to come.) Unlike most religions, and in degree unlike any, Islam is a proselytizing religion. Spreading the "true faith" provided a large measure of the energy behind the Muslim conquests of vast areas of the world stretching from Spain to Indonesia. These conquests and the movement of people associated with them brought Islam to what would ultimately become Pakistan.

Muslim rule in India was established by an immigrant elite which was periodically reinforced and occasionally threatened by further immigration. The Muslims did not rule India from a distant homeland as did the British, nor were they members of a dominant group within the Indian social community. They ruled by the imposition of or threat of unlimited military force and by arrangement of patronage relationships involving political office which were made available to non-Muslim petty chiefs.[2] For much of Moghul India, the political system rested not on legitimizing cultural support, but rather on coercion and self-serving contractual arrangements. The servants of the Empire served only because it was in their personal interest to do so. There was no ideological linkage between ruler and ruled as in, say, the Chinese empire, which rested on the common idelogical bond of Confucianism with both rulers and masses sharing a common commitment to the rationale of the system. Likewise, the Tsarist system of Russia was predicated on the "faith" the masses had in the paternalistic intentions of the Tsar, a faith that was very difficult to shake.

Many people were converted to Islam because of its spiritual attractions. Those outside the Hindu caste system converted in hopes of improving their social status. Others adopted the faith under duress. Among this latter group there was often found only a superficial commitment. Especially in areas remote from political and spiritual centers such as Eastern Bengal, Islamization was limited. Here the population had been influenced and converted by Muslims "not themselves well versed in the law of Islam or personally committed to teaching its requirements."[3] The result was varieties of Islam which contained Hindu rites and rituals and other accretions. Often Islam did not absorb or eliminate local cultural patterns but fused with them. Over time, local and regional variations in religious practice made Islam in South Asia less than uniform. Commitment to local culture endured and failure to allow for it eventually proved troublesome for Pakistan. According to one view, it was not the Muslim conquests of the subcontinent as such that account for the existence of Pakistan. According to this line of reasoning, Pakistan would not have come into existence if it had not been for the Sufi movement. Sufis are mystics who have a strong spiritual commitment to Islam and who think salvation will come about more as a result of faith than other ways. If Pakistan's existence were a function of Muslim conquest alone, then it would include a much larger area. In actuality it exists only in those areas where Sufism met with success."[4]

The two main sects of Islam are the Sunnis and the Shias. Most Pakistanis are Sunnis, as are most other peoples in the Islamic world, but there is also a significant Shia community that enjoys power disproportionate to its numbers. Only in Iran and Iraq do the Shias constitute a majority of the population. Another sect that has figured in Pakistan's politics are the followers of Mirza Ghulam Ahmad, or Ahmadiyas, whose beliefs are radically orthodox. They are called Ahmadiyas after Mohammed, who was also called Ahmad rather than after the name of the sect's founder. This group pursues vigorous proselytism and believes that an inspired reformer will appear every 1,000 years.[5]

Much of the population of West Pakistan is linked ethnically or culturally with peoples outside the area, sometimes even outside the subcontinent. This is not true of Bengal, the population of which does not bear evidence of significant migration. In contrast, many groups in the West wing derive their ancestry from outside, and some, like the Syeds, claim descent directly from the Prophet through his daughter Fatima or through Ali. The Quraish claim descent from the tribe of the prophet. While these people may not all be immigrants, the intermarrying among Arabs and populations converted to Islam and the taking of Arab names indicate at least a spiritual descent. The Moghuls, who ruled India for several centuries, came from Central Asia with the invading armies of Babur or came later after his conquest. The Pathans, the sturdy people of the hill areas of the Northwest, are mostly indigenous but moved southward during the conquests of Mahmud of Ghazni and his successors. Afghans conquered northern India on several occasions, and people of Afghan descent "spread over much of northern India as government officials and mercenaries."[6]

Muslims did not adjust to British rule and as a result remained politically retarded. They did not adapt to the new institutions and practices of the Raj nor use them as an avenue to modernization and political growth. Nor did they use the British as a counterpoint against which they could sharpen their nationalistic ideology and organization, something the Hindu community did effectively. Several writers have commented on this situation. According to Freeland Abbott, the fear of Christian conversion led the Muslims to withdraw into themselves and leave the Hindus to benefit from British opportunities. This tendency to keep away from Christians "fostered distrust and promoted wishful thinking as the Muslims romanticized the days of the Moghuls, drew into themselves, and refused to cooperate with the new rulers of India."[7] The upper classes of the Hindu community associated closely with the British fairly early and benefitted most from reforms enacted

in the latter part of the 19th century. More traditional Hindus eventually sought a rejuvenation of their
religious communal identity. This revivalism ultimately
estranged other communities because there was no room
for them in the Hindu scheme of things. Even as late
as the latter part of the 19th century, the Muslim community was backward "in all spheres of life" compared
to other communities.[8] To the missionaries who were
instrumental in spreading Western education, the avenue
by which Indians would participate in their own governance, the Muslims were unwilling subjects. "Finding
Hindus easier to locate, existing in greater numbers
and easier to convert, they concentrated their efforts
on them."[9] While this assessment was addressed to the
Calcutta region specifically, by the time the British
had reached other Muslim areas to the west, the pattern
had been set.

Aziz Ahmad, echoing Freeland Abbott, observes that
the Muslims avoided positions in the Raj that would
have given them higher status and political importance.

> "The Muslims of India are still content in
> their poverty and plight, trading on the names of
> their ancestors, or doing menial jobs or begging
> or just starving. Honest work in professions or
> crafts they regarded as beneath their dignity;
> trade and agriculture they find too complicated,
> and service under the British is, of course,
> according to their myopic theologians, repugnant
> to religious law."[10]

Although recruited in large numbers into the military, Muslim units played little part in the political
awakening of the community. Also absent from the movement that would eventually result in a separate Muslim
state was any significant role played by religious
leaders. In fact, they were the most vocal opponents
to the establishment of an independent state. It is
curious that the leaders of the Pakistan movement sought
to create a political entity whose distinctiveness
would be based on Islam, but the spiritual exponents of
the religion would play no role in the process. This
ambiguity over the relationship of religion to the state
has plagued Pakistan to the present day.

The "Idea" of an Islamic State

The idea of an Islamic state is as old as Islam
itself. But from the beginning there has been a problem defining the political dimensions of this state.
Neither the Prophet nor the Quran provide guidance in
the matter. While it was assumed the successors of the
Prophet would possess both religious and secular authority, there have been arguments ever since concerning

what the latter entailed, not that Muslims all agree on the first issue for that matter. Moreover, it is not clear how the caliphs, i.e., the Prophet's successors, should be chosen. While the first four were selected from among the companions of the Prophet, their successors often gained office through force. As Islam spread, matters of secular authority became even more entangled. For the most part, authority was vested in some sort of ruler or monarch whose claim to that authority was theoretically tenuous, that is, there was little rational justification for it. While in many places in the Islamic world the dynastic principle endured for a considerable time, all dynasties faced potential (and not arguably illegitimate) overthrow by force.

The point of departure of Islamic political thought is the absolute sovereignty of God. By extension God is the source of all law which in actuality comes in the form of His revealed word and through the Prophet Mohammed. It is not possible to produce legislation independent of God's law nor is it possible to modify it "even if the desire to effect such legislation or change in Divine Law is unanimous."[11] Government can legitimately enforce only the laws of God. Laws that do not conform to this prescription are not binding.

Secular authority, which is only an extension of divine authority, rests with the "whole community of Muslims including the rank and file."[12] The actual exercise of authority, which must always be consistent with God's will, is entrusted to those who have a thorough understanding of Islamic law. But this does not include everybody but only those whose opinions are correct by virtue of their long study and contemplation. While authority resides in the community of Muslims, this is not an unqualified acceptance of popular sovereignty, as "the great mass of the common people are incapable of perceiving their own true interests."[13] Only Muslims possess the right of political participation. Others "are not entitled to have any hand in shaping the fundamental policy of the state."[14] Non-Muslims or Zimmis are entitled to live within the state and enjoy rights and privileges but they are, nevertheless, wards of the state.

In addition to the possibility of disobedience to unIslamic law, there is also a classical dilemma in Islamic political thought concerning the legitimacy of rule that has been illegally acquired. If power has been seized by illegal means, can this action be offset by the justice of subsequent rule? Can an illegitimate ruler gain legitimacy by just rule? If such illegal actions are condoned as acceptable, then there is no legitimate reason why others cannot use the same means to gain power themselves.[15] In contemporary times, the succession of regimes in Pakistan illustrates this problem. The tendency to regard illegal accession to power as not unacceptable has consistently frustrated the process of institutionalization.

Pakistan's "founding fathers" could not draw upon a rich theoretical tradition in their efforts to combine Islamic political ideas with 20th century South Asian realities. Drawing specifically on the grandeur of the Moghul period and the political significance of the Muslim minority status, Sir Syed Ahmad Khan, Mohammed Iqbal, Mohammed Ali Jinnah, and others developed a case for an independent Muslim state.

Sir Syed Ahmad Khan, while not himself an original thinker, brought considerable freshness to Islamic ideas. He tried to relate the rational/pragmatic approach of Europe to the conditions of the non-Western world. The Western acceptance of the inevitability of change and faith in man's ability to determine its direction meant that by applying such a philosophy in countries like his own, things could be made better. Sir Syed "believed that man's knowledge was expanding and that it would not be confined within previously established limits. He read the Quran in a manner supporting his belief in expanding knowledge."[16] Through expanding knowledge and especially education, Sir Syed felt the lot of the Muslim community could be improved.

By arguing that modern education was not incompatible with Islam, Sir Syed and others of the Muslim intelligentsia encouraged a collective and unified approach to Muslim education. They extended the discussion of the nature and purpose of education using as their medium the language of Islamic conviction. Thus, by emphasizing the common denominator of Muslim identity, these reformers were able to fuse Islam with modern ideas through education.[17]

In the latter part of the 19th century, most Muslims lacked a well-defined sense of common identity and common cause. To encourage this and promote mobilization, Sir Syed started the Society for the Educational Progress of Indian Muslims which founded the Mohammedan Anglo-Oriental College at Aligarh in 1875. Aligarh would figure prominently in the nationalistic movement in the years to come. He also founded the Mohammedan Educational Conference in 1886, whose objectives were to encourage the study of Western sciences and literature and to revive Muslim religious education. Whereas these educational endeavors seemed harmless enough, they did serve in the long run to mobilize the Muslim population. However, the efforts were pursued in a way designed to avoid provoking the British as the Congress movement was doing.[18]

One area in which Muslim sensibilities were provoked was languages. The Indian subcontinent is a mosaic of languages with 14 major tongues and 600 or more dialects. With the ascendency of Islam, Urdu became the dominant language in Muslim areas eclipsing indigenous languages. With the advent of the British, the status of Urdu eroded due to non-Muslim assertiveness. In many areas, with the exception of the Northwest, Urdu declined under the British. In contrast, in the Northwest, the importance of Urdu was enhanced during this period. In 1900, however, without consulting Muslim opinion, the Lieutenant Governor of the United Provinces issued orders which permitted the optional use of Hindu script in court documents and required a knowledge of both scripts by court officials. This action stimulated fears among Muslims of a loss of ground of Urdu to Hindi. As time went on, the language issue became one of the points of dispute between the Muslim and non-Muslim communities.[19]

Mohammed Iqbal, a poet by trade, was one of the first to formulate a concept of Muslim nationalism. Initially he defined Indian nationalism in territorial terms, that is, including both Hindus and Muslims within a geographical area. This was consistent with the prevailing Indian nationalist sentiment in general and the Congress in particular, which were under the influence of moderate and cosmopolitan figures. When more radical politicians took over control of the Congress and the role of Hindu revivalists assumed a greater importance in its ideology, the Muslims and Iqbal found the nationalist movement less congenial. This led him to develop his views of Islamic nationalism, which in turn produced the concept of an independent state for the Indian Muslim community. He tacitly excluded the Bengalis from his conception of this community. In his view the salvation of Islam and India lay with the "virile and martial races of Punjab, NWFP, Baluchistan, and Sind."[20]

Iqbal's world view was simple: it consists of two parts, East and West. The West he saw as materialistic and decadent, lacking a moral structure by means of which human happiness could be achieved and the condition of the poor masses improved. The East, in contrast, was exploited and humiliated by the West but possessed the philosophy and moral fiber to achieve ultimately the betterment of the human condition.[21]

Iqbal's special contribution to Muslim thought was the enlargement of the scope and authority of popular consensus or ijma. But the question arises, how far can ijma be extended to the unschooled masses or to a political elite untutored in religious law? Modern Islamic systems like Pakistan, Egypt and Turkey have attempted to have it both ways: inclusion of "the people" as a response to demands for broader participation in politics but tempered by constraints imposed by the ulema. "This problem has been Pakistan's chief dilemma in constitution-making and legislation."[22]

Iqbal figured that the real problem facing the

Muslim leadership was the poverty of the Muslim masses. The way to deal with this problem was to create a Muslim state which would achieve "the enforcement of the law of Islam." The solution is Islam, but it must be applied correctly. "If this system of law is properly understood and applied, at least the right of subsistence is secured to everybody." This is not a radical or revolutionary step, "but a region to the original purity of Islam."[23]

The Indian National Congress had been working since its creation in 1885 to promote the methods and subject matter of Western education. By so doing it soon became a vehicle for the articulation of nationalist sentiments. This nationalism became increasingly an expression of Hindu sentiments because they were being presented with great vigor and enthusiasm while those of the Muslim community were not. Thus the Muslim community came to feel the need for its own organization. This organization became a reality after the Muslim deputation visited Lord Minto in Simla and received his recognition that Muslims constituted a distinct community. On December 30, 1906, the members of the Mohammedan Educational Conference meeting in Dacca turned themselves into the All-India Muslim League.[24]

In the 1920's the Muslims, apart from occasional outbursts accusing the Hindus of unfair tactics, had no political philosophy with which to face the future. "The revelation of their divisions and factious impotence merely encouraged the Congress leadership to brush them aside as men who had no political goods to deliver and who, therefore, could be discounted as a force in India."[25]

Liaquat Ali Khan told the constituent assembly in March 1949 that "Pakistan was founded because the Muslims of the subcontinent wanted to build up their lives in accordance with the teachings and traditions of Islam."[26] But as Abbott observes, there was no agreement before or after the creation of Pakistan as to what "in accordance with the teachings and traditions of Islam" might mean.[27]

But support for the creation of Pakistan was far from unanimous. The two colleges created in the 19th century to further Muslim educational needs--Aligarh and Deoband--were divided on the issue. Aligarh reflected more modern and progressive thinking, particularly that of Syed Ahmad Khan, its founder, and supported the idea of an Islamic state. The Deobandi school, which was more conservative and traditional, held reservations about Pakistan. They did not trust the Westernized intellectuals who were leading the campaign for an independent state. The commitment of this group to Islam was also suspect. Other opponents included Maulana Maududi, a leading Muslim theoretician, who

refused to support the Pakistan movement because he
believed that a nationalist movement could not be
Islamic. Abul Kalam Azad, a leading scholar and the
first education minister of independent India, did not
subscribe to the two-nation theory, preferring instead
a commitment to the unity of India. The Ahmadiyas, an
Islamic sect that does not accept the finality of the
prophethood of Mohammed, looked to the British as pro-
tectors, and did not support the Pakistan movement.[28]

The driving force behind the Pakistan movement was
the Muslim middle class, many of whom were educated in
Aligarh. "It is questionable whether the leaders of
the Muslim League even viewed the problem as fundamentally religious, however willing they may have been to
appeal to religious sentiment."[29]

Mohammed Ali Jinnah, popularly regarded as the
founder of Pakistan, played a critical role in revita-
lizing the Muslim League prior to World War II and
carrying through the crusade for a separate state. He
returned to India in 1935, after having left to settle
in England in 1931 in bitterness at his rebuff both at
the hands of Congress and Muslim groups. 1935 was a
momentous time in India, as the first national elections were to be held that year. The All-India Muslim
League was in decay and unable to collect annual sub-
scriptions. Jinnah "was a nonentity in Indian
politics." Despite these handicaps, he transformed the
Muslim League into an effective mass movement which
would ultimately achieve the goal of an independent
state.[30]

As leader of the Pakistan movement, Jinnah necessarily possessed considerable power and prestige. Upon
achieving independence, he sought to continue his status by becoming Governor General. He made it clear
that it was not his intention to associate his own personal popularity with the integrity of the institutions
of Pakistan's new government. Whether or not the parliamentary system of government and the other institutions of the political system actually worked and how
well would not be directly attributable to Jinnah, as
he did not become part of them. He possessed power
personally and exercised it accordingly. This seriously inhibited the institutionalization and legitimation of the regime, a condition which was compounded
by Jinnah's early demise. "Jinnah conducted the
affairs of the government of Pakistan as he had been
accustomed to conduct those of the Muslim League."[31]

The Pakistan movement was confronted with the need
to adapt a complex and conservative system of belief to
a rapidly changing social and political context. In
this connection it is difficult for Muslims, rather more
than it is for others, to overcome fatalism. For
Muslims there is no such thing as free will; everything
is determined by God. Human actions happen to the

extent they are willed by God; if they do not happen,
that is also God's will. This may be overly simplistic,
but there is a problem coming to terms with change.
This is due in part to the denial of the law of causa-
tion. There is no necessary connection between cause
and effect. Nothing must <u>necessarily</u> happen or follow
from an antecedent. Instead there is the law of <u>aada</u>
or custom. Things happen because of habit from which
other things follow. But this succession of events is
not necessary, i.e., they are not caused.[32] This may
explain why Muslim politics is often mercurial and
inconsistent. There is a tendency to refect the proposition that to get from A to B, it is necessary to
follow a certain course. In order to achieve a working
political arrangement, certain institutional patterns
must be accepted or certain changes in institutional
patterns must be made. If political results are not
satisfactory, there is a tendency to revolt, riot or
assassinate. This is rather like a physicist who, not
getting the results desired form an experiment, blows
up the laboratory.

Theorists of the Islamic state draw little enrichment from other political philosophies. Despite the
emphasis upon community, consensus, and rule of law,
Islamic thinkers dismiss Western democracy. Authoritarian doctrines, such as fascism, have little to
offer, but communism would seem to have much in common
with the Islamic state. Both oppose the accumulation
of wealth by a privileged class and adhere to the idea
that the economic structure of the state should be used
to secure social welfare. Both are committed to equal
opportunity and hold the collective interest superior
to the individual. Social perfection is to be achieved
through social revolution.[33] But, of course, the ideal
of social perfection provokes markedly different
strategies for its achievement. For the communist it
is the Marxist-Leninist classless society. For the
Muslim it is the realization of the ideals of Islam.
While devout Muslims abhor communism as a "godless
doctrine," lack of agreement and cooperation among
them, especially those of strong traditional loyalties,
has prevented their working constructively toward the
realization of common Islamic goals. The tragedy of
Islam has been an inability to balance or synthesize
spiritual and material values. Islam has been able to
"recreate elements of a renaissance, but not of a
reformation."[34]

The movement to create an independent state and
the record of that state since 1947 shows a discon-
tinuity between its conceptual source--Islam--and the
actual functioning of political institutions. These
institutions are not of Islam in the sense they are
derived from it but are viewed in terms of their consistency with Islam. The state is always outside Islam

to a greater or lesser extent and thus never completely legitimate.

Pakistan's National Identity

While the antecedents of the Pakistan movement go back to the early Islamic conquerors of the subcontinent, organizationally the movement did not gain momentum until the founding of the Muslim League in 1906. In the same year, demands for separate seats in provincial legislatures for the Muslim constituency were granted in the Montagu-Chelmsford reforms. In 1908 the poet Iqbal articulated for the first time the idea of a separate homeland for Muslims. The suggestion was taken up by students at Cambridge University who called for an independent state for which they coined the name Pakistan. The distinction between Muslim and Hindu communities as a basis for two separate states was widely accepted in Muslim League circles by 1938. The idea was reiterated during the Sindhi provincial meeting of the League and finally adopted as the official League position in the Lahore Declaration of March 23, 1940. The Lahore Declaration, which was later cited by East Pakistan as a precedent for their demand for provincial autonomy, called for independent states based on Muslim numerical majorities and did not specifically envisage one single state.[35] The British recognized the possibility of partition as early as 1942. But apart from a general concern for domination by the Hindu majority, the great majority of rural Muslims did not share common characteristics of race, language, or culture.[36]

The politicization of the Muslim community came about as a consequence of three developments: various efforts at Islamic reform and revival during the late 19th and early 20th centuries, the impact of Hindu-based nationalism, and the democratization of the government of British India.[37] The Muslim community was faced with the need to catch up with other groups and to capture for itself a place in the rapidly developing national political arena. To achieve this an identity was developed based on communal awareness.

According to Binder, the concept of Pakistan as articulated in the Lahore Declaration was neither nationalistic nor Islamic. It was not nationalistic because it was aimed at Indian nationalism, and it was not Islamic because Islam was not taken as the basis of the political organization nor as defining its goals. In fact, "the resolution . . . can be perfectly well explained without reference to Islam, though not without reference to Muslims."[38]

The two-nation theory which stressed political communities defined in terms of Hindus and Muslims was no more than a tool of "political expediency."[39] Jinnah was opposed to a role for religion in politics. His successors resisted attempts by the clergy to achieve political influence while at the same time using religion and religious leaders for political purposes. Pakistan grew out of the political frustration experienced by League leaders for a share of political power. The two-nation theory and Islamic ideology matured under the impetus of this frustration rather than the other way around. The ideology of Pakistan "had no intellectual content until the ulema joined the Pakistan movement. No theoretical discussion, critical examination or detailed analysis of the bases of this ideology, or its implications for the state it was to give birth to, were allowed."[40]

Pakistan came into existence before its ideological base had been fully developed. Its essence, the "community of Islam" idea was, in practice, little more than a catch-word or slogan. The Muslim League considered the political universe to consist of a united India until 1940 when it began working for a separate state. Up until that time the Muslims were a special interest group or constituency within India rather than a distinctive separatist movement. Moreover, the eventual justification for this movement was communal rather than religious; that is, it was negative non-Hinduism clothed in the language of Muslim theological consciousness. The Pakistan movement, with an inchoate political philosophy, was closely tied to the Muslim League, a party that was led by politicians "who were almost totally secular."[41]

Having achieved independence on the basis of Islamic identity, it was not possible to ignore religion and develop an entirely secular political structure. Somehow the essentials of Islam had to be recognized and incorporated into a constitutional framework. To this end the Constituent Assembly appointed a Basic Principles Committee which in turn appointed a Board of Islamic Learning or Ta'limat-i-Islamiyya in 1949. This Board was to render advice on how to make the new constitution consistent with the principles of Islam. The Board attempted to translate the concept of the classical caliphate into the structure of the modern state. It recommended a presidential system with the choice of president in the hands of the leaders of the religious community, i.e., the ulema. A committee of experts would advise the president and the legislatures at the national and provincial levels. Most of these recommendations were rejected by the Assembly with the exception that the president be a Muslim. The views of the Board indicated the sense of the religious leaders that the political power of the state ought to be to a large extent in their hands.[42]

Attempts to incorporate Islam into a modern constitution proved consistently frustrating. Politically,

there were few contemporary lessons to draw upon.
Theories of the Islamic state are medieval in origin
and conception, ill-suited for the 20th century. Sayeed
notes: "it has never been made clear what concrete
shape this idea of an Islamic State should take."[43] It
is supposed to be based on the Islamic way of life, but
it may be asked in what specific political ways this
differs from the Christian, American, or Social
Democratic way of life. The political resurgence of
Islam witnessed most recently in Iran with the fall of
the Shah and the regime of the ayatollahs suggests that
the Islamic way of life differs most particularly in
that the superficial manifestations of "immortality"
present in Western societies are missing from Islam.
There is, of course, more substance to the issue than
that, but the problem has always been and remains defining the "political" dimensions of an Islamic state.

The case against following Western precedents was
strongly put by Maulana Maududi. Maududi and the party
he founded--the Jama'at-i-Islami--took an anti-Western
and anti-scientific position. In his view, the Islamic
state would operate at the highest moral level, i.e.,
as defined or revealed by God through his Prophet and
in the Quran. Western government and politics serve as
an inappropriate model because they have rejected trans-
cendant authority resulting in "the visibly growing
anarchy of Western society."[44] In the view of Maududi
and other traditionalists, Western man sees himself as
independent of God in secular matters, and thus his life
lacks a firm moral foundation. Since Islam is the only
correct basis for morality, acheivement of this morality
can only come about by avoiding Western practices.[45]

Maududi was concerned that Pakistan would be governed by a Westernized elite whose conception of government would be that of an "irreligious state like Turkey
and not that of an Islamic State." He felt that only
those versed in the Quran, the Sunnah, Islamic Law, and
Islamic history and also possessing "unstinted devotion
and loyalty to Islam and a deep awareness of account-
ability before God" should be entrusted with authority
in an Islamic state.[46]

To its members, the League was the manifestation
of Pakistan; it gave expression to the state. It was,
therefore, treason to oppose it. "During the national
liberation period the League, as the embodiment of Muslim nationalism had demanded total submission of Muslims
to its programme and leadership."[47] As time went on,
the League took on an increasingly West Pakistan character due to the fact that its leaders came from there
and also because it contained the capital city, first
Karachi and then Islamabad. The development of a
Pakistani nationalism with a broader base than Islamic
ideology was aborted by the military coup of 1958.
Qureshi suggests the Awami League could have been the

vehicle for promoting a greater sense of national identity and unity. "With the adroit handling of West
Pakistan by Suhrawardy and the work done by Mujib and
Bhashani in East Pakistan, the Awami League became a
popular national organization, poised for sure victory
in the prospective elections of 1959."[48] But the
elections were not held. Instead the military took
over, and the arena of political bargaining shifted
from political parties and parliament to the inner councils of the bureaucracy whose effectiveness rested on
the support of the army.

The abolition of the Constitution and the postponement of the first general election seem to
have been the main destroyers of the fledgling
Pakistani nationalism, for East Pakistan never
again became reconciled to the location of power
of the State in West Pakistan since this power was
used to deny East Pakistan what it considered its
rightful share of government.[49]

After the coup by Ayub Khan, the secularization of
Pakistan's politics proceeded rapidly. The new rulers
would make little effort to build the institutions of
the state upon the foundations of Islam, although lip
service was still paid to the importance of religion.
The new constitution written to Ayub's specifications
did not even include the term "Islamic state," although
as a result of public pressure it was later added by
amendment.
  Ayub's seizure of power was testimony to the fact
that Pakistan had not in 10 years of trying found its
political footing. The philosophical orientation of
the new government was secular, and its methods included
attempts to reorganize governmental structure and
improve administration. But the underlying social and
ideological differences that had produced a decade of
frustration had not been resolved. Thus, the new regime
was grafted onto a fragmented and only partly developed
base. Fundamental constitutional controversies and the
struggle for power which had been taking place in the
relatively open arenas of the press and the National
Assembly were shifted to the closed environment of the
military and the civil bureaucracy. This would ultimately prove insufficient, because the administrative
and military elites were ill-suited by temperament and
orientation to seek solutions that would satisfy important constituencies. Political dialogue took the form
of covert palace intrigue, which would eventually result
in a huge gap between the government and the society.[50]
  Ayub came to power threatening to purge the Civil
Service of Pakistan, and a few were actually dismissed.
The CSOP may have been initially frightened by the prospect of having its power diminished, thus encouraging

a cooperative spirit toward the military. The bureaucracy may also have viewed the Ayub "revolution" as preferable to a more sweeping upheaval from below. Initial efforts at administrative reform and reorganization improved efficiency. But the power of the CSOP was not diminished. In fact, "no administrative reorganization dared attack its privileged position."[51] The end result was an alliance between the small bureaucratic and military elites which would dominate the political process for the next decade.

Another institution which could have been useful for the development of a broader ideological base was the educational system. Inherited from the British, education offered significant potential for modernization. Moreover, education was already highly politicized and involved in the Pakistan movement. As has already been noted, Aligarh and Deoband were centers of development of Muslim political ideology. "Yet neither education nor the educational community were really used for the development of Pakistani nationalism."[52]

The lack of many capable political leaders would not only be a hindrance to governing but would restrict the growth of a rich heritage of heroes and myths, a necessary ingredient for any nationalism.[53] Misfortune such as the death of Jinnah early in the life of the country to be followed shortly by the assassination of Liaquat Ali removed the most renowned political leaders. No others of equal stature emerged to fill the gap. Politicians "played the game of parochialism exclusively for the advancement of personal or group interest."[54]

The events of 1971 probably dealt the concept of Muslim nationalism in Pakistan a serious and perhaps mortal blow. By its actions, East Bengal rejected the religious basis of nationalism. In other areas of the country such as Sindh, provincialism has lingered expressing itself, for example, in the Urdu-Sindh language riots. Likewise, local identity is important in the Northwest Frontier Province and Baluchistan.[55] But many national leaders have regarded provincialism as a threat and have never seemed able to build on it, preferring instead to work against it. The national government has tried to create a national identity by decree. One such effort occurred in 1956 when the four provinces of West Pakistan were merged into "one unit." According to Qureshi this "forcible merger. . . seems to have been a colossal mistake."[56] Persistent resistance to Bengali nationalism was an even greater mistake.

NOTES

1. Wayne Wilcox, "The Wellsprings of Pakistan," in Lawrence Ziring, et. al., (eds.) Pakistan: The Long

<u>View</u>, Durham: Duke University Press, 1977, pp. 25-34.

2. Peter Hardy, <u>The Muslims of British India</u>, London: Cambridge University Press, 1972, pp. 11-14.

3. <u>Ibid</u>., p. 27.

4. Ahmed Abdulla, <u>The Historical Background of Pakistan and Its People</u>, Karachi: Tanzeem Publishers, 1973, p. 172.

5. Donald Wilbur, <u>Pakistan: Its People, Its Society, Its Culture</u>, New Haven: Human Relations Area File, 1964, p. 13.

6. <u>Ibid</u>.

7. Freeland Abbott, <u>Islam and Pakistan</u>, Ithaca: Cornell University Press, 1968, p. 110.

8. Manvoorudin Ahmed, "Iqbal and Jinnah on the 'Two Nations' Theory," in C. M. Naim (ed.), <u>Iqbal, Jinnah and Pakistan; The Vision and the Reality</u>, Syracuse: Maxwell School of Citizenship and Public Affairs, 1979, 48-9.

9. Abbott, <u>Islam and Pakistan</u>, p. 111.

10. Aziz Ahmad, <u>Islamic Modernism in India and Pakistan; 1857-1964</u>, London: Royal Institute of International Affairs, 1967, p. 99.

11. S. Abul Maududi, <u>The Islamic Law and Constitution</u>, Lahore: Islamic Publications Ltd., 1980, p. 138.

12. <u>Ibid</u>., p. 139.

13. <u>Ibid</u>., p. 141.

14. <u>Ibid</u>., p. 147.

15. Kemal A. Faruki, <u>The Evolution of Islamic Constitutional Theory and Practice</u>, Karachi: National Publishing House, 1971, p. 70.

16. Abbott, <u>Islam and Pakistan</u>, p. 147.

17. Hardy, <u>The Muslims of British India</u>, p. 94.

18. <u>Ibid</u>., p. 138.

19. <u>Ibid</u>., p. 143.

20. Naim, "Afterward," in <u>Iqbal, Jinnah, and Pakistan</u>, pp. 177-78.

21. Saleem M.M. Qureshi, "Iqbal and Jinnah: Personalities, Perceptions, and Politics," in <u>Ibid</u>, p. 14.

22. Aziz Ahmad, <u>Islamic Modernism in India and Pakistan</u>, p. 155.

23. Quoted in <u>Ibid</u>., p. 163.

24. Hardy, <u>The Muslims of British India</u>, p. 164.

25. <u>Ibid</u>., p. 211.

26. Quoted in Abbott, <u>Islam and Pakistan</u>, p. 183.

27. <u>Ibid</u>.

28. <u>Ibid</u>., pp. 183-5.

29. <u>Ibid</u>., p. 185.

30. Hardy, <u>The Muslims of British India</u>, p. 223.

31. Saleem M. M. Qureshi, "Iqbal and Jinnah: Personalities, Perceptions and Politics," p. 14.

32. Aziz Ahmad, <u>Islamic Modernism in India and Pakistan</u>, p. 263.

33. <u>Ibid</u>., p. 204.

34. <u>Ibid</u>., p. 272; John L. Esposito, "Pakistan:

56

Quest for Islamic Identity," in John L. Esposito (ed.),
Islam and Development: Religion and Sociopolitical
Change, Syracuse: Syracuse University Press, 1980, p.
159.
    35. The Lahore Declaration stated: "Resolved that
it is the considered view of this session of the All-
India Muslim League that no constitutional plan would
be workable in this country or acceptable to Muslims
unless it is designed on the following principle, viz
that geographically contiguous units are demarcated into
regions which should be so constituted with such territorial readjustments as may be necessary, that the areas
in which the Muslims are numerically in a majority in
the northwest and eastern zones of India should be
grouped to constitute Independent States in which constituent units shall be autonomous and sovereign."
    36. Saleem M. M. Qureshi, "Pakistan Nationalism
Reconsidered," Pacific Affairs, (Winter, 1972-3) p. 557.
    37. Leonard Binder, "Pakistan and Modern Islamic
Nationalist Theory," The Middle East Journal, 11
(Autumn, 1857) 382.
    38. Leonard Binder, "Pakistan and Modern Islamic
Nationalist Theory, Part II," The Middle East Journal,
12 (Winter, 1958), 51.
    39. Qureshi, "Pakistan Nationalism Reconsidered,"
p. 561.
    40. Ibid., p. 562.
    41. Ibid., p. 558.
    42. Aziz Ahmad, "Activism of the Ulama in Pakistan,"
in Nikki R. Keddie (ed.) Scholars, Saints, and Sufis;
Muslim Religious Institutions in the Middle East Since
1500, Berkeley: University of California Press, 1972,
pp. 260-1.
    43. Khalid B. Sayeed, "The Jama'at-i-Islami Move-
ment in Pakistan," Pacific Affairs XXX (March, 1957),
59.
    44. Hamid Algar, "Islam and the Intellectual Chal-
lenge of Modern Civilization," in Altaf Gauhar (ed.),
The Challenge of Islam, London: Islamic Council of
Europe, 1978, p. 294.
    45. Freeland Abbott, "The Jama'at-i-Islami of Paki-
stan," The Middle East Journal 11 (Winter, 1957), p. 50.
    46. Sayeed, "The Jama'at-i-Islami Movement in Paki-
stan," p. 59; Maududi, The Islamic Law and Constitution,
p. 222.
    47. Qureshi, "Pakistan Nationalism Reconsidered,"
p. 563.
    48. Ibid., pp. 563-4.
    49. Ibid., p. 564.
    50. Albert Gorvine, "The Civil Service under the
Revolutionary Government in Pakistan," The Middle East
Journal, 19 (Summer, 1965) 324.
    51. Ibid.
    52. Qureshi, "Pakistan Nationalism Reconsidered,"

p. 565.

53. R. M. MacIver, The Web of Government (rev. ed) New York: The Free Press, 1965, p. 30. "Myth is the all-pervading atmosphere of society, the air it breathes."

54. Qureshi, "Pakistan Nationalism Reconsidered," p. 568.

55. Ibid., p. 569.

56. Ibid.

4
Constitutional Problems:
Government in Concept

Frustrations of Constitution Making

The problems of defining Pakistan as a political entity manifested themselves during the prolonged efforts to draft a constitution. It had been much easier to think of the advantages of an independent state for Muslims than it was to delineate the institutional characteristics of such a state.

The task of writing a constitution establishing and defining the political order proved to be difficult. While India took three years to produce its constitution, Pakistan took 10. India is still using its original constitution; Pakistan's first constitution lasted less than three years. Two subsequent constitutions also failed. During the period when the first constitution was being drafted, political confusion was a constant companion. There were frequent leadership crises, growing tension between the two wings, and the intractable problem of Kashmir.

Like many countries, Pakistan had its founding father. Mohammed Ali Jinnah enjoyed immense personal popularity and dominated the political scene. Jinnah's role was much like that of Jawaharlal Nehru in India. But unlike Nehru, Jinnah did not become Prime Minister. He chose instead the office of Governor General, in effect the successor to the viceroy. In this way, Jinnah may have tried to place himself above politics. But by this action, the prestige of the country's strongest political figure was withheld from the fledgling government. The Governor General could only be a transitional figure or a symbolic head of state; to make more of the office would only complicate the process of institution-building. Jinnah established a precedent whereby personality was more important than institutions. Moreover, during the 1950's the political activism of the Governor General in competition with the Prime Minister would add to political confusion. To make matters worse, Jinnah's demise in 1948 deprived the country of his charisma and leadership and placed the burden of governance on a political arrangement that had only been defined in barest outline. A second jolt was received in October 1951 when the second most prestigious political figure after Jinnah, Prime Minister Liaquat Ali Khan, was assassinated.

The years following the deaths of Jinnah and Liaquat Ali were marked by fragmentation and intense individual efforts to achieve power. Liaquat Ali was succeeded by Khwaja Nazimuddin who had succeeded Jinnah as Governor General. Ghulam Mohammed became the new Governor General. In 1953, during the political crisis of that year, the Governor General dismissed the Prime Minister. Ghulam Mohammed himself appointed the next Prime Minister, Mohammed Ali, and also chose most of his cabinet. Mohammed Ali, like Nazimuddin, was a Bengali. This maneuvering among East and West Pakistani politicians was a small part of a larger constitutional issue: the determination of the relative importance of the two wings of the country.

In the early 1950's the Bengalis began protesting that their status in the federation was inferior to that of the West wing. Despite the fact that many top offices in the government fell to Bengalis during that time, they contended that the affairs of the country were controlled by West Pakistan. There was a fundamental disagreement over the direction of economic policy. The Bengalis pointed to chronic poverty and generally backward economic conditions in East Pakistan and demanded that national resources be used to bring the standard of living up to that of the West wing. In the West, on the other hand, it was argued that national resources should be invested in those areas which would bring the greatest return in the shortest period of time. In general, the Bengalis felt that they were being treated as second class citizens. Even as early as the first Constituent Assembly, a Bengali Delegate stated:

> Sir, I...said that the attitude of the Muslim League coterie here was of contempt toward East Bengal, toward its culture, its language, its literature, and everything concerning East Bengal...In fact, sir, I tell you that far from considering East Bengal as an equal partner, the leaders of the Muslim League thought that we were a subject race and they belonged to the race of conquerors.[1]

In the midst of this uncertainty, Pakistan attempted to draft a constitution. Like India, Pakistan's constitutional heritage is derived from the British colonial experience. By a process that began during the latter part of the 19th century, the British moved slowly toward institutionalization of self-rule in the subcontinent. In measured steps, India's participation in its own government was increased through a system of consultative assemblies or councils, members of which were at first mostly official government nominees. In the Indian Councils Act of 1909, representation of important Indian interests was increased, six special constituencies were created for Muslims in the Imperial Legislative Council, and similar "reserved seats" were established in some of the provinces.[2] In the Government of India Act of 1919, self-government was accepted as the goal of British policy. The Act created a bicameral legislature at the national level and set in motion a federalizing process by providing for the division of authority between the national legislature and the provincial assemblies. The Government of India Act of 1935 firmly established the federal principle and set the constitutional pattern to be followed by India and Pakistan. This Act provided the initial constitutional framework for Pakistan until the enactment of the constitution of 1956. The drafting of the constitution was assigned to a Constituent Assembly selected by the provincial assemblies meeting as electoral colleges. One member was chosen for every one million people. Representatives from princely states were selected by the rulers of the states. Since the Muslim League dominated the areas included in Pakistan, only those persons sympathetic to the League were selected.[3] While the Constituent Assembly was to function in an independent Pakistan, the provincial legislatures had been elected in 1945-46 and at that time had no idea that they would be called upon later to select a Constituent Assembly.

The Constituent Assembly, consisting of 69 members later raised to 79, first met in Karachi on August 10, 1947. It was assigned a dual responsibility--to draft a constitution and to serve as a legislative body--until a government was created under the new constitution. The same people were involved in each activity, including the same officers, but the rules of procedure were different.

Although small in numbers, the Assembly often had poor attendance. Since short sessions were frequent, members traveling great distances--from the Northwest Frontier Province or East Bengal--did not find it worth their while to spend the many hours necessary for traveling back and forth in order to attend the meetings. Moreover, many members of the Assembly were officeholders in other parts of the government, such as ambassadors, provincial officials, and bureaucrats. It was common for the various provincial legislatures to select from among their own membership to serve in the Constituent Assembly. This meant a confusing overlap of various responsibilities. The deliberations of the

Assembly received very little exposure in the press, and the public was thus uninformed about the constitution-drafting process. A base of popular support for the eventual constitution was not developed.[4]

It was soon evident that the differences between the East and West wings would create serious obstacles. The representatives from East Pakistan were particularly concerned that the constitution provide a government, especially a legislative branch, that would recognize and accommodate its numerical majority. There was also the issue of different languages and disagreements over which would be the national language. Many in West Pakistan, including the Muslim League, strongly favored Urdu as the national language. The point was urged by Jinnah himself:

> But let me make it very clear to you that the State language of Pakistan is going to be Urdu and no other language. Anyone who tries to mislead you is really the enemy of Pakistan. Without one State language, no nation can remain tied up solidly together and function.[5]

This meant that Bengalis would have to learn what amounted to a foreign language in addition to their native language--Bengali--plus English.

In March 1949 the Assembly adopted an "objectives resolution" which stressed the importance of Islam as the source of constitutional principles. The ultimate sovereignty of Allah was acknowledged "and the authority which he has delegated to the State of Pakistan through its people for being within the limits prescribed by him is a sacred trust...." This suggests two things: a tentative commitment to popular sovereignty but limited in ways prescribed by Allah. The second clause described a "sovereign independent state of Pakistan" apparently meaning sovereign in the sense of the community of nations. The third clause stated that the "principles of democracy, freedom, equality, tolerance, and social justice as enunciated by Islam shall by fully observed." Again the delineation of these concepts takes place within the context of Islam. The fourth clause states "Muslims shall be enabled to order their lives in the individual and collective spheres in accord with the teachings and requirements of Islam as set out in the Holy Quran and the Sunnah." The spiritual and secular lives of Pakistani Muslims (and necessarily non-Muslims) would be governed by the tenets of Islam. Non-Muslims are covered in a clause which stated: "adequate provision shall be made for the minorities freely to profess and practice their religions and develop their cultures." Here there is a practical problem of who decides what is "adequate." The remaining clauses provided for a federal system with the provinces having autonomy; safeguards for minorities, backward, and depressed classes; and an independent judiciary.[6]

In September 1950 the Committee issued an "interim report" calling for a bicameral federal legislature with equal representation in the upper house for the two wings and representation based on population in the lower. Representatives in either chamber were to serve five-year terms. The head of state would be selected by the legislature. Provincial governments would parallel the national, except they would have unicameral legislatures. The report also recommended Urdu as the national language. In July 1952 the "final report" was presented. Changes included equal representation of the two wings in the legislature and no national language was mentioned. To insure the Islamic integrity of government, an ulema of five authorities on Islamic jurisprudence would pass on the religious legality of all laws except those involving money. Ulemas would function at both the national and provincial levels.[7]

Agreement on constitutional language remained elusive, and political confusion mounted. The Governor General, Ghulam Mohammed, who drew his authority from the Government of India Act of 1935, as did the Constituent Assembly, attempted to move the process along by changing the cabinet. The new Prime Minister, Mohammed Ali Bogra, tried to break the impasse by again suggesting the compromise of equal representation in the upper house and proportional representation in the lower in order to meet the objectives of the East wing. Also, he suggested the President and the Prime Minister should come from different wings, and the Supreme Court, rather than a religious group, should pass on the Islamic integrity of legislation.

Meanwhile, the Constituent Assembly passed the Constitution Amendment Act of 1954 which gave all constitution-making authority to itself, prohibited federal courts from passing on laws enacted by the Assembly, and withdrew the authority of the Governor General to dissolve the Constituent Assembly. Acting as a legislature, the Assembly took other actions objectionable to the Governor General, in particular the repeal of the Public and Representative Offices (Disqualification) Act, which was much favored by the Governor General and provincial governors as a tool to control government officials. PRODA provided that government officials found guilty of misconduct in office could be disqualified by order of the Governor General from holding any public office for a period not to exceed 10 years. In response the Governor General dismissed the Assembly on October 24.

Later the Supreme Court not only upheld the Governor General's action but went even further and declared all 44 acts passed by the Assembly invalid be-

cause they had not received the assent of the Governor
General as provided under the Indian Independence Act
of 1947, Section 6. These 44 acts were in effect
amendments to the interim constitution, the Government
of India Act of 1935. The Court further held that as a
legislative body, the Constituent Assembly was acting
unconstitutionally, thus making all laws invalid. The
same applied to provincial legislation. Ghulam Mohammed
tried to validate 33 of the 44 acts, but there was some
question if he had the authority to do so. Consequently, he validated them under his emergency powers,
pending approval by a new Constituent Assembly which he
then set about creating. The Court upheld such "temporary" actions and on May 25, 1955, the Governor General
called for elections to the second Constituent Assembly
to consist of 80 members equally divided between the
two wings.[8] Meanwhile, the political situation became
increasingly unstable. In the elections of 1954, the
Muslim League in East Bengal was repudiated, resulting
in another round of personnel changes.

The second Constituent Assembly, like the first,
was indirectly elected. All members from the East were
selected by the Provincial Assembly, itself chosen in
March 1954. This election marked a major turn of
events. The Muslim League, which had commanded a majority in the East Pakistan Assembly, was reduced to 10
seats and all but destroyed as an effective party. In
the West a variety of selection procedures were used.
Thirty-one members were chosen by the Assemblies. Four
were elected by the Tribal Advisory Council of the
Northwest Frontier Province. Municipal governments
chose two persons.[9]

While the second Constituent Assembly involved
many new faces and reflected some of the changes in the
political environment, it functioned much like its predecessor. The same people served simultaneously as
members of a Constituent Assembly engaged in a constitution-writing process and as members of a national
legislature conducting ordinary legislative business.
Functioning as a legislature was nearly as unsuccessful
in the second Assembly as it had been in the first.

The second Constituent Assembly first met on July
7, 1955, and immediately passed the Validation of Laws
Act of 1955 which repassed 38 Acts of the first
Assembly. The Governor General, General Iskander Mirza,
assented to these in October. The most important Act
of this body was the West Pakistan Act of 1955 which
replaced the four units of the West with the "one-unit
scheme." The tribal areas remained under central
government jurisdiction. With the problem of gross
disproportion between the East Wing and the smaller
provinces in the West removed, a constitution was
enacted on January 9, 1956. The Governor General gave
his assent on March 2, and the constitution came into

effect March 23. The Awami League opposed it on the grounds that the central government should have authority only over foreign affairs, defense and currency.

The Constitution of 1956

The preamble of the constitution restated the principles of the "objectives resolution" of 1949. Similar language would be contained in the 1962 and 1973 constitutions. Under the 1956 constitution, a strong executive-type regime was established. The President, who had to be a Muslim at least 40 years of age, served a five-year term and could be re-elected once. The President was not to be chosen directly by the voters but rather by an electoral college consisting of the members of the National and Provincial Assemblies. The President could be impeached by a three-fourths vote of the National Assembly. The Prime Minister, who held the real power, and other ministers of the cabinet were appointed by the President from among members of the National Assembly. The independence of the President was restricted by the requirement that he act in accordance with the advice of the cabinet. He possessed veto power over legislation which could be overridden by a two-thirds vote of the members of the National Assembly present and voting. Alternatively, he could suggest amendments to bills which required a majority of the total membership of the Assembly for approval. No money bills could be introduced in the Assembly except on the recommendation of the President. When the Assembly was not in session, the President was authorized to issue ordinances which carried the force of law. However, these ordinances expired after six weeks from the beginning of the Assembly session. The President possessed the authority to issue a proclamation of emergency if the security or the economic life of the country were threatened or if internal disturbances proved to be beyond the capacity of provincial governments to control. Under an emergency proclamation the President could suspend fundamental rights. Such proclamations had to be laid before the National Assembly after two months but could be extended for up to four months more by the Assembly.

The legislative branch, a unicameral body called the National Assembly, consisted of 300 members equally divided between the two wings of the country. Ten additional seats were reserved for women for a period of 10 years after the promulgation of the constitution. The term of office for members of the Assembly was five years unless dissolved by the President. At least two sessions were to be held each year with no more than six months between sessions. At least one session per year was to be held in Dacca, East Pakistan.

The constitution envisaged an independent judiciary consisting of a Supreme Court and provincial High Courts. The Supreme Court, composed of a Chief Justice and six judges, was appointed by the President. Judges could be removed by a two-thirds vote of the National Assembly for misbehavior or infirmity. The Supreme Court had original jurisdiction to issue declaratory judgments on "any question as to the interpretation of the constitution" involved in disputes among governments in the federal system. Provincial High Courts, whose members were also appointed by the President, handled appellate matters from lower courts and were also authorized to consider matters of constitutionality.

The constitution contained a lengthy list of fundamental rights to be guaranteed by the judiciary which could issue orders requiring compliance. For the most part, however, the significance of these civil rights was compromised by language in most clauses stating that the right is "subject to any reasonable restrictions imposed by law." Moreover, under emergency powers of the President, fundamental rights could be suspended. Access to public places could not be denied on the basis of race, religion, caste, sex or place of birth, although "nothing in this Article shall prevent the making of special provision for women."

Pakistan has consistently defined itself as a federal system. Under the 1956 constitution, this federation consisted of only two provinces, an arrangement which no doubt accounts for much of the political difficulty that would follow. The constitution provided three separate lists of authority: federal, concurrent, and provincial. There were 30 items under the federal list, including such things as defense, foreign affairs, coinage, ports, and similar matters of national interest. The 19 items on the concurrent list included the substantive areas of public policy, like civil and criminal law and economic activities. There were 94 items on the provincial list, including public order, land and other forms of ownership, education, and issues of general public welfare. Such substantial provincial authority apparently free from federal interference was not a feature of later constitutions.

In the event of conflict between national and provincial laws, the national prevailed. An exception was where action taken under the concurrent list, while in conflict with an act of the National Assembly but approved by the President, could prevail in the province concerned. The National Assembly could take specific action to repeal or amend such provincial acts, however.

The structure of the provincial governments parallelled that at the national level. The Governor was appointed by the President and served at his pleasure. The Governor in turn appointed the provincial cabinet and Chief Minister. Each Provincial Assembly consisted of 300 members plus 10 seats for women reserved for 10 years.

All of Pakistan's constitutions have contained the injunction that no law shall be enacted which is repugnant to the Quran or the Sunnah. However, no precise mechanism was spelled out in the 1956 constitution giving effect to this provision. The constitution called for the establishment of a commission to recommend measures for bringing existing laws into conformity with Islam and to suggest legislative efforts to give effect to the injunctions of Islam. Other Islamic features of the constitution included the designation of the country as an Islamic Republic and the assignment of ultimate sovereignty to Allah.

The constitution could be amended by a two-thirds vote of the National Assembly, provided this included at least a majority of the total membership.

The constitution was deemed in force on February 29, 1956. Although no ratification procedure was prescribed, legitimation of the document was provided by the statement: "we the people of Pakistan in our Constituent Assembly. . . do hereby adopt, enact, and give to ourselves this Constitution." While this is a fairly clear and straightforward statement of popular sovereignty, it was limited by Islamic Provisions.

While it took 10 years to draft the constitution, it lasted little more than two and a half years. The new order came into being at a most difficult time. After a period of favorable economic activity brought on mainly by the Korean War, Pakistan's import-export balance declined, as did agricultural productivity. Corruption and nepotism were rampant, and quarrels over provincial autonomy worsened. Under these conditions, the constitutional process never worked properly. Elections were postponed, and in the midst of unending bickering, President Iskander Mirza, himself an army man, declared martial law and appointed General Ayub Khan Chief Martial Law Administrator on October 9, 1958. (Of all offices in the political history of Pakistan, this has proven to be the most durable.) Mirza probably delayed too long in reaching an understanding with the army, which might have allowed the constitutional process to survive. But by the time he acted it was too late. On October 27 Ayub staged a coup and assumed the presidency himself. Iskander Mirza was flown off to pensioned exile. On February 17, 1960, President Ayub appointed a commission to draft a new constitution.

The Constitution of 1962

Political instability during the 1950's had created conditions whereby the army, willingly or not, was drawn into the political process. Military intervention of some sort appeared necessary to rescue the country from political chaos. The armies of India and Pakistan are closely identified with the British tradition of high professional standards and a non-political orientation. Praetorianism does not come naturally to such military systems. Wheeler notes: "the imposition of martial law in 1958 was in large part a preventive action on the part of General Ayub Khan and his colleagues who stopped the process of political decay before it could undermine the integrity of the army itself."[10] Whether it was necessary to scrap the constitution was another matter. This action did, however, start an unfortunate precedent.

Mohammed Ayub Khan, a graduate of Sandhurst and temperamentally and in physical appearance very much a product of the British Army, abrogated the constitution of 1956 and suspended all political activity. Political parties were declared illegal, the national and provincial assemblies were dissolved, and a campaign was launched against corruption and misconduct by former government officials. Measures were taken to stimulate industrial growth and to increase agricultural productivity. The success of the latter effort in East Pakistan contributed to Ayub's strong showing in the election of 1965.

Ayub felt that Pakistan's political inexperience and peculiar problems demanded something less than full-fledged democracy. His scheme for a stable and workable political structure was called Basic Democracy. This system, set forth in the Basic Democracies Order of October 27, 1959, called for the establishment of a multi-tiered political arrangement based upon several thousand local political units or Basic Democracies selected by popular elections. Each Basic Democracy comprised a constituency of between 1000 and 1200 people. The first election of Basic Democrats took place in December 1959 and January 1960.

The Basic Democracy system was composed of four tiers. Basic Democrats were elected to the lowest level called Union Councils in the rural areas and Town and Union Councils in urban areas, hereafter referred collectively as Union Councils. Each of these units was composed of approximately 15 members, 10 of whom were elected Basic Democrats. The remaining five members were appointed by the government. These units were intended to play an active role in administration of public affairs. They were assigned the task of agricultural, industrial and community development within their jurisdiction. In addition, they had the responsibility of maintaining law and order, and each Council possessed some judicial powers to take care of minor civil and criminal cases. To enable these units to perform their duties, they were given the power of taxation to raise funds at the local level.

In addition to these rather extensive and ambitious responsibilities, the elected members of the Union Councils served as an electoral college for the selection of the President and the members of the National and Provincial Assemblies. This system of indirect election was employed in the presidential and assembly elections of 1964-65.

The next highest level was the Thana Councils in East Pakistan and the Tehsil Councils in West Pakistan. These Councils were not as important in a functional sense as the Union Councils, in that they were not assigned specific responsibilities. To the extent that they operated at all, they seemed to perform more of a coordinating function. Membership of the Thanas and the Tehsils was composed of an equal number of government appointees and representatives of the Union Councils, all of whom were chairmen of the respective bodies.

The third rung of the Basic Democracy system was composed of the District Councils. These were assigned the responsibility of maintaining public services such as primary schools, roads, bridges, and related matters. Further, the District Councils were entrusted with the responsibility of promoting economic development, particularly at the village level. The District Councils were composed of an equal number of government appointees and elected members, at least 50 percent of the latter coming from among the chairmen of the Union Councils drawn from the Tehsil/Thana level.

The highest level in the four-tiered system was the Divisional Councils. But these were not assigned any particularly distinct activities. The Divisional Councils were composed of 45 members and like the District Councils were composed of half government appointees and half elected members. Of the non-official members, at least 50 percent were chairmen of Union Concils drawn from the district level.

The Basic Democracy scheme of Ayub Khan was a gradualist approach to the development of a democratic political system. In a sense, the scheme was a combination of traditional panchayat government and Jeffersonian democracy. The emphasis upon local initiative and autonomy was probably a realistic appraisal of political and economic realities. Accordingly, an attempt to build funtional democratic institutions at this level makes a great deal of sense. Ayub recognized that any attempt to move quickly into a completely democratic arrangement would probably run into difficulty due to Pakistan's political immaturity. The experience from 1946 to 1958 suggested that a workable democratic order would not be achieved merely by the promulgation of a constitution.

On February 17, 1960, Ayub appointed a Constitution

Commission and gave it explicit instructions on the type of order he wanted, including the Basic Democracies. Ayub had recieved a mandate from the Basic Democrats on February 14, 1960, to carry out such a constitutional process and to accept the result upon completion, which he did on March 1, 1962.

The constitution created a Republic of Pakistan excluding the word "Islamic" which had been contained in the 1956 document. However, the term was inserted as a result of the First Amendment Act of 1963, a significant victory for the ulema and a defeat for those favoring secularization of politics. In the new constitution, elements of the 1956 document were combined with the Basic Democracies framework to which were added practices drawn from parliamentary and presidential systems.

The executive was even stronger than that envisaged under the 1956 constitution. The President was chosen by the Basic Democrats functioning as an electoral college. The term of office was five years, and the incumbent had to be a Muslim at least 35 years of age. Should the President, for whatever reason, decide to resign, he could do so by informing the Speaker of the National Assembly in writing. It is significant to note that Ayub violated this principle himself when he resigned in 1969, turning power over to the army. The President could be removed by action of the National Assembly. First, one-third of the members must move for removal for violation of the constitution or gross misconduct. Three-fourths of the total membership of the Assembly must then approve. Should fewer than half of the total membership vote in favor of removal, then the original one-third would cease to be members of the Assembly.

The President had complete executive authority. He appointed the Council of Ministers, who were not members of the Assembly, and the advice of this body was in no way binding on him. Very little legislation could be introduced in the Assembly without his consent. During time of war or internal disturbances, he had the power to declare an emergency. Ordinances issued during an emergency were not subject to Assembly disapproval. The President was authorized to suspend fundamental rights during an emergency.

The legislative branch consisted of a single chamber National Assembly made up of 156 members equally divided between the two wings. Three seats were reserved for women. The term of office was five years, although the Assembly could be dissolved sooner by the President. The President possessed the usual veto powers, but an added feature made it possible in the event of disagreement between the President and the Assembly for the President to refer the matter to the electoral college in the form of a question capable of

a yes or no answer. A presidential veto could be overridden, in which case the bill would also be referred
to the electoral college. If two-thirds of the Assembly
disapproved amendments proposed by the President, they
were also referred to the electoral college. Ordinances
issued by the President during a period when the Assembly was not in session were subject to Assembly approval
and could last no longer than 180 days unless approved.
All proposals for expenditure of money originated with
the President, and the Assembly only had power to refuse
or decrease an amount, not increase it.

The judicial system was little changed under the
1962 constitution, except the Supreme Court did not
have authority over matters of constitutionality. "The
validity of a law shall not be called in question on
the ground that the legislature by which it was made
had no power to make the law." The President, who
appointed judges, could also remove them as well as
ministers without giving reasons.

Fundamental rights were spelled out in a lengthy
section, although it was more general than the 1956
version. Again, rights were "subject to any reasonable
restrictions imposed by law." New provisions included
guarantees of distinct language, script, or culture.
As a concession to East Pakistan, Urdu and Bengali were
both recognized as national languages.

The 1962 document was much less specific than its
predecessor had been in defining national and provincial authority. The national government had its authority spelled out, while the provinces retained everything else. The most critical feature was that most
taxing power was held by the center.

The provincial governments also reflected the considerable importance of the President. Each Provincial
Assembly had 155 members, of whom five seats were reserved for women. The President appointed the Governor
and could remove him without giving reasons. While the
Governor possessed veto powers over provincial legislation, in the event of override by the Assembly, he
could refer the matter to the National Assembly. If
the National Assembly, with the concurrence of the
President, supported such a call by the Governor, the
Provincial Assembly could be dissolved. But the Assembly could not be dissolved otherwise.

Initially the constitution had little to say about
Islam apart from establishing a Council of Islamic Ideology which was only advisory in "enabling and encouraging the Muslims of Pakistan to order their lives in
all respects in accordance with the principles and concepts of Islam." An Islamic Research Institute was
also provided which assisted the Council and also acted
on its own to disseminate Islamic ideas. Over the life
of the 1962 constitution, the Council, which was dominated by conservatives, and the Institute, which

espoused modernist views, were frequently in conflict.[11] However, the First Amendment Act of 1963 gave the Council added responsibility for examining all laws extant before 1963 with the view of bringing them into conformity with Islam. The repugnancy clause was reinstated, and the Council was to advise which laws failed to meet the test. The amendment required that facilities be provided to enable Muslims to live their lives in accordance with Islam, and Islamiyat (religious instruction) should be compulsory.

The constitution could be amended by two-thirds vote of the National Assembly and concurrence of the President. If the Assembly favored an amendment but the President did not, the issue could be referred to the electoral college for final decision. During its 10-year lifespan, the 1962 constitution was amended on four occasions.

The constitution came into force when the National Assembly held its first meeting on June 8, 1962. Like its predecessor, there was no ratification process. Instead, the constitution was "enacted" by Ayub Khan under a mandate given him by the people on February 14, 1960. On that occasion the Basic Democrats had voted in favor of his request for authority to draft a new constitution.

The political arrangement devised by Ayub Khan was intended to be both a political system capable of growing and developing and at the same time an organizational vehicle for economic development. The various levels of the system plus their key role as an electoral college recognized existing political influences and leaders. The Basic Democrats could be influential at the level of the village or town--a universe with which they were familiar. As political questions grew broader in scope, the people became less and less familiar with their dimensions, and under the Basic Democracy system their influence was reduced. National problems would be handled by the government, which was only indirectly responsible to the voters. This is how the system was supposed to operate, in theory, at least.

While everyone seems to want one, very few countries are able to make a legislative system work effectively. The National Assembly was hampered by lack of experience, and its members were unable to engage in the persuasive and coalition-building efforts necessary in law-making. The Assembly also had limited financial power, which, of course, reduced its overall significance. Finally, it was dominated by the government party, which was unwilling to tolerate or deal constructively with an opposition.[12]

Pakistan's politics were dominated by uncompromising and self-serving political elites that had very little popular support. Members of the National Assembly from West Pakistan were predominantly land-

quality was missing. Ultimately unable to withstand stress, the system collapsed.

The Constitution of 1973

The constitutional crisis of 1970-71 ended in complete disaster.[14] The immediate result of free elections and democratic politics was the independence of Bangladesh. Now Zulfiqar Ali Bhutto, the party he headed--the Pakistan People's Party--and an elected assembly set about the task of picking up the political pieces and putting the country back together again. While the 1962 constitution had been abrogated by General Yahya Khan when he took over from Ayub Khan, the civil war had interrupted the process of writing a new one. Nevertheless, the National Assembly, that is, the 150 seats allocated to the West wing which had been elected in 1970 on the basis of Yahya's Legal Framework Order, now served as the Constituent Assembly. On April 14, 1972, this group met to begin work on Pakistan's third constitution in 25 years.

While this work was going on, an interim constitution based on martial law regulations prevailed. This interim arrangement provided for a presidential system at the national level and a parliamentary system at the provincial level. The President possessed considerable power, although there were provisions to override his veto and for his impeachment. In the provinces, no-confidence votes against the chief ministers were disallowed unless a successor was named.

The Assembly met again in August, but the drafting committee had not completed its work. Two issues delayed the process: whether the system should be presidential or parliamentary and the extent to which the provinces should enjoy autonomy. It would be a severe test of Bhutto's political skills to gain the strong central government he wanted and to enlist the support of opposition parties at the same time. Bhutto acceded to the demand that the executive, in theory at least, be responsible to the legislature. In return he extracated a provision which made it very difficult for no-confidence motions to succeed. Legislative control over budget matters were also restricted.

The result was a constitution that differed in some fundamental ways from its predecessors. It called for a parliamentary system, departing from the strong presidential format used before. A greater measure of provincial autonomy was envisaged than had existed before, although this proved illusory. Bhutto would increasingly view provincial autonomy as tantamount to separatism. A strong commitment to political rights was not fulfilled either because of Bhutto's efforts to extend the authority of the central government and his suspicion of political opposition. Finally, the

1973 constitution for the first time made Islam the
state religion of Pakistan.

The new order followed the conventional parliamentary pattern. The head of state was the President
chosen for a five-year term by the national legislature.
The office had no specific powers except the granting
of pardons. In this and in every other activity, the
President was required to act on the advice of the Prime
Minister. The President could be removed by a two-
thirds vote of the parliament.

The actual executive power was in the hands of the
Prime Minister selected by a majority of the National
Assembly. The Prime Minister in turn selected all
other ministers who themselves had to be members of
parliament, but only one-fourth could be members of the
Senate. All must be Muslims. A no-confidence vote in
the Prime Minister must name another member of the
Assembly as successor. No-confidence resolutions could
not be moved during the budget debate. For 10 years or
until the second general election, whichever was longer,
a member of a party who voted for a no-confidence resolution without the majority support of his party had his
vote disregarded. This measure was intended to give
added stability to the government and to promote party
solidarity.

As with previous constitutions, the executive was
given special powers. When parliament and the provincial assemblies were not in session, the President and
the provincial Governors could issue ordinances which
expired after three months, or sooner if disapproved by
the legislature. If the President (meaning the Prime
Minister) decided that security was threatened or internal disturbances were beyond the capacity of provincial governments to control, he could declare an
emergency. While the authority of the parliament remained intact during an emergency, the provincial
governments including the High Courts, could be taken
over by the central government. Fundamental rights
could also be suspended. Emergencies were to be sub-
mitted to parliament within 30 days and expired in two
months unless approved. If the National Assembly stood
dissolved at the time of a declaration of emergency, it
could be approved by the Senate, in which case it could
last four months.

For the first time, the legislative branch consisted of two houses--the National Assembly and the
Senate. The latter added somewhat to the importance of
the provinces. The Assembly consisted of 200 members
elected by universal franchise and apportioned among
the provinces on the basis of population. For 10 years
or until the second general election, whichever occur-
ed later, 10 additional seats were allocated to women.
Six additional seats were allocated to non-Muslim
minorities. These 16 seats would be filled by persons

lords, whereas those from the East were mainly lawyers
and businessmen. While the traditional landed gentry
had all but disappeared in East Pakistan, feudal families still dominated the social, political and economic
life of the West wing. These same families derived the
greatest benefits from the economic development of the
country. For such a small group of people, and from
one wing of the country at that, to enjoy disproportionate advantages would eventually lead to trouble.

The failures in political development were exacerbated by successes in economic development. During the
Ayub years especially, Pakistan had been a showpiece of
economic growth among emerging nations. Industrialization proceeded rapidly, and by 1968 manufactured goods
were earning considerable foreign exchange. During the
late 1960's steps were made to redress the economic
imbalances among the provinces. Economic growth especially favored the Punjab and Karachi. The electoral
system contained within the Basic Democracy scheme
worked in at least one election, that of 1964-65. But
a combination of modernization and political ineptness
brought an end to the Basic Democracy experiment and
the regime of Ayub Khan in 1969.

As is often the case, economic growth, even growth
as large as that experienced by Pakistan, does not satisfy popular demands. Instead, as standards of living
improve and as economic and social mobility increase,
demands accelerate. The more Pakistan industrialized,
the more it was confronted by unrest among the workers.
The more the educational system was expanded and educational opportunities increased, the more student difficulties occurred. As strictures on political activities
were relaxed, the more chaos resulted in the political
arena. It was particularly unfortunate that the opposition parties refused to accept the verdict of the
1965 election. A characteristic of underdeveloped
political systems is the unwillingness to accept and
live with defeat. Instead of accepting the verdict of
the 1965 election and working to build a more effective
opposition to Ayub's rule through the mechanisms of
legitimate political activity, the opposition to Ayub
took the form of violence, disorder, and extra-legal
actions. Administrative effectiveness was hampered by
a tendency toward overcentralization. Efforts by Ayub
to shift more responsibility to provincial levels met
with some success, but the process was slow.[13]

On paper the Ayubian system looked good. There
was strength at the center to insure stability, a
measure of democracy which could grow over time, and
some discretionary authority at the provincial level.
But the system did not evolve or grow because the people
who ran it and derived benefit from it prevented it
from doing so. While in many respects political activity during Ayub's tenure was effective, a dynamic

chosen by the elected members of the Assembly. A curious arrangement, to say the least, this would have Muslims selecting representatives of non-Muslims. The term of office was five years unless the Assembly were dissolved earlier.

The Senate consisted of 63 members, of whom 14 were elected by each Provincial Assembly, five were chosen by the members of the tribal areas serving in the National Assembly, and two from the federal capital were chosen in a manner determined by the President. Selection from the provinces was by a system of proportional representation, using the method of a single transferrable vote. The term of office was four years, and the Senate was not subject to dissolution.

All bills originating under Part I of the Federal list, which included important ones like defense, currency, and education, had to originate in the Assembly. The Senate had 90 days to accept, reject, or amend bills passed by the Assembly. Failure to act within the 90 days was taken as acceptance. The Assembly did not have to accept action by the Senate. All bills introduced under the Concurrent List and those under Part II of the Federal List could originate in either house. The most important of the latter concerned industrial development. Bills of this type which were rejected or amended by either house were reconsidered in a joint session and could be passed by a majority vote of the total membership of the joint session. Money bills were only considered by the Assembly, and all such bills required the prior consent of the government, i.e., the Prime Minister and the cabinet.

The judiciary, following earlier precedents, consisted of a Supreme Court, High Courts and various inferior courts. The Supreme Court had the usual original jurisdiction on cases of dispute between governments or issues involving fundamental rights. It also had appellate jurisdiction, including cases certified by a High Court as involving a "substantial question of a law as to the interpretation of the Constitution." Judges were appointed by the President after consultation with the Chief Justice and, in the case of the High Courts, with the Governor and the Chief Justice of the High Court. Since confirmation was not required, this arrangement gave the executive considerable leverage over the judiciary. Judges could be removed on recommendation of the Judicial Council for misconduct as defined by a code of conduct developed by the Council.

Pakistan has always been nominally a federal system but has never really functioned as one. Under the 1973 constitution, the importance of the provinces was enhanced somewhat. This has been a persistent constitutional issue which led eventually to the succession of the East wing. But the smaller provinces of the West wing have also tried to avoid domination by the Punjab, the traditional center of power. This would be a major issue during the Bhutto years and remains so today. After 1972 the central government retained its dominance. The provinces did not have their own constitutions or independent judicial systems. In dividing constitutional authority, 67 subjects were placed under the control of the center, and 47 were held concurrently with the provinces. All other matters were reserved to the provinces. The constitution was silent on which authority would prevail in the event of a conflict over concurrent powers. As it turned out, the provinces enjoyed little autonomy.

In structure, the provincial governments paralleled that at the national level. The Governor possessed only symbolic powers, like the President, and was required to adhere to the advice of the Chief Minister. The size of the provincial assemblies varied: Baluchistan had 40, Northwest Frontier Province had 80, Punjab had 240, and Sind had 100. The size variation reflects populations in each province. As at the national level, proposals concerning money were required to come from the government. For 10 years or the second general election, whichever came later, money requests were considered agreed to unless a majority of the total membership of an Assembly voted against or approved a reduction. The Assembly could not increase the amount contained in a bill.

There was the familiar lengthy list of fundamental rights set out at the beginning of the constitution. One innovation was the statement: "Steps shall be taken to ensure full partcipation of women in all spheres of national life." But there were the usual qualifiers "subject to any reasonable restrictions imposed by law." As experience would tell, fundamental rights would fare no better under Bhutto than they had under previous regimes.

The Islamic provisions of the 1962 constitution, as amended, were retained. Pakistan would be known as an "Islamic Republic," and for the first time Islam was declared the state religion. No law would be allowed which was repugnant to the Quran or the Sunnah. An Islamic Council, appointed by the President and consisting of 8 to 15 members, would review existing laws in light of the repugnancy clause. It would also advise on ways to give legislative effect to the injunctions of Islam. Legislative bodies were required to reconsider laws the Council deemed repugnant to Islam.

The constitution could be amended by the parliament. Such bills originated in the Assembly and if approved by two-thirds of that body together with a majority of the Senate, went into effect. The Senate could reject an amendment by so voting or not acting

within 90 days. The constitution required no ratification procedure, and it automatically came into effect
on August 14, 1973. It was amended seven times up to
the fall of Bhutto.

Conclusions

Each of Pakistan's three constitutions differed
in important respects. The first involved a strong
federal model. The second envisaged "guided democracy"
and a strong executive. The third established a
parliamentary system. Despite these outward differences
in form, there were a number of substantive consis-
tencies. Each acknowledged the ultimate sovereignty of
Allah. Thus the highest seat of authority is not the
people, nor is the constitution the highest law of the
land; Islam is. This is further demonstrated in the
repugnancy clause which prohibits any law contrary to
the Quran and the Sunnah. A serious constitutional
problem arises here. Secular authority seems to derive
its legitimacy from spiritual law. Not only is there
the practical problem of determining the nature of the
latter, but this arrangement deprives the constitution
of its fundamental status in the political system.
On a related point, the people, although receiving
authority from Allah, play no direct role in the constitutional process. On no occasion was a constitutional convention selected with the specific task of
constitution-writing. Such bodies always doubled as
legislatures. But most significant was the fact that
none of the three constitutions required popular ratification. They were put in effect by government proclamation. Amendments likewise required no popular vote.
Each constitution could be amended by the legislatures
with, in the 1962 version, the concurrence of the
President. It is true that many constitutions do not
require direct public involvement for their creation or
amendment. It does seem reasonable, nevertheless, to
conclude that this tenuous link between the people and
the constitutions of Pakistan may account in part for
their ineffectiveness. If the public had been more
actively involved in the process of constitution-
making, they might have taken the results more seriously.
The federal relationship was another issue common
among the three constitutions. The federation consisted at first of five units, then changed to two, and
finally became four after the secession of East Pakistan. Not only is this a small number of units for a
workable federation, but the units were grossly disproportionate in size and political importance. The population of Bengal exceeded the combined populations of
all the provinces of the West wing. Baluchistan and
the Northwest Frontier Province are dwarfed by Punjab.

While the division of authority under each constitution recognized provincial spheres, in practice the national government could interfere and dominate in several ways. Except in 1973, the provinces did not have the benefit of representation in one house of a bicameral legislature, a common feature of federations, which could have helped protect their integrity.

Considerable attention was paid to fundamental rights, but their significance was compromised by qualifications. The importance of these provisions was further limited by the fact that the judiciary was not powerful enough to protect them. The frequent use of emergency powers was a further source of erosion.

In each constitution, irrespective of its form, the executive dominated the legislature. The first two constitutions designed executive-type systems. While the 1973 constitution called for a parliamentary arrangement, the power of the legislature to restrict the Prime Minister was severely limited.

One might speculate that the weakness of the provincial governments, the legislatures and the courts contributed to political failure by not providing constructive channels for bargaining and decision-making. The executive served not only as a magnet attracting political power but also was the focus of attention of the opposition. Unfortunately the focus on executive power resulted in the constitutions themselves being identified with specific persons or governments.

The pattern of throwing out the constitution with a rejected government is among the most pernicious practices in Pakistan's political history. The 1973 document was not abrogated after the 1977 military coup, but General Zia did, on his own "authority" as Chief Martial Law Administrator, amend it extensively. This exercise destroys the very essence of a constitution which exists, after all, to protect against just such arbitrary use of power.

NOTES

1. The Constitutional Assembly of Pakistan, Debates, Vol. 1, p. 530, quoted in Keith Callard, Pakistan: A Political Study, New York: The Macmillan Co., 1957, pp. 172-3.
2. Smith, The Oxford History of India, p. 332.
3. Muneer Ahmad, Legislatures in Pakistan: 1947-58, Lahore: University of Punjab, 1960, p. 14.
4. Callard, Pakistan: A Political Study, pp. 80-4. Also see Wayne A. Wilcox, Pakistan: The Consolation of a Nation, New York: Columbia University Press, 1963, pp. 165-97.

80

5. Quaid-I-Azam Speaks, Karachi, n.d., p. 133, quoted in Callard, Pakistan: A Political Study, p. 182.

6. Hamid Yusuf, Pakistan in Search of Democracy, 1947-77, Lahore: Afrasia Publications, 1980, p. 34.

7. Louis Dupree, "Constitutional Development and Cultural Change, pt. VI: The First Pakistani Constitution of 1956: American Universities Field Staff Reports, South Asia Series, Vol. IX, No. 8, 1965, pp. 2-5.

8. Ibid., pp. 6-10.

9. Muneer Ahmed, Legislatures in Pakistan, 1947-58, pp. 17-8.

10. Richard S. Wheeler, The Politics of Pakistan: A Constitutional Quest, Ithaca: Cornell University Press, 1970, p. 147. Also see Wayne A. Wilcox, "Pakistan Coup d'etat of 1958," Pacific Affairs 38(Summer, 1965) 142-63.

11. Fazlur Rahman, "Islam and the New Constitution of Pakistan," Journal of Asian and African Studies, VII (July & October, 1973) p. 201.

12. M. Rashiduzzaman, "National Assemblies of Pakistan under the 1962 Constitution," Pacific Affairs 42 (Winter, 1969-70) 481.

13. A.M.A. Muhith. "Political and Administrative Roles in East Pakistan's Districts," Pacific Affairs 39(Fall/Winter, 1967) 282-4.

14. See Chapter 6.

5
Institutional Problems: Government in Action

Economic Problems

At the time of partition, Pakistan's economy was basically agricultural. With no major industries and an inefficient commercial system together with limited natural resources, the country faced an economic future that was not promising. Jute and cotton were major cash crops, but they were subject to the vagaries of the world market. A further difficulty was the fact that these crops were limited to the East wing, which did not have the textile mills to produce finished products. The textile industry had developed under the British, but with partition the mills were located in India and the crops in Pakistan.[1]

During the early 1950's, significant gains were made in some areas but losses occurred in others. The textile industry grew as a result of increased international demand brought on by the Korean War. But with the end of the conflict, exports and foreign exchange dropped sharply. Pakistan enjoyed an agricultural surplus until 1952, when it became necessary to import large amounts of food grains. Economic difficulties were a major factor in the political disorders of the late 1950's. Once the political process was made operational under Ayub Khan, important economic gains were registered. But this was not to last long.

The 1965 war was a crushing blow to Pakistan's ambitions and brought in its wake a host of destabilizing political developments. There was dissatisfaction with the Tashkent agreement which ended the war and established the status quo ante bellum. The army, which was experiencing widespread discontent and wounded pride due to its frustrating lack of success in the war, found a ready scapegoat in President Ayub and his government. (A similar fate awaited President Yahya Khan in 1971 after he accepted the Indian ceasefire ultimatum and surrendered the army in East Pakistan.) These factors, together with mounting political and

economic discontent, resulted in increasing turmoil
from 1965 until Ayub's fall in 1969.

During this period the divergency of interests
within the country and especially between the two wings
became increasingly evident. The East Pakistanis had
joined in the struggle for Kashmir, but after the frustrations of the 1965 war they were inclined to accept
the Tashkent settlement and to focus on solving domestic
problems, such as the correction of economic imbalances.
This attitude clashed with the view of some leaders in
the West wing who wanted to continue pressing for a
suitable settlement of the Kashmir issue. The policies
of the government, as a result, encountered increasing
opposition in both wings.

The effectiveness of the political process steadily
deteriorated from 1965 to 1969. Among political parties
and student groups in both wings there was dissatisfaction with Basic Democracies on the grounds that they
were ineffective, inoperable, and undemocratic. Experience with the form but not the substance of representative government was not enough. Moreover, the system
tended to entrench the status quo and did not give the
newly emerging urban-industrial groups the power they
demanded. The process of gradual growth of democratic
institutions envisaged under Ayub's constitution of
1962 had been too slow. Political control remained concentrated in relatively few hands within the administrative structure and in the person of the President.
Moreover, charges of corruption were levelled against
the government. The mounting public outcry against
inefficiency and corruption eroded the government's
effectiveness.

Many of the problems for which the government was
blamed were actually beyond its control. During the
war the United States stopped economic and military
assistance, helping to arrest the impressive economic
development of the previous years. There were signs
toward the end of the decade that growth was resuming,
but by then the political damage had been done. The
army was frustrated over the suspension of military aid.
Increased government spending necessitated by the suspension of foreign aid rapidly depleted meager foreign
exchange reserves, placing the country in a weakened
position internationally.

After the war, the decision to finance refitting
the military through higher taxes fell heaviest on the
politically uninfluential elements of the public.
Savings were to be effected by cutting "social over-
head," i.e., public health, welfare, education, and
social facilities. Yet at the same time capital investments benefitting large farmers, export/import traders,
industrialists, and the military continued.[2]

The concentration of economic power in the hands
of a very few people was a double-barrelled problem.

Embassy gave a special rate to tourists of more than Rs. 10 to the dollar.

The rupee could have simply been devalued to reflect its true worth. This alternative was avoided because it would have increased the price of everything Pakistanis imported, although making exports cheaper. Also, at that time few countries allowed their currencies to "float" to their market value. By keeping the rate fixed against the dollar, Pakistan perpetuated the fiction that its economy was stronger than it really was. This is not unimportant, since much economic activity is predicated on confidence, a most elusive and artificial concept.

In 1967-68, exports declined, weakening Pakistan's foreign exchange position, while the rising cost of living diminished the domestic buying power of the rupee. The floating value of the bonus voucher, which reflected these economic factors, provided a cushion for exporters. However, this benefitted only a handful of the more powerful economic interests who were in a position to speculate. To compound economic woes, there were a couple years of poor harvest in the late 1960's.

Although there were signs of economic improvement by 1968, the political atmosphere remained gloomy. In 1967, six opposition parties joined to form the Pakistan Democratic Movement. The elements of this movement had only one common ingredient—opposition to President Ayub Khan and his system of Basic Democracies.

The government seemed particularly insensitive to the growing opposition in the East wing. In 1963, for example, Ayub had appointed Abdul Monem Khan governor of the province. Monem Khan "could not have been a worse choice" because of "his repressive rule and pervasive corruption."[6] In January 1967, relations between East and West Pakistan were further estranged by the Agartala conspiracy. Twenty-nine persons in East Pakistan were arrested and accused of plotting secession. India was charged with complicity in the plot and with sending arms to the secessionists. However, the government's case was shoddy; nothing was ever proven, and the charges were ultimately dropped. But the affair provided East Pakistani nationalists with yet another opportunity to put forth the claim that they were being treated like second class citizens.

The government's emphasis upon economic growth rather than correcting the problems of maldistribution of existing assets worsened the problems of integration. While there was increased emphasis upon the East Pakistan economy through added public sector investments, the disparity in per capita income between the two wings continued to widen. While East Pakistan's economy grew, that of West Pakistan grew faster. That West Pakistan was in a better structural position to achieve

economic growth did not impress the B[...] view, insufficient governmental effo[...] to improve the East wing's capabilit[...] cally. There were sound reasons to [...] two economies, an idea that strength[...] of the autonomists "for it lent a m[...] to their otherwise vague ideologic[...] demands, and helped mobilize the supp[...] strata of Bengali society behind thei[...]

Perhaps the most serious polit[...] weakness of the Ayub period was the [...] power in too few hands. This elite c[...] two score families who followed narr[...] political and economic practices. M[...] families became high ranking milit[...] moved from there into prosperous busin[...] family connections. Top bureaucrat[...] with the same family and "old boy" s[...] triad—business, military, bureaucracy[...] entirely in West Pakistan.[8] Moreover[...] and nepotistic practices restricted in[...] by precluding access to economic or [...] It also restricted the development of [...] at a time when Pakistan required the [...] in all areas of endeavor. From a p[...] view, the restrictions on access to [...] serious as non-elites vented their[...] violence against the regime.[9] Notes [...]

The rapacity which made the[...] most enterprising, aggressive, [...] wing industrialists and entrepre[...] twenty-two millionaire families, [...] These families, the Adamjees (ju[...] the Saigols and Valikas (textile[...] the Haroons Dawn newspaper and [...] the Habibs, Hyesons, Fancys, Daw[...] owned two-thirds of the nations [...] assets and four-fifths of its ba[...] ance.[10]

Violence and Disorder

In February 1968, President Ayub[...] heart attack. His incapacity and leng[...] demonstrated the extent to which the [...] was anchored in the person of the [...] momentum of the government was lost. O[...] including Bhutto's Pakistan People's [...] their anti-government activities. Bhut[...] popular among young intellectuals and[...] fessionals such as lawyers, and thos[...] mitted to a favorable settlement [...] question. The PPP did not encompass[...]

The fact that only a handful of families controlled the bulk of the economic resources was a cause for discontent and opposition. Ayub was blamed for failure to bring economic democracy to the country. On the other hand, the members of the economic elite looked with great disfavor upon any government effort to curtail their advantages. Ultimately the powerful families together with their military and bureaucratic allies would conspire to bring down the Ayub regime.

As early as 1959, government agencies were taking note of the narrow concentration of wealth in that 60% of all bank credit went into only 222 accounts. In 1963, 89 of the 119 non-government-controlled companies on the Karachi Stock Exchange had 50% of their shares in fewer than 20 hands. Ayub showed his concern by stating in the Third Five-Year Plan that it would be the policy of his government to prevent excessive concentration of wealth.[3]

One of the first efforts to reduce the power of the traditional elites was the land reform of 1959. An indication of the dimension of the problem is the fact that in the Punjab almost 20 percent of the cultivable land was controlled by only one-half of one percent of the population. Although rather modest, the reform did transfer some land from large to middle-sized estates. A limit of 1000 acres of ordinary land and 500 acres of irrigated land was imposed. This action had more psychological than economic effect. But middle-sized landowners were encouraged in their support of the government, a not unimportant fact, since many of them were army officers.[4]

In order to stimulate exports and to increase foreign exchange earnings, a bonus voucher scheme was introduced on January 1, 1959. Ordinarily exporters were not allowed to earn foreign exchange; such earnings had to be converted into Pakistani rupees at the official rate. In addition to the Rs. 4.76 per dollar earned at the official rate, exporters were given bonus vouchers rated at 20-40% of the value of the exports. These vouchers could be used to import items that were on a special list that exempted them from licensing restrictions. It had been the general practice of the government to restrict imports by limiting them through licensing. Thus under the new scheme, exporters could increase their net gain by using bonus vouchers to import goods that otherwise would be restricted. Moreover, there was a market for bonus vouchers, and their value ranged from 160-180% of their face value. Importers were, however, required to match their bonus vouchers with an equal amount in cash. This mechanism not only stimulated exports and foreign exchange earnings but also provided a safety valve for the overpriced rupee.[5] The rate of Rs. 4.76 to the dollar was as much as two or more times its market value. The American

Embassy gave a special rate to tourists of more than
Rs. 10 to the dollar.

The rupee could have simply been devalued to
reflect its true worth. This alternative was avoided
because it would have increased the price of everything
Pakistanis imported, although making exports cheaper.
Also, at that time few countries allowed their currencies to "float" to their market value. By keeping the
rate fixed against the dollar, Pakistan perpetuated the
fiction that its economy was stronger than it really
was. This is not unimportant, since much economic
activity is predicated on confidence, a most elusive
and artificial concept.

In 1967-68, exports declined, weakening Pakistan's
foreign exchange position, while the rising cost of
living diminished the domestic buying power of the
rupee. The floating value of the bonus voucher, which
reflected these economic factors, provided a cushion
for exporters. However, this benefitted only a handful
of the more powerful economic interests who were in a
position to speculate. To compound economic woes,
there were a couple years of poor harvest in the late
1960's.

Although there were signs of economic improvement
by 1968, the political atmosphere remained gloomy. In
1967, six opposition parties joined to form the Pakistan Democratic Movement. The elements of this movement
had only one common ingredient--opposition to President
Ayub Khan and his system of Basic Democracies.

The government seemed particularly insensitive to
the growing opposition in the East wing. In 1963, for
example, Ayub had appointed Abdul Monem Khan governor
of the province. Monem Khan "could not have been a
worse choice" because of "his repressive rule and pervasive corruption."[6] In January 1967, relations between East and West Pakistan were further estranged by
the Agartala conspiracy. Twenty-nine persons in East
Pakistan were arrested and accused of plotting secession. India was charged with complicity in the plot
and with sending arms to the secessionists. However,
the government's case was shoddy; nothing was ever proven, and the charges were ultimately dropped. But the
affair provided East Pakistani nationalists with yet
another opportunity to put forth the claim that they
were being treated like second class citizens.

The government's emphasis upon economic growth
rather than correcting the problems of maldistribution
of existing assets worsened the problems of integration.
While there was increased emphasis upon the East Pakistan economy through added public sector investments,
the disparity in per capita income between the two
wings continued to widen. While East Pakistan's economy
grew, that of West Pakistan grew faster. That West
Pakistan was in a better structural position to achieve

economic growth did not impress the Bengalis. In their view, insufficient governmental effort was being made to improve the East wing's capability to grow economically. There were sound reasons to view Pakistan as two economies, an idea that strengthened the position of the autonomists "for it lent a material foundation to their otherwise vague ideological and political demands, and helped mobilize the support of the various strata of Bengali society behind their cause."[7]

Perhaps the most serious political and economic weakness of the Ayub period was the concentration of power in too few hands. This elite consisted of a mere two score families who followed narrow and nepotistic political and economic practices. Many sons of these families became high ranking military officers and moved from there into prosperous businesses, maintaining family connections. Top bureaucrats were recruited with the same family and "old boy" school ties. This triad--business, military, bureaucracy--was based almost entirely in West Pakistan.[8] Moreover, its self-serving and nepotistic practices restricted institutional growth by precluding access to economic or political power. It also restricted the development of managerial talent at a time when Pakistan required the very best effort in all areas of endeavor. From a political point of view, the restrictions on access to power proved most serious as non-elites vented their frustrations by violence against the regime.[9] Notes one observer:

> The rapacity which made the fortunes of the most enterprising, aggressive, or corrupt West wing industrialists and entrepreneurs, the famous twenty-two millionaire families, was inexcusable. These families, the Adamjees (jute and textiles), the Saigols and Valikas (textiles and chemicals), the Haroons Dawn newspaper and car assemblies), the Habibs, Hyesons, Fancys, Dawoods, and others, owned two-thirds of the nations entire industrial assets and four-fifths of its banking and insurance.[10]

Violence and Disorder

In February 1968, President Ayub Khan suffered a heart attack. His incapacity and lengthy convalescence demonstrated the extent to which the political process was anchored in the person of the President. The momentum of the government was lost. Opposition groups, including Bhutto's Pakistan People's Party, increased their anti-government activities. Bhutto was especially popular among young intellectuals and students, professionals such as lawyers, and those strongly committed to a favorable settlement of the Kashmir question. The PPP did not encompass all opposition groups and it had little support in East Pakistan. But Bhutto and the PPP were the most visible and active in the political arena.

On November 14, 1968, many opposition politicians were arrested in Lahore and charged with inciting the people, especially students, to disorder and for encouraging the use of violence. But demonstrations continued and became even more violent, and on one occasion President Ayub Khan was fired upon while addressing a meeting in Peshawar. Ayub blamed the political parties for creating the trouble and for encouraging the use of violence by "lawless elements." His solution was to arrest the "ringleaders of lawlessness."[11]

One of the most consistent and certainly the most consistently disruptive political forces in Pakistan has been students. Students in the East wing were politically active before independence and after 1947 continued to support various causes and especially those involving provincial issues. In 1952 there were demonstrations demanding that Bengali be equal to Urdu as national languages. The government was then attempting to make Urdu the official national language. The massive demonstrations and violence forced a compromise on the issue. The main driving force behind this protest was the students. West Pakistan was not spared language problems. After the overthrow of Ayub in 1969 and again during the civil war of 1971, there was a move to establish Sindhi as the official language of Sind. This proposal was strongly resisted by immigrants into the province, especially to the industrial area around Karachi where riots occurred over the issue in 1972. The non-Sindhi-speaking population feared they would be unable to compete for jobs if Sindhi were made the official language of the province.[12]

As a result of the tradition of agitational politics and the nature of the educational system, the youth of Pakistan have become "politically overdeveloped."[13] One study showed as many as 80% of the students to be politically active.[14] Student political activity would become even more widespread during the Bhutto years when the educational system, especially universities, was greatly expanded. West Pakistan experienced major student disorders which began November 7, 1968, in Rawalpindi and continued until Ayub resigned in February 1969. The students mixed demands for extensive social and political change with reforms in university administration and curriculum. A large anti-government demonstration on January 2 was marked by the display of black flags and black armbands to protest the Ayub regime. In East Pakistan, student anti-government disorders coincided with renewed demands from the Awami League and Sheik Mujibur Rahman for greater autonomy.

In Bhutto's opposition to Ayub, students found a leader and a cause. He called for an end to Basic Democracy and free elections based upon universal adult suffrage. Widespread student violence in November resulted in Bhutto's arrest in Lahore on the 14th. But the violence continued and open criticism of Ayub spread, coming even from former supporters like retired Air Marshal Asghar Khan.[15]

As pressure against him continued to mount, Ayub expressed his willingness to compromise on several major issues. First, he agreed to release many of the political prisoners detained during the course of the disturbances, including Bhutto. Second, he agreed to cancel emergency regulations which had expanded police powers. While he made it clear that the many demands advanced by the opposition were not acceptable, he did display a willingness to discuss the possibility of constitutional reforms. These included the direct election of the President and the members of both national and provincial assemblies. Further, the opposition wanted the elimination of state of emergency powers, which at the discretion of the President gave him almost dictatorial control. The immediate restoration of all civil rights and freedoms was also demanded. In effect, the opposition wanted the dismantling of Ayub's Basic Democracy, an end to strong executive rule, and the creation of parliamentary government.

To work out differences between himself and the opposition, Ayub proposed a roundtable conference. One immediate problem arose from the fact that Sheik Mujibur Rahman was in jail facing charges that he was plotting with India to make East Pakistan an independent state. Its strength dictated the participation of the Awami League in any such roundtable conference, and the fact that Mujib was its head meant that he should be the League's representative. An original suggestion to give Mujib temporary parole to attend the conference was rejected by Mujib, who demanded that all charges be dropped not only against himself but against the others accused in the conspiracy. Bhashani's National Awami Party and Bhutto opposed the round table conference idea, Bhashani calling for "politics of the street."[16]

Apparently the army was unwilling to shore up the Ayub government by quelling the disturbances or by some other display of support. On February 21, Ayub attempted to blunt the opposition by announcing that he would not seek re-election in 1970. Considering the length of his tenure, over 10 years, and the state of his health, this was not a dramatic move. Accordingly, the announcement had little effect, and the disorders continued. Confronted with the fact that the opposition continued to grow no matter how many concessions he made, the army intervened again. The scenario was almost an exact replay of 1958. As its price for taking action, the army and its chief of staff, General Agha Mohammed Yahya Khan, demanded the resignation of President Ayub. On February 25 he resigned as President of Pakistan, thus ending probably the most stable and productive period in the country's history.

When General Yahya Khan formally assumed power on March 25, 1969, anarchy reigned in East Pakistan. Students and radical groups held sway. The Basic Democracy system and the administrative structure, especially law and order, simply had ceased to exist. Workers commandeered their places of employment demanding wage increases. In rural areas "hundreds" of people were killed in the violence. Prices soared out of sight as capital fled the country. Attempts to convert rupees into hard currencies contributed to spiraling inflation.[17]

Yahya Khan, who was then 52, was a classic product of the British military tradition, just like Ayub had been. Having obtained their military training under the Raj, these people were, and many still are, more British than the British. A stiff, no nonsense "soldier's soldier," Yahya had no experience and less inclination for politics. He reluctantly accepted the responsibility of cleaning up the mess Pakistan was in but looked forward to an early transfer of power to non-military authorities. One can only assume that Yahya was sincere in his motives during the troubled times that were to follow. His decision to use military force against East Pakistan is at once a measure of his lack of political imagination and an indication of the desperate state of the country's politics.

Party Activities

The development of political parties has been handicapped by two factors. As is true in many countries, the search for compromise is not a governing norm of Pakistan's political culture. The political process has not been marked by broad and continuous participation using political parties as the vehicle for mobilization and aggregation of interests. Instead, the political process has been factionalized with a patrimonial style of leadership.[18] The desire to maximize gains on behalf of vested interests tends toward an unwillingness to sacrifice a limited amount in return for some measure of gain. Political leaders and groups are satisfied with nothing less than the totality of their demands. As a result, political problems are not resolved by the continuing give and take process of bargaining, but sooner or later result in deadlock.[19]

A second obstacle in the development of political parties has been the extensive involvement of the mili-

tary in the political process. Military men have dominated the political scene much of the time, but they are
by nature and training ill-disposed toward the kinds of
relationships that exist in political parties. They
are more comfortable with the hierarchy of command that
characterizes a military relationship. Mohammed Ali
Jinnah, the leading political figure at the time of
independence, did not cultivate a strong party system.
He relied instead on the strength of his own charismatic
appeal. Political parties in Pakistan have not developed as vehicles for obtaining organized political
power. Nor have they been used as electoral vehicles
for the mobilization of popular support. Both are
functions necessarily performed by political parties.

Among all the political parties that have been
active over the years, only two have enjoyed any particular long term success. The Muslim League, the party
of Jinnah, was the vehicle of self-government immediately after independence. As leader of the Muslim independence movement, the League was in a position to
become an effective organizational vehicle in independent Pakistan, as did the Congress in India. But its
strength deteriorated rapidly in the early 1950's. The
League was unable to retain its cohesion nor could it
strengthen itself through competition, as opposition
parties were suppressed. The League eventually fragmented into several branches, none of which was able to
command a significant following. It was revived in a
modified form by President Ayub Khan, who tried to
create a party to support his government, but this was
largely ineffective.

The Awami Muslim League, founded in Dacca, East
Pakistan, in June 1949, grew up in opposition to the
Muslim League. It was composed of people disenchanted
with the League's politics plus those whose political
ambitions had not been satisfied by membership in the
League. Maulana Hamid Khan Bhashani became the first
President, Shamsul Huq was Secretary General, and
Sheikh Mujibur Rahman was appointed Joint Secretary but
succeeded Huq as General Secretary in 1952. H. S. Suhrawardy soon joined the party and shared the leadership.
On November 16, 1953, the Awami League issued an election manifesto in anticipation of the provincial elections scheduled for March 1954. Among other things,
the manifesto demanded regional autonomy and socialist
economic measures.[20] The Awami League and other opposition parties formed a united front and captured 223
seats in the East Pakistan Provincial Assembly. The
Muslim League collapsed, winning only 10 seats. Fazlul
Huq, leader of the Krishak Sramik Party representing
the middle peasantry and a member of the united front,
became Chief Minister. But on May 30, Governor General
Ghulam Mohammed decided the situation was too unstable,
so he declared Governor's rule in East Pakistan. This

meant that politicians who opposed the government faced the threat of arrest. Many politicians took this opportunity to look after their own personal health. Suhrawardy flew to Zurich to consult with his physician, while Bhashani went to meet his in London.[21]

The Awami League had taken an active part in the language dispute in 1952, protesting the government's efforts to make Urdu the national language. The League demanded that Bengali also be considered a national language. Initially the Awami League was an all-Pakistan party, but by 1955 the demands for recognition of Bengali and greater autonomy for East Pakistan plus the decision to allow membership in the party for non-Muslims caused a split between the East and West wing branches of the party. Bhashani proposed in April 1955 that the Awami League open its membership to non-Muslims, of which there were a large number in East Pakistan. This broadened the base of the League in East Pakistan, but at the same time it alienated some Muslims, particularly in the West wing. The upshot of this was to compromise the significance of the Islamic state idea in East Pakistan and to create a non-communal Bengali party whose basis ultimately would be Bengali nationalism. The inflexibility of the Muslim League in refusing to admit non-Muslims was one of the factors leading to its early demise.

In 1955 the Awami League split over the issue of foreign policy. Suhrawardy favored an alliance with the United States, whereas Bhashani wanted a completely independent and non-aligned foreign policy. In July 1957 the National Awami Party was formed by the Bhashani dissidents, calling for an alliance of all leftist and provincial groups committed to the dismemberment of the one-unit scheme in West Pakistan and an independent and non-aligned foreign policy.

On October 7, 1958, the constitution was scrapped with the imposition of martial law. President Iskander Mirza expressed doubts that Pakistan could sustain a parliamentary system of government. He observed that the experience since independence had been one of successive crises, opportunistic maneuvering among politicians, and a generally unsatisfactory level of performance. The politicians were not serving the interests of the country, and the people were disenchanted with them. Any further attempts to run the country through elections and legislative bodies would be unrewarding and would instead result in further chaos. Accordingly, he called upon the military to assume control, arguing that it was the only alternative.

Politicians' activities were restrained by the Public Officers (Disqualification) Order of 1959. Political activity was further limited by the Elective Bodies (Disqualification) Order which gave politicians the option of staying out of politics or of being tried for misconduct, by means of which they could be cleared. Most were unwilling to risk this alternative. Restrictions were also placed on the press. The ban on parties was extended in the constitution of 1962 and was augmented by the Prohibition of Unregulated Activity Ordinance which followed the constitution by two months. Under these circumstances, elections to the provincial and national assemblies were held in May and June of 1962. There were thus no political parties and little political activity prior to the elections. The candidates were left to campaign on their own without the benefit of party organization. There were no organized discussions of the policy agenda facing the country or programs offered to deal with various problems. The legislators to be chosen by this election were left with no coherent guidance from the voters. The candidates' manifestoes "used the emotionally attractive but highly vague and elusive cliches and catchwords which had been the prevalent political currency prior to the 1958 coup."[22]

A bill permitting parties passed the National Assembly on July 14, 1962, and was signed by Ayub Khan two days later, reflecting his desire for "broad based political parties." The return of party activity permitted the holding of public meetings which were attended by thousands of people. At these meetings criticism of the regime soon became strident. Rather than involving discussions of policy alternatives and electoral strategies, the meetings turned into attacks on the political order itself. These meetings and the attacks on the political order occurred despite the fact that the Political Parties Act stated: "No parties shall be formed with the object of propagating any opinion, or acting in a manner, prejudicial to the Islamic ideology, integrity, or security of Pakistan."[23]

Under the Political Parties Act, several parties were revived. Ayub's attempt to resurrect the Muslim League under the banner of the Convention Muslim League produced little more than an official party handpicked by government ministers. It did not adopt a program until February 1963, in which it favored, among other things, Islamic ideology, an Islamic social order, and equal rights for women. The party program was vague on specific policy questions.

Those former members of the Muslim League who did not regard Ayub's Convention group as genuine or representative of the people established the Council Muslim League on October 27, 1962, with Khwaja Nazimuddin as its president. The party opposed Ayub's 1962 constitution on the grounds that it was fundamentally undemocratic.

The first party to be revived under the new law was the Jama'at-i-Islami on July 16, 1962. The Jama'at, possessing a solid organization, devoted leadership, and a loyal albeit a limited following, co-opted the religious issue and preempted the constituency of the traditionalist religious leaders, i.e., the ulema. The latter were reduced to taking individual propagandistic stands on specific constitutional and policy issues. They lacked organization and did not constitute a theological movement. The government was able to co-opt many important ulema by befriending them and extending patronage.[24] The Jama'at called for an Islamic state based on the Quran and the Sunnah, a democratic government, and an executive subordinate to the legislature.

The Nizam-i-Islam, organized on August 6, favored "conformity of all existing laws to Islamic texts," amendment of the 1962 constitution, restoration of legislative powers, fundamental rights and direct elections.

Of all the pre-martial law political parties, the Awami League had been the hardest hit, losing most of its leadership under various ordinances and orders.[25] Even its founder, H.S. Suhrawardy, did not favor its revival. The party did not return as a political force until after Suhrawardy's death in December 1963.

On October 4, 1962, Suhrawardy announced the formation of the National Democratic Front, which consisted of most opposition parties. It had a one-point program--democratization of the constitution. The NDF "stood against accepting any office in the government." Suhrawardy had not favored reviving the old Awami League, but after his death, the Working Committee of the League decided to do so with immediate effect. Within two weeks, on January 11, 1964, Mujib announced the revival of the party in the East wing. The party was officially revived on January 25 as a national political party.[26]

The Council Muslim League, the Jama'at, and the Nizam "show strong dedication to Islamic ideology, whose implementation is the cardinal principle of their programs."[27] The NDF, the Awami League, and the National Awami Party, revived August 31, 1963, were avowedly secular and pragmatic. Only the Convention, and to some extent the Council Muslim Leagues, showed interest in substantive policy issues. "The other parties show a lack of practical policy declarations. Their demands fit the struggle of movements to gain concessions from colonial or authoritarian rulers. The political dialogue was a rehash of the proclamations of intentions and aspirations current around the time of Partition."[28]

Qureshi notes the truncated nature of party politics:

> Politics in Pakistan has never been based upon philosophy or program; it has almost always remained confined to and a prisoner of personalities. Ever since Partition there has been no other

motive of alliances than personal gain and soon after the political game could be played again, partisan politics reverted to its normal centers of gravity.[29]

Despite the support of the President, the Convention Muslim League did not become an effective political party. Part of the problem was Ayub's suspicion of political parties. Because of this, his party did not become a mechanism for mobilizing popular support, nor did it serve as a channel of communications for informing the people of government activities. According to Wheeler: "The Muslim League became simply a device to maintain government control of the assemblies and to recognize and reward the government supporters."[30]

Ayub attempted to enlist the support of erstwhile critics from the East wing such as Khwaji Nazimuddin and H.S. Suhrawardy, but both refused.[31] While he assumed the titular role of party leader, he left the actual working of the party to others. But the party did not develop organizationally because of Ayub's unwillingness to make room at the top for talented and loyal followers. He preferred instead to keep as much power as possible for himself. A broad leadership did not develop, as potential successors to Ayub were denied a share of decision-making powers.[32]

Not only were Pakistan's plans frustrated in the 1965 war with India, but the war further estranged the East wing. For the people of East Pakistan, the war brought home the extent to which politicians of the West were willing to go in jeopardizing their security and welfare in pursuit of a solution to the Kashmir problem. It was in the aftermath of this experience that Sheik Mujib put forward his six-point program in February 1966, calling for a federal form of government based upon the Lahore Resolution of 1940. The six points became the core of the Awami League's philosophy and increasingly became the focus of political relations between the two wings. (See chapter 6 for a discussion of the six points.)

In April 1967, opposition to the Ayub regime was broadened and strengthened by the formation of the Pakistan Democratic Movement. This group, composed not only of the East Pakistan Awami League but political parties from the West, accepted the Awami League's six points. In addition to the League's platform, the new list of demands included one for the incorporation of all the other points into a constitution. But within four months, disputes over the program of the Pakistan Democratic Movement resulted in a split within the Awami League. The more militant group was headed by Sheik Mujib.

In 1968, relations between the two wings were further polarized by the announcement of a conspiracy on

the part of certain East Pakistan political leaders and
the government of India to achieve independence for East
Pakistan.   This was known as the Agartala Conspiracy
case, for which Sheik Mujib was brought to trial in Dacca
in June.   The whole affair served the interests of Mujib
and the Awami League.   Instead of removing Mujib from
the scene and discrediting the Awami League as the
central government might have hoped, the Agartala Conspiracy proved awkward and embarassing for Ayub.   Mujib
was sent to jail, which established his credentials as
a victim of oppression, and publicity given to the case
popularized the League's six-point program.

Mujib's popularity in East Pakistan increased considerably as a result of his arrest.   Ayub, or at least
his provincial governor in East Pakistan, Monem Khan,
may have hoped to discredit Mujib politically by impli-
cating him in Indian subversion.   It is not improbable
that Mujib was conspiring with Indian officials.
Indeed, both India and Pakistan had been actively promoting subversion against one another since 1947.
Pakistan intelligence service agents had observed a
close associate of Mujib meeting regularly with P.N.
Ojha, First Secretary of the Indian Mission in Dacca.
The substance of these conversations were then evidently
communicated to Mujib.   After the creation of Bangladesh, Mujib claimed to have been working for East
Pakistan's secession for some time.[33]

The changing political landscape during the 1960's
is reflected in the career of Bhutto.   Bhutto served in
Ayub's cabinet from October 1958 until June 1966, during
the last three and a half years of which he had been
foreign minister and deeply involved in the confrontation with India in 1965.   Critical of the Tashkent settlement, he left the government and became its critic
and an outspoken advocate of democracy.   In November
1967 he founded the Pakistan People's Party, which had
particular appeal to students.   It was the students who
were most active during the violence of 1968, and
Bhutto's support of their activities was a factor
leading to his arrest in November of that year.

As violent resistance to the Ayub government
mounted, the demands of the students esclated in proportion.   In order to protest a variety of grievances,
including many involving universities, the students
staged a number of strikes.   In December 1968 Ayub
agreed to meet at least some of the students' demands.
A particular student grievance was the university ordinance whereby degrees could be withheld for improper
political activities.[34]   This ordinance was withdrawn
on December 8.   In January 1969, violence reached the
point where shootings occurred.   In response, students
escalated their demands to include investigation of
police conduct, compensation for victims of shootings,
immediate release of those arrested in the disturb-

ances, and amnesty for all engaged in demonstrations. The more the government moved to suppress the demonstrations, the more the demonstrators escalated their demands and increased pressure on the government.

Students in East Pakistan were particularly busy. By February 1969, the East Pakistan Student All Party Committee of Action was probably the most active political force in that part of the country. The Committee issued a list of 11 demands calling for parliamentary democracy with a weak central government, nationalization of most large-scale commercial and industrial enterprises, special tax rates and wage considerations for peasants and workers, more investment in East Pakistan, withdrawal from the American alliance system, and amnesty for all political prisoners. In addition, there were 14 demands relating to education.[35] The Awami League and the students united in a common cause against the central government. The six-point program of the Awami League and the 11-point program of the students were compatible, and during the constitutional crisis of 1971, Mujib mentioned the two programs together as the basis of East Pakistan's demands for a new constitutional order.

Ayub resigned on March 25, 1969, and asked the Chief of Staff of the Army General Mohammed Yahya Khan to impose martial law. This is a commentary on how much faith Ayub placed in his own constitution which called for the Speaker of the Assembly to take over until a new President has been elected.

Within about three months of Yahya's takeover, political order had been restored. He then undertook extensive political and economic reforms. Government economists acknowledged growing economic disparities especially between the two wings, and in June 1969 measures were initiated designed to improve economic conditions. However, admission by the central government that disparities existed and initiation of efforts to remove them did not have the effect of mollifying the Bengalis. Instead, these measures served to intensify their rhetoric.[36]

The return to martial law in 1969 was viewed by East Pakistanis as indefinitely postponing the realization of their demands for greater autonomy. But Mujib and the Awami League were not willing to seek compromise. Their demands were not negotiable. On November 29 Ayub announced sweeping political changes.[37] Presidential and Assembly elections were scheduled for October 5, 1970. These elections, in line with Awami League demands, would be based upon the one-man, one-vote principle, giving the East wing a majority voice. Yahya agreed to the dissolution of the one-unit scheme for West Pakistan and promised that a new constitution would incorporate the idea of maximum provincial autonomy. Finally, unrestricted political activity was restored effective January 1, 1970. These actions allowed for the unrestrained operation of the processes of democracy for the first time in the country's history.

While Yahya's ultimate intention may have been to establish a regime based on democratic principles, he relied almost entirely on the military in the meantime. He took charge of Defense and Foreign Affairs himself. General Hamid, the Chief of Staff, was in charge of the Home Ministry. The Air Chief of Staff, Nur Khan, had the Ministries of Education, Labor, and Health and Social Welfare. The Navy Chief controlled Finance, Planning, Industry, and Commerce.[38]

Events of 1965

1965 was a watershed year. The bickering and quarreling that had inhibited political development during the earlier years had been replaced by the relative progress and stability of the regime of Ayub Khan. Economically, Pakistan had enjoyed one of the brightest records of growth among all underdeveloped countries, although the benefits of this growth accrued more to the West than to the East wing. Considerable international stature had been gained, largely as a result of the alignment with the United States. In return for participation in CENTO and SEATO, Pakistan was rewarded with extensive American military and economic assistance.

The elections of 1964 and 1965 indicated a growing maturity of the political system. An articulate opposition to Ayub had emerged and contested his re-election as President. The Basic Democracies system functioned successfully in the elections, giving confidence and reinforcement to the regime. For the first time, the political system rested on an expression of popular legitimacy, insofar as one election, by indirect means, could so determine. However, the system suffered from serious problems, thanks in large measure to the self-serving activities of the political and economic elites. Also, there were many who refused to accept the system and demanded a greater voice in the affairs of the country. There remained an unwillingness to live with the deficiencies of the political system and an even greater unwillingness to cooperate in correcting them.

One of the conditions necessary for a successful constitution is the ability to evolve or adapt. In Pakistan, constitutional law was evolving through practice and judicial interpretation. It appeared that firm constitutional foundations for a strong executive system were being laid.[39] Combined with a strong bureaucracy, this arrangement could have become increasingly efficient. But it was absolutely necessary that the basic mechanisms of leadership selection and decision-making remain intact. They did not.

A coalition of opposition groups called the Combined Opposition Party, including the Awami League and several other smaller parties, was formed in 1964 to oppose the re-election of Ayub Khan. The COP was formed through the efforts of former Prime Minister Khwaja Nazimuddin. The party put forward as its candidate Mohammed Ali Jinnah's sister, Fatima Jinnah. As a candidate, Miss Jinnah had several strong points. In the first place, the fact that she was the sister of Quaid-i-Azam--the founder of Pakistan--with the magic name of Jinnah gave her the advantage of recognition. Moreover, she had never held public office before so was untainted by any charge of scandal. Corruption has traditionally been a key issue and would be a charge levelled against Ayub Khan. Miss Jinnah did not have any strong ideological bent, which meant that she could campaign on most any issue in a way that might be effective. Her disadvantages as a candidate were a general lack of experience with politics and campaigning and the fact that she was 71 years old.

The membership of the opposition to the Ayub government reflected the growing gap between the modern and the traditional sectors of society. The modern sector, i.e., intellectuals, students, industrial workers, bar associations and other professional groups, largely opposed Ayub. This, of course, meant that the urban areas were opposed to Ayub's rule, even if they were not enthusiastic about the alternative party and its candidate. Ayub received massive support from the rural areas--the traditional sector of society. Although Ayub could not be described as adhering to traditional values, he drew his strength from those who did. Thus his bid for re-election polarized the issue of modernity vs. tradition, urban vs. rural.

The presidential election was conducted within the Basic Democracy framework. The 200 to 600 voters in each constituency did not actually vote for President, but chose Basic Democrats who served as electors. Eighty thousand Basic Democrats, 40 thousand from each wing, selected the President. The elections were held in the West wing from October 31 to November 9 and in the East wing from November 10 to November 19. The result gave an impressive endorsement to Ayub Khan, as he received a majority of the votes in both wings,[40] although he did less well in the East.

Presidential Election Results

	Ayub Khan	Fatima Jinnah
West Pak.	28,939 (73.3%)	10,257 (26.7%)
East Pak.	21,012 (52.9%)	18,434 (46.5%)
National	49,951 (62.7%)	28,691 (36.0%)

Source: Sharif al-Mujahid, "Pakistan's First
          Presidential Elections," Asian Survey XI
          (June, 1965) 292.

On March 21, 1965, the elections for the National
Assembly were held.   Again the election was indirect,
with the Basic Democrats choosing the Assembly members.
The election was a resounding victory for Ayub's Convention Muslim League which won 120 seats, while the
Combined Opposition Party won only 11, 10 of which
were from the East wing.   The only other party to win
seats was the National Democratic Front in the East
wing, which won five seats.   The remainder went to independents.   Although the Pakistan Muslim League won only
54.8% of the vote, it captured 80% of the seats.   In
contrast with the presidential election, the balloting
was much closer for the Assembly.   In the East wing,
the Muslim League won only 49.6% of the votes.   It
received 61.3% in the West wing.   The difference
suggests the substantial personal popularity of President Ayub Khan.[41]

The results of the elections strengthened the
government of Pakistan and encouraged it to adopt a
more assertive posture on the Kashmir issue.   Another
factor was the increasingly cordial relations between
Pakistan and China.   In 1963, the two countries reached
an understanding concerning each others border claims
and initiated air service between themselves.   Developments in India suggested a political weakening of that
country.   India was deprived of the strong and effective
leadership that had guided it since independence with
the death of Jawaharlal Nehru in May 1964.   Nehru's
successor, Lal Bahadur Shastri, was not a commanding
figure and possessed far less influence than had his
predecessor.   During 1964 and 1965, India experienced
considerable domestic turmoil due in part to several
years of poor harvests and food shortages.   Political
disorders resulted from the adoption of Hindi as the
official language of India in January 1965.

For several years, India had been consolidating
its hold on Kashmir and in fact no longer considered it
disputed territory.   Beginning in 1961, India began
publicly declaring Kashmir to be an integral part of
the Indian union.   This action virtually eliminated any
hope for a negotiated settlement favorable to Pakistan.
This combination of circumstances prompted the leaders
of Pakistan to force the Kashmir issue.

In early 1965 a series of incidents occurred between Indian and Pakistani troops along the Kashmir
ceasefire line.   Meanwhile, major engagements occurred
in another disputed border area--the Rann of Kutch.
This piece of ground, which has no resource value but is
strategically important, lies along Pakistan's south-

east border with India.   For most of the year it consists of dry mud flats with some isolated scrub growth.
During the monsoon season it is completely flooded and
impassable. The Rann was part of an area where the two
countries had never agreed as to the precise delineation
of the boundary. The Indians, relying upon some British
decisions, claimed the whole of the Rann, while Pakistan
claimed that the boundary should run through the middle
of the Rann on the grounds that it is either a boundary
lake or an inland sea. According to international law,
the Pakistanis argued, when a body of water of this
type constitutes a part of an international boundary,
then the boundary line is considered to run through the
middle of the body of water.[42]

The Rann of Kutch boundary dispute was one of the
legacies of partition that had not been resolved. The
Indians, figuring the boundary gave them the entire
Rann of Kutch, had moved military and border personnel
into the area to enforce their claim. But Pakistan,
also seeking to enforce its claim, did the same. Given
the presence of military units of both countries in the
same area, confrontation is not surprising. The fighting began in February 1965 and soon escalated into a
major conflict.

Neither side appeared willing to increase its
military involvement, recognizing that the fighting
might escalate out of control. The impending monsoon
season may also have moderated desires to press forward
militarily.   Accordingly, both sides agreed to a
British-mediated ceasefire effective June 30, 1965.
The status quo as of January 1, 1965, was to be restored
and the border decided by arbitration.[43] This brief
conflict was a prelude to the fighting over Kashmir.

The situation in Indian-held Kashmir began to
deteriorate rapidly in 1965. Sheik Abdullah, leader of
the dominant party in Kashmir, was becoming less responsive to the wishes of Delhi. On May 8 he was arrested
and removed by the Indian government to internment in
South India. Supporters of Abdullah and groups advocating the union of Kashmir with Pakistan protested vio-
lently.   Resistance spread rapidly, and anti-Indian
guerilla activities soon occurred with much encouragement from the Pakistani side of the line of control.
Direct involvement by Pakistani personnel increased
steadily, resulting eventually in clashes with Indian
troops.

Confronted with the growing Kashmir crisis, Prime
Minister Shastri was persuaded by his military advisers
to take action to stop infiltration from Pakistan. In
mid-August the Indian army attacked various positions
in the north of Kashmir. Pakistan reacted in September
by sending armored units into the southern areas of
Indian-held Kashmir with the intention of cutting their
main lines of communication.

India escalated its military effort on September 6 by sending three columns into Pakistan. The Kashmir problem had finally given rise to a general war. In addition to armor and infantry, both sides launched air attacks against population centers.

In spite of some initial success on both sides, neither could hope to attain complete victory. Pakistan's forces were unable to attain their objectives. Although having a tactical advantage, the costs involved in pressing forward encouraged India to accept a ceasefire.

Western reaction to the war was to suspend military assistance to both countries. This suspension came eventually to include other forms of assistance in the hope of pressuring them to agree to a ceasefire. The suspension of military aid fell most heavily upon Pakistan, which relied almost exclusively on the United States for military equipment. India was slightly better off, having received aircraft and armor from Britain, France and the Soviet Union. The Pakistanis were particularly distressed by the reaction of their allies. They seemed to have entertained the idea that participation in the American alliance system meant that CENTO and SEATO allies would offer support should they get into a military confrontation with India. Not only was this support not forthcoming, but the allies were exerting pressure on Pakistan to stop fighting.[44]

Arranging for a lasting ceasefire was not easy. The United States and Britain could not play active roles because they had lost favor with Pakistan. China was unacceptable to India. The United Nations, through its Secretary General U Thant, met with only limited success in arranging a ceasefire. However, a Security Council resolution demanding a ceasefire was agreed to by both belligerents on September 23. Although the major hostilities had stopped, incidents continued along the ceasefire line for several months.

The Soviet Union was in a position to mediate the dispute, and on September 4 Premier Kosygin offered his good offices for negotiations. Although Pakistan was not enthusiastic about Russian mediation, both sides did agree to direct negotiations. The parties met in the Soviet Union at Tashkent on January 3, 1966. After an initial period of failure when the conference reached a point of imminent collapse, a sudden and dramatic announcement on January 10 revealed that agreement had been reached. On the following day, Prime Minister Shastri died.

The Tashkent Declaration oddly enough had little to say about Kashmir itself.[45] The Declaration consisted mostly of promises by both sides to attempt permanent resolution of their mutual difficulties. They agreed to conduct continuing discussions at high ministerial levels on a variety of matters. A stipulation

that both sides should withdraw to the established
international boundaries of the 1949 Kashmir ceasefire
line was implemented in late February. Although discussions did occur in the months to follow, they produced little of any consequence. Soon each side accused
the other of violating the principle and spirit of the
Declaration of Tashkent, and the situation by late 1966
had returned pretty much to the status quo ante.
Pakistan's failure to acquire Kashmir by military
means would prove momentous for two reasons. First,
Pakistan had tried every approach to gain control of
Kashmir from diplomacy to United Nations intervention
to war without success. From 1965, the incorporation
of Kashmir into India was a fact, although some Pakistanis refuse to accept it as such even today. Second,
Ayub's opponents would interpret the Tashkent agreement
as surrender and would use it to discredit him. But
his government was not all that would be brought down.
The Kashmir debacle would result in the loss of legitimacy of the regime itself, bringing on another constitutional crisis.

NOTES

1. Richard Nations, "The Economic Structure of
Pakistan and Bangladesh," in Robin Blackburn, ed.,
Explusion in the Subcontinent, Baltimore: Penguin Books,
1975, p. 254.
2. Wayne A. Wilcox, The Emergence of Bangladesh:
Problems and Opportunities for a Refined American
Policy in South Asia, Washington: American Enterprise
Institute for Public Policy Research, 1973, p. 13.
3. Lawrence J. White, Industrial Concentration and
Economic Power in Pakistan, Princeton: Princeton Univer-
sity Press, 1984, pp. 42-3.
4. Burki, p. 1132; Lawrence Ziring, The Ayub Khan
Era; Politics in Pakistan 1958-1958, Syracuse: Syracuse
University Press, 1971, p. 19; Talukder Maniruzzaman,
"Group Interests in Pakistan Politics, 1947-1958,"
Pacific Affairs, 39(Spring/Summer, 1966) 85.
5. White, Industrial Concentration and Economic
Power in Pakistan, pp. 117-18.
6. Hamid Yusuf, Pakistan in Search of Democracy,
1947-77, Lahore: Afrasia Publications, 1980, p. 62.
7. Rounaq Jahan, Pakistan: Failure in National
Integration, New York: Columbia Univeristy Press, 1972,
p. 87.
8. Louis Dupree, "The Military is Dead: Long Live
the Military," AUFS Report, XIII #3 (SA Series) 1969.
9. White, Industrial Concentration and Economic
Power in Pakistan, p. 35.

102

10. David Loshak, Pakistan Crisis, London: Heinemann, 1971, pp. 27-8.
11. Richard S. Wheeler, The Politics of Pakistan;
A Constitutional Quest, Ithaca: Cornell University
Press, 1970, p. 147.
12. Theodore P. Wright, Jr., "Muslims from India
in the Pakistani Legislative Elite" paper delivered at
the annual meeting of the Association for Asian Studies,
April 1, 1973, p. 9.
13. Ziring, The Ayub Khan Era, p. 71; Also see
Douglas Ashford, National Development and Local Reform;
Political Participation in Morocco, Tunisia, and
Pakistan, Princeton: Princeton University Press, 1967,
p. 258.
14. Jahan, Pakistan; Failure in National Integ-
gration, p. 41.
15. Phillips Talbot, "Pakistan Turns a Corner,"
AUFS Fieldstaff Report XIII #1 (SA Series), 1969.
16. Wayne A. Wilcox, "Pakistan in 1969: Once Again
from the Starting Point," Asian Survey X(February,
1970), 73-81.
17. Loshak, Pakistan Crisis, pp. 32-3.
18. Gerald A. Heeger, "Politics in the Post-Military State: Some Reflections on the Pakistan Experience," World Politics, 29(January, 1977) 254.
19. For a discussion of the importance of political
institutions in bridging and mediating the competition
and conflict among social groups see, Reuven Kahane,
Legitimation and Integration in Developing Societies:
The Case of India, Boulder: Westview Press, 1982.
20. Mohammed Ayoob and K. Subrahmanyan, The Liberation War, New Delhi: S. Chand & Co. (Pvt.) Ltd., p. 54
21. Dom Moraes, The Tempest Within: An Account of
East Pakistan, Vikas Publications, 1971, p. 33.
22. Qureshi, "Party Politics in the Second Republic
of Pakistan," The Middle East Journal, 20 (Autumn,
1966), 457.
23. Ibid., p. 470.
24. Aziz Ahmed, "Activism of the Ulama in Pakistan," in Scholars, Saints, and Sufis: Muslim Religious
Institutions in the Middle East Since 1500, Nikki R.
Keddie (ed.), Berkeley: University of California Press,
1972, p. 264.
25. Qureshi, "Party Politics in the Second Republic
of Pakistan," pp. 461-8.
26. Ibid., p. 469.
27. Ibid., p. 471.
28. Ibid., p. 471-2.
29. Ibid., p. 472.
30. Wheeler, The Politics of Pakistan: A Constitutional Quest, p. 147.
31. Lawrence Ziring, The Ayub Khan Era: Politics
in Pakistan, 1958-69, Syracuse: Syracuse University
Press, 1971, p. 38.

32. Rounaq Jahan, Pakistan: Failure in National Integration, pp. 128-31.

33. Choudhury, The Last Days of United Pakistan, pp. 22-5.

34. G.S. Bhargava, Pakistan in Crisis, New Delhi: Vikas Publications, 1969, p. 16.

35. Wheeler, The Politics of Pakistan: A Constitutional Quest, p. 273; Bangladesh, My Bangladesh. pp. 149-50; M. Rashiduzziman, "The National Awami Party of Pakistan," Pacific Affairs XLIII (Fall, 1970) 402.

36. Wilcox, "Pakistan in 1969: Once Again from the Starting Point," p. 75.

37. Wheeler, The Politics of Pakistan: A Constitutional Quest, p. 309.

38. Choudhury, The Last Days of United Pakistan, p. 50.

39. Ralph Braibanti, "Pakistan: Constitutional Issues in 1964," Asian Survey V(February, 1965) 79-87.

40. Sharif al-Mujahid, Pakistan's First Presidential Elections," Asian Survey V(June, 1965) 280-94.

41. Sharif al-Mujahid, "The Assembly Elections in Pakistan," Asian Survey V(November, 1965) 538-51.

42. "The Rann of Kutch Dispute," Pakistan Horizon, XVIII(Fourth Quarter, 1965) 377.

43. The three-man arbitral tribunal was composed of judges from Yugoslavia, Iran, and Sweden. In February 1968, after two years of fact gathering and deliberations, the tribunal awarded 90 percent of the Rann to India and the remainder to Pakistan. Although receiving the smaller portion, Pakistan accepted the decision. In India, in contrast, there was considerable dissatisfaction. A motion of no confidence was introduced in the Lok Sabha against Prime Minister Gandhi's government.

44. Cf. Frank Trager, "The United States and Pakistan: A Failure of Diplomacy," ORBIS IX(Fall, 1965) 613-619. Trager argued that the failure of the United States to support Pakistan in the interest of courting favor with India undermined the American position in relation to both countries. His argument that the main issue concerning the United States in South Asia is the strategic threat from the north would seem to be supported by the Soviet invasion of Afghanistan.

45. M.S. Rajan, "The Tashkent Declaration: Retrospect and Prospect," International Studies 8(July, 1966-April, 1967), 1-28 and Der Sharma, Tashkent: A Study in Foreign Relations with Documents, Varanasi: Gandhian Institute of Studies, 1966.

6
Problems of Democracy

The Legal Framework Order

The elections of December 1970 were a new experience for the people of Pakistan. For the first time they were allowed to choose members of the government themselves. The National Assembly elections on this occasion were to be by direct vote rather than through the mechanism of indirect representation under Ayub's Basic Democracy scheme. Never before had popular attitudes been allowed to affect directly the course of political events, an experience that would ultimately prove to be devastating.

Ideally, the introduction of representative democracy would be the culmination of the process of political development and growth that had occurred since August 1947. Unfortunately there had been little real progress in dealing with fundamental constitutional problems. Two attempts to find a workable constitutional arrangement ended in failure, although the 1962 constitution lasted nearly 10 years. The procedure to be followed in 1970 was the same as that used before. After the constitution had been drafted, the National Assembly would become a legislative body operating within the constitutional limitations of the document just drafted.

On November 28, 1969, President Yahya Khan addressed the country and outlined how authority would be transferred from the military to a civilian government. He recognized that some sort of mechanism was necessary for the transfer of power, since the 1962 constitution had been abrogated with the assumption of martial law. Accordingly, he decided to establish such a mechanism by decree under his authority as Chief Martial Law Administrator. This was the Legal Framework Order promulgated March 30, 1970, under which the elections for the National Assembly were held.

In his speech of November 28, Yayha discussed Pakistan's problems. He accepted the fact that there

were serious disparities in growth and the distribution
of social income between the two wings and within the
West wing. "Apart from the political and constitutional
problems, the most disturbing to my mind and the one
that affects the lower income group in particular is
the rise in cost of certain essential commodities."[1]
He also acknowledged the existence of corruption among
government officials. "Investigations carried out by
the Government during the past few months have resulted
in the identification of certain serious cases of corruption, misuse of office, and misconduct among Class I
gazetted officers."[2]

Yahya seemed prepared to deal with the fundamental
constitutional problems facing the country. The two-
unit scheme whereby the East and West wings were considered on a constitutional parity was abandoned in
favor of four provinces in the West wing and one in the
East. The one-unit arrangement for the West wing was
looked upon by the Bengalis as giving the West undue
influence in the federal government. A second major
demand from East Pakistan concerned representation.
The parity system had, in effect, denied East Pakistan
the political strength due it as a consequence of its
larger population and had placed the smaller provinces
in the West wing under the dominance of Punjab. Yayha's
call for elections in his November 28 speech accepted
the one-man, one-vote principle, which ultimately resulted in a majority for East Pakistan in the National
Assembly. A third issue was critical, and the inability
to find a satisfactory solution resulted in the Civil
War. In all federal systems, including the United
States, the question of center-state relationships
sooner or later becomes critical. In Pakistan the
relationship between the two wings had always been
chronically difficult. On the question of center-state
relationships, Yahya favored increased provincial autonomy.

> As regards the relations between the Center
> and the Provinces, you would recall that in my
> July Broadcast I pointed out that the people of
> East Pakistan did not have their full share in the
> decision-making process on vital national issues.
> I also said then that they were fully justified in
> being dissatisfied with this state of affairs. We
> shall therefore have to put an end to this posi-
> tion. The requirement would appear to be maximum
> autonomy to the two wings of Pakistan as long as
> this does not impair national integrity and soli-
> darity of the country.[3]

In 1947 a transitional political framework was
afforded by British law and colonial acts. In 1970
the same function was performed by the Legal Framework

Order. The difference lies in the fact that British laws had over 100 years of tradition and acceptance whereas the LFO was purely a product of martial law. In the LFO, Yahya tried to define constitutional parameters. It was a constitution in itself because it provided limitations and injunctions which had to be followed in the subsequent constitutional drafting process. For example, the LFO provided guidelines on the number of assembly seats and types of electoral constituencies, provided for reserved seats for women, stipulated that Pakistan be based upon Islam, and required a list of fundamental rights and an independent judiciary. The National Assembly was given 120 days in which to complete its work. If it failed it would be disbanded and new elections called.

By issuing the LFO, Yahya, and by implication Pakistanis in general, acknowledged a distrust of the constitution-making process. The constituent assembly could not be allowed to write a fundamental law which would contain unacceptable provisions. But unacceptable to whom? At issue is the basic question of sovereignty: Where is authority located? If the people are sovereign, then there can be no logical constraints on their law-making authority, although it is customary to make it difficult for them to exercise it. If they are not sovereign, then who is? Pakistan, and many other political systems for that matter, has never satisfactorily answered this question. Yahya issued the LFO under his authority as Chief Martial Law Administrator. But that authority is merely that of usurpation, of military power. Absent is a rationalization of this authority, a legitimizing justification.

At the root of this issue is an unwillingness to accept the implications of the constitution as the "fundamental" or highest law of the land. To do so would compromise the political status of Islam in the minds of many. But on the other hand there has been no inclination to establish a theocratic state, one where Islam is the highest law of the land and rule is in the hands of the clergy. With only a half-hearted commitment to constitutionalism, it is not surprising that there have been repeated failures.

Mujibur Rahman and the Awami League

The political philosophy of Mujibur Rahman reflected two fundamental areas of discontent. The first was economic; the economic development of East Pakistan had been not only neglected but exploited to the benefit of the dominant groups in the West wing. In fiscal policy, the advantage of West Pakistan had nearly always been the determining factor. Many policies benefitted the West at the expense of the East, such as currency valuation. The extreme over-valuation of the rupee

aided the expansion of industry in the West but caused
hardships for the East. Industrial development and
foreign trade benefitted the West and was a disadvantage
to the East in the long run. Government policy contributed to this development. Agricultural exports from
East Pakistan earned foreign exchange which was invested
in industrial projects in the West. Moreover, the
banking system tended to be concentrated in the West.
Transportation and shipping were headquartered in and
benefitted the West. Pakistan International Airlines,
the national carrier, had its central offices in the
West, and the services of the airline reflected the
interests of the West more than those of the East.

Mujibur Rahman was born on March 17, 1920, of a
middle class family in Bengal. He attended Maulana Azad
College in Calcutta, graduating in 1947. He also
studied law at the University of Dacca. While a student, Mujib was influenced by H. S. Suhrawardy who was
then a leader of the Muslim League. In 1949 Mujib
broke with the Muslim League and together with Maulana
Bhashani founded the East Pakistan Awami League.

Sheik Mujib attacked the concentration of economic
power in the hands of a small West Pakistani elite. In
his view this elite had increased their grip on the
economy of East Pakistan to the detriment of the people.
Accordingly, he favored the nationalization of banks,
insurance companies, and the jute trade. "The shares
of big industries and factories should be distributed
among the workers. For 23 years the poor people have
been exploited by the pot-bellied gentlemen."[4] With a
nationalized industrial scheme, the larger population
of East Pakistan would have had greater influence or
even control over the economy in a one-man, one-vote
political system. Mujib also expressed concern about
the distribution of wealth. The per capita income of
the East wing was much less than that of the West wing.
He therefore advocated more social welfare and a
greater effort by the national government to provide
food, shelter and clothing for the people. There should
also be tax advantages for small landholders, and
"excess land" owned by the rich should be redistributed
among landless peasants.[5] He argued that the efforts
of the national government to overcome poverty were
minimal. Natural disasters such as typhoons which
often plagued East Pakistan met with only half-hearted
measures from the government. The slow response of the
government to the disastrous typhoon of 1970 was particularly galling.

> The generous assistance received from abroad
> only underlines the tardiness and callousness of
> our own rulers. At a time when Pakistan is enjoy-
> ing a bumper wheat crop it is ironic that the first
> shipment of food grains to reach us came from

abroad. While we have a substantial army stationed
in East Pakistan, it is left to the British Marines
to bury our dead. We have army helicopters but we
have to wait for helicopters to come for relief
operations from the United States, France, and
other countries. Assistance from China, the U.S.,
the U.S.S.R., and the U.K. arrived within days of
the disaster, while it took our government 10 days
to allot relief assistance. The value of Chinese
and U.S. aid at market value exceeds that of the
central government.[6]

Mujib's second area of disagreement with the policies of the government concerned foreign affairs.[7] He
preferred non-alignment over that of close affiliation
with the Western bloc. The position entailed the withdrawal of Pakistan from the Central Treaty Organization
and the Southeast Asia Treaty Organization. Participation in American alliances had not produced significant
advantages for Pakistan but had occassionally created
problems. The policy of collaboration with the West
resulted in the alienation of other governments, particularly the Soviet bloc. This is not to say that
Mujib's sympathies were with the communists at the
expense of the noncommunist world, but rather that he
felt the degree to which Pakistan had followed Western
policies had unnecessarily alienated other governments.
Accordingly, a more balanced approach in international
relations would be more to Pakistan's advantage.
      Mujib advocated a more flexible approach toward
India. He recognized the fact that there are substantial areas of disagreement with India, particularly
Kashmir and the Farakka Barrage, the latter affecting
the East wing. India's attitude over Kashmir was not
acceptable, and the development program pursued by the
Indian government in the lower Ganges was detrimental
to the interests of East Pakistan. India had not lived
up to previous commitments on Kashmir and seemed inclined to divert and use the water of the Gangetic basin
without consideration for the interests of its eastern
neighbor. Nevertheless, Mujib believed that the possibility of accommodation with India existed. He reasoned that Pakistan's belligerence had contributed to
the difficulty of reaching such an accommodation.
      Pakistan's hard line attitude toward India, espe-
cially over the Kashmir issue, according to Mujib,
served the interests of India and a small clique in
West Pakistan, particularly the military. The interests
of the country as a whole suffered as a result. The
Kashmir issue, since it came to be defined largely in
military terms, served the interests of the military
and certain capitalists in West Pakistan who exploited
the war syndrome to further their economic gains.
Accordingly, as Mujib saw it, the Kashmir issue had

been inflated in order to further military control over
the political system and to divert resources into those
sectors of the economy which benefitted from military
and related industries.

In one area, at least, Mujib seemed largely in
agreement with the national government and the political
leaders in the West wing. This was the trend toward
closer ties with China. Mujib's attitude toward China
did not seem intended to play China off against India,
as is the case with West wing leaders, but rather was a
manifestation of his non-aligned posture in foreign
policy.[8] The Chinese, however, did not respond by
endorsing or supporting Bengali nationalism. Despite
the fact that China's ideology would seem to require
support of such national movements and the geopolitics
of the area around East Pakistan favored Chinese involvement, the government of China strongly and forth-
rightly supported the national government, including
the attempted suppression of the Awami League secession
in 1971.

The party of Sheikh Mujib, the Awami League, had
been a factor in the politics of Pakistan almost since
independence, first against the Muslim League and later
against the rule of Ayub Khan. The Awami League became
an important force in East Pakistan politics with the
election of 1954 when the Muslim League was all but
eliminated. In the early days, the Awami League was
headed by H.S. Suhrawardi and Maulana Bhashani. Bhashani
left the party to form the National Awami Party and
Sheik Mujib took over control after the death of Suhrawardi.[9]

The full extent of the Awami League's popularity
in East Pakistan was not evident prior to the elections
of 1970. Actually, the strength of the party grew
rapidly during the campaign. The appeal of the six-
point program and the party's opposition to the national
government grew as a result of the ineffective response
made to the typhoon disaster of November 1970. The
inability or unwillingness of the government to move
quickly and effectively to aid the victims of the storm
and its apparent indifference to the plight of the East
Bengalis worked to the advantage of the Awami League.
The Awami League's six-point program was widely regarded
as an attempt to establish a strong bargaining position
in anticipation of the constitution drafting process.
There was not only the hope but the expectation that
the Awami League would be willing to compromise on at
least some of its demands.

The thrust of the Awami League's six-point program
was the creation of an institutional arrangement whereby
the domination of national economic and political life
by the West wing would be impossible. In the almost 24
years of Pakistan's history, the East wing was exploited
to the benefit of the West wing, and the national gov-

ernment was the vehicle of this exploitation. Accordingly, the six-point program was intended to eliminate or neutralize the machinery of the national government. The first point called for a constitution truly federal in nature. That is to say, the national government would have only specifically delegated authority, with the states or units within the federation retaining the bulk of political and economic powers. Moreover, the federal or national government would be strictly parliamentary with a weak executive. The legislative body would be supreme in national affairs. The legislature would be selected on the basis of direct elections by universal adult franchise, giving the East wing majority control.

The second point dealt specifically with the powers of the federal government. In only two areas would it have authority--defense and foreign affairs. All other matters, either expressed or reserved, would reside with the federated provinces. The remaining points of the program so significantly circumscribed the activities of the national government and its ability to perform them that even defense and foreign affairs would be indirectly controlled by the states.

The third point dealt with currency. The Awami League demanded two separate currency systems, one for each wing. These currencies would be independently based but be freely convertible with one another. An alternative method provided one currency, but with two separate national or reserve banks to regulate the flow of capital between the two wings. The Awami League intended to prevent capital from being generated in one wing and then invested in the other. They wanted the wealth generated by the East Pakistan economy to be reinvested there.

The fourth point dealt with taxation and revenue collection. It called for the vesting of powers of taxation and revenue collection strictly in the hands of the federating states; the federal government would have no power of taxation. Funds necessary to meet the obligations of national government programs would come through a system of grants made by the states. The state, apparently, would be free to determine to what extent the federal government received funds. The amount appropriated would be based upon a system of sharing, presumably by ability to pay. This appears to be an arrangement simliar to the system of financing in the United Nations.

This point is tantamount to a demand for independence. The power of taxation in any political system determines the ability of governmental units to perform their functions. Denying the central government any power to raise revenue independent of the states means ultimately that the central government has no power. A federal system requires that authority be divided

between a central government and the states. Each
possesses authority to perform certain activities, which
means there must be the ability to perform these
activities. An arrangement whereby the central government has the authority to raise an army and maintain
the national defense but the states alone have the
authority to pay for this army is not a federation.
Without the ability to raise the necessary resources to
effect policy, the constitutional system is in reality
a confederation. In other words, aiblity must be com-
mensurate with authority.[10]

The fifth point dealt with the removal of economic
disparities that had grown up over the years between
the two wings. The Awami League called for a series of
unspecified economic and legal reforms designed to eliminate this disparity. This point did not call for
specific actions, but rather it demanded recognition of
the disparities between the two wings and a commitment
to their removal. The campaign manifestoes of most parties in 1970 and statements by President Yahya Khan indicated acceptance of this demand.

The final point dealt with the military and was
one of the most serious differences between the two
wings. The Civil War, of course, pointed out the role
of the military in the East-West relationship. The aim
of the Awami League's sixth point was to eliminate the
military as an agent of the national government, that
is, a national government representative exclusively of
West Pakistan. The Awami League wanted a national
military of extremely modest proportions based on equal
representation of the two wings. In addition, it wanted
a separate military force composed only of East Pakistanis and governed by the authorities of East Pakistan.
There would be a similar setup in the West wing. A
modest national military would be sufficient for international problems affecting the entire country. Provincial armies would prevent the use of national forces
by one wing against the other. But taken together,
these forces would be sufficient for defense.

The various policies articulated by the Awami
League and its leader Sheik Mujib in effect reverse
the pattern of development of the previous 24 years.
Economically, nationalization of industry was favored
over capitalism. Politically, regional autonomy was
advocated over a strong national government. In foreign
policy, non-alignment was viewed as preferable to close
ties with the United States. Culturally, Bengali
nationalism eclipsed Islam.

Bhutto and the Pakistan People's Party

Bhutto's popularity began to rise in 1965. The
results of the war and the Tashkent agreement produced
a rift between Bhutto and President Ayub. Bhutto had

been a member of Ayub's government and a trusted lieutenant, but with the failure of the war, Bhutto joined
the opposition. The existing opposition parties did
not reflect his political ideas, so he formed his own
party--The Pakistan's People's Party--on November 30,
1967. The principal supporters of the PPP were students
and urban intellectuals who were frustrated because of
their lack of involvement in the regime of Ayub Khan.
Those who rallied to Bhutto's standard included J.A.
Rahim, who adhered to socialist principles and was the
real ideological force behind the party. Other top
leaders were Mabashir Hasan, Mairaj Mohammed Khan, Abdul
Hafiz Pirzada, Bhutto's cousin Mumtaz Ali Bhutto, Sheik
Mohammed Rashid, Mustafa Khar, and Mohammed Ali
Kasuri.[11] Bhutto's stronghold was Lahore, and the PPP
became the dominant party in the whole of Punjab. In
addition, the party acquired considerable influence in
Sind.[12]

In 1970 the PPP was a relatively new party. It
had not been in existence long enough to make enemies
among the voters or for its politicians to make mistakes
which might cause embarrassment at election time.[13] The
party also enjoyed effective leadership. Bhutto in
particular was an attractive and skillful political
figure. He had been on the political scene long enough
for many people to know him, but he broke with the
government in time to avoid being associated with its
failures. Moreover, he had a keen sense of awareness
of the shifts in public opinion and was able to move
with these changes with great finesse.

But it was not long before there was a falling out
among the leaders. Bhutto was less committed to the
achievement of the party's ideological program than
were some other party leaders. Rahim and others sought
a compromise with Sheikh Mujib and the Awami League, but
Bhutto refused to go along. By 1974 Bhutto dominated
the PPP and "converted Rahim's socialist dream into a
cultist police state."[14] Rahim was arrested and beaten
up by police.

The program of the Pakistan People's Party called
for Islamic socialism. In its election manifesto the
party promised to rid the country of social, economic,
and political ills. These problems would be corrected
once the evils of capitalism, especially class conflict,
had been rooted out and an Islamic version of socialism
created. "The struggle in Pakistan is not between Muslim and Muslim but between exploiters and the exploited,
between oppressors and the oppressed."[15]

A vehicle of social change advocated by Bhutto and
the PPP was the nationalization of basic industries.
However, nationalization would not be extended to all
industrial enterprises. "We do not propose to nation-
alize industries that are functioning competitively and
whose control in private hands is not detrimental to

the security of the state."[16] Corruption in government,
inflation, problems of rural economic development, and
university reform were among other problems drawing
attention. The party manifesto did not offer specific
remedies for the chronic constitutional crisis.
In matters of foreign policy, the issue of Kashmir
was central for the PPP. Bhutto split with Ayub over
Kashmir, and his position remained one of no compromise
on the subject: Kashmir should be part of Pakistan,
"Pakistan without Kashmir is a body without a head."[17]
The party called for avoiding the entanglements of great
power politics, presumably reflecting disenchantment
with American failure to support Pakistan in its
quarrels with India. The party welcomed support from
any country on the issue of Kashmir.

The Election Results

The elections to the provincial and national
assemblies which Yahya scheduled for October 5, 1970,
would return power to civilian control. Originally the
LFO called only for elections to the National Assembly.
Provincial elections were to follow framing of a constitution. Mujib proposed they be held simultaneously,
and the idea was accepted by Bhutto and Yahya.
There was no shortage of political parties contesting the election, although most of them had rather
limited followings. The Muslim League, the instrument
of Pakistan's founding, was fragmented into three parts:
one--the Council Muslim League--claimed to be the true
inheritor of Jinnah's mantle. The second--the Convention Muslim League--was Ayub Khan's attempt to use the
Muslim League as his own political vehicle. The
third--the Qayyum Muslim League named after its leader
Abdul Qayyum Khan--was a rallying point for conservative West Pakistan interests. There were several
"Islamic" parties with the Jama'at-i-Islami the best
known and the only party with extensive local organization in both wings.[18] Others included the Jamiat-ul-
Islam and the Markaziv Jamiat-ul-Ulema-i-Pakistan. The
Pakistan Democratic Party, an attempt to form a coalition of anti-Ayub groups, had some measure of success
in the 1964-65 elections. The strengths of these
parties was confined almost exclusively to the West
wing. The Awami League had at one time drawn strength
from the West wing but was now primarily an East wing
party. The National Awami Party represented the "old
guard" left and had split into three factions: a
Baluchistan faction, a group under Wali Khan with
support in the Peshawar plain, and another in East
Pakistan under Maulana Bhashani. The newest party was
the PPP.[19]
In the East wing, the campaign involved an appeal
for an independent Bangladesh. Students paraded with

maps and flags depicting the creation of an independent state. The authorities reacted with remarkable calm apparently unwilling to threaten the electoral process. Governor Ahsan may also have contributed to an undue sense of optimism by his statements that the process would succeed.[20]

Three hundred seats in the National Assembly were contested in the general assembly. In addition there were 13 seats reserved for women who would be chosen by the elected members of the Assembly. Of the 300 general seats, 162 were allotted to East Pakistan and 138 to the four provinces of West Pakistan allocated as follows: Baluchistan 4; Northwest Frontier Province 25; Punjab 82; and Sind 27. Twenty-five political parties plus independents contested these seats presenting 1570 candidates. This gives an average of slightly more than five persons contesting each seat. Thirteen of the parties contested no more than six seats. Eight parties contested more than 100 seats, with the Awami League presenting the largest number of candidates--169.

The results of the election were startling in several respects.[21] First, the Muslim League was all but eliminated as an electoral force. The combined totals of the various Muslim League parties were extremely modest despite the fact that they each contested more than 100 seats. The Council Muslim League won seven out of 119 seats contested. The Qayyum branch won nine out of 132 seats contested. The Convention Muslim League--the party of former President Ayub--won two out of 124 seats contested.

The second significant result was the overwhelming victory of the Awami League in East Pakistan. The Awami League contested 162 seats in East Pakistan and seven in West Pakistan. Of the 169 seats contested, 160 were won all in the East wing. The only other seats won in the East wing were one by an independent and one by the Pakistan Democratic Party headed by Nurul Amin.

A third important consequence of the election was the victory of the party of Zulfiqar Ali Bhutto. The party contested 119 seats, all of them in the West wing, and won 81 seats. The party's strongest showing was in Punjab with 62 victories. The fact that the PPP won 81 seats out of the 138 allocated to the West wing shows the strength of the party and of Bhutto personally. It is also important to note that no seats were contested by the PPP in East Pakistan.

The results of the Provincial Assembly elections followed the same pattern as the national voting. Each provincial assembly had 300 seats. The Awami League captured 288 seats in the East Pakistan Assembly. The PPP did not win a majority in the West wing but did win 144 seats. Its closest rival was a branch of the

Pakistan Muslim League with 24 seats. The remainder of the seats were scattered among several other minor parties, including 53 independents.

The election vividly described the political condition of Pakistan. The Awami League had won practically all the seats in the East wing, while the PPP had won the greatest number in the West wing. The National Assembly, which was charged with the task of drafting a new constitution, was hopelessly divided between regionally-oriented parties.

The Hijack Incident

On January 30, 1971, a twin engine Fokker Friendship of Indian Airlines flying from Srinagar to New Delhi was hijacked by two Kashmiris and directed to fly to Lahore. This incident served to illustrate the highly volatile nature of Pakistan's politics and the style of its politicians. The two hijackers claimed to be freedom fighters, whose seizure of the aircraft was intended to dramatize the cause of Kashmir's liberation from India.

Initially there was some indication that the airport authorities were prepared to return the passengers and crew to India immediately and perhaps even to arrest the hijackers. But this course of action was abandoned in the face of growing turbulence over the issue. Students from Punjab University gathered in large numbers and moved on the airport to demonstrate their support for the hijackers, but police broke up the procession by the use of tear gas and a lathi charge. Another development further inflamed the situation when Bhutto visited the scene and had a short conversation with one of the hijackers. He congratulated them on their effort and stressed the continued importance of the Kashmir freedom struggle. The hijackers were made into instant political heroes.

The Government of Pakistan seized this opportunity to breathe some life into the dormant Kashmir issue. While Pakistan attempted to exploit the propaganda value of the incident, India held most of the cards. Moreover, by its failure to return the plane, its crew and luggage, Pakistan was violating a United Nations resolution it had previously supported.

The right wing Jan Sangh party in India condemned Pakistan and the Indian government's handling of the affair. The problem arose in the first place, according to the Jan Sangh, because of the failure of the Indian government to deal effectively with Kashmiri saboteurs and "fifth columnists."

The passengers and crew were allowed to return to India, but the hijackers kept the airplane in return for which they demanded the release of several of their colleagues from Indian jails. India refused, and at

8:35 on the evening of February 2 the plane was blown up by the hijackers, or "commandoes," as the Pakistan press had taken to calling them.[22] India immediately took retaliatory measures by banning all Pakistani military overflights of Indian territory. Meanwhile, rioting broke out in New Delhi on February 3 around the Pakistan High Commission. The High Commission employees greeted the demonstrators by throwing rocks at them. This fracas resulted in 22 injuries, 10 of them Indian policemen involved in attempting to disperse the crowd. India claimed the hijacking and the destruction of the plane could not have been accomplished without the "connivance and assistance" of the Pakistan authorities.[23]

In East Pakistan, Sheik Mujibur Rahman's reaction was in sharp contrast to that of Bhutto. Mujib condemned the destruction of the plane and called for a thorough government investigation of the affair. Bhutto, on the other hand, maintained that the government of Pakistan was not responsible and that the hijackers being Kashmiris were merely struggling against Indian imperialism, thus entitling them to asylum.[24]

On February 5, further rioting involving Pakistan High Commission employees and Indian demonstrators occurred. High Commission personnel moved outside the compound and engaged demonstrators with stones and sticks. Meanwhile, the Indian government banned all Pakistani flights over Indian territory. This action severed the direct connection between East and West Pakistan, consisting of 82 flights a week. Indian flights over Pakistani territory were also rerouted.[25] As a result of this action, Pakistan was forced to maintain communications with the East wing by flying via Ceylon, thus doubling the distance.

Rioting around the High Commission in New Delhi worsened, with injuries mounting into the hundreds. The Delhi police were forced to use large quantities of tear gas to prevent mobs from storming the Commission buildings. On February 6, Pakistan asserted that hijackers were not Indian nationals and thus not subject to Indian law. Pakistan also requested an end to the suspension of overflights, arguing that the whole affair was India's fault.[26]

By making a cause celebre out of the hijacking, the Pakistanis had done themselves great injury. India's ban on overflights caused India little inconvenience but was a great hardship for Pakistan.

The Awami League became increasingly critical of the hijacking episode and of Bhutto's role in it. They saw in the hijacking and the status accorded the hijackers an attempt on the part of the Western ruling elite, and Bhutto in particular, to create a new Kashmir crisis which might somehow nullify the election or result in a postponement of the National Assembly or both.

The hijack incident illustrates the grandstanding that has been characteristic of the style of Pakistan's politicians. Taking advantage of the inept handling of the affair by the government, Bhutto, Mujib, and others fanned public emotions. Second, the incident demonstrated the importance of Kashmir in the politics of West Pakistan but not necessarily that of the East wing. The failure of the military effort in 1965 and the Tashkent agreement were used by the opposition to bring down Ayub Khan. Now Kashmir was being used again, but this time not only would Yahya Khan be brought down, but the country would be dismembered.

Failure to Find Compromise

From the National Assembly Elections in December 1970, through March 1971, negotiations took place among Yahya Khan, Z.A. Bhutto, and Sheik Mujib, during which the East Pakistanis were unyielding. The Awami League insisted that their six points be the basis of a new constitution. For their part, the leaders of West Pakistan demanded at the very least the possibility of compromise on some of the points. Leaders of West Pakistan did not have a list of specifics to be included in the constitution, except that it should provide for a federal system and the continued unity of the country. Differences between the two wings over the future constitution were not resolved before the scheduled meetings of the National Assembly. Occasional rumors in the press that possibilities for compromise might exist were denied by Mujib. He regarded the election as a referendum on the six points, and they were "as such beyond the scope of adjustment."[27]
Yahya reiterated frequently his commitment to the transfer of power to civilian authority, but he would not allow any constitutional wording which would threaten the unity of the country. Bhutto stated on several occasions that four of the six points would be acceptable in principle if the Awami League would yield on the points dealing with foreign trade and foreign aid. However, he rejected the overall thrust of the program because it would result in a central government virtually without power. To pressure Yahya and the Awami League, Bhutto threatened to boycott the Assembly. On February 15 he announced the Pakistan People's Party would not attend the National Assembly "simply to endorse a dictated constitution." There must be "an understanding that there is room for compromise and adjustments. We must have scope for adjustment. There must be a consensus of the federating units in the framing of the constitution."[28]
Bhutto was playing a weak hand. He did not command the monolithic support in the West wing that Sheik Mujib enjoyed in the East. Some West Pakistanis were

inclined to blame Bhutto for the constitutional and political difficulties, suggesting that he was exploiting the crisis for his own advantage.

As leader of the largest minority party in the National Assembly, Bhutto was faced with two options. While he had little sympathy for East Pakistani separatism, he did appear sensitive to conditions in the East wing. He could have accepted the will of the majority party to show his commitment to democracy and hope the Awami League would accept compromise. It is highly improbable that Yahya Kahn would have accepted a constitution dictated by the Awami League which would have resulted in an autonomous East wing. Bhutto could have played along, established his credentials as a firm believer in democracy and allowed the President to assume all the blame for rejecting the results of the 1970 election. On the other hand, Bhutto could have refused to cooperate in the National Assembly venture on the grounds that the Awami League intended to dictate a constitution which would divide Pakistan, a proposal unacceptable to the Pakistan People's Party and most West Pakistanis. As it turned out, Bhutto pursued both of these strategies, altering his position when circumstances required. Up until the 11th hour crisis in March, he seemed to favor the second option by his threatened boycott of the National Assembly. Considering the timing and the fact that the Awami League had made no concessions, Bhutto's agreement to attend the session raises the interesting question of whether or not he was privy to the decision to use the army in East Pakistan.

While the East Pakistanis were unified on the subject of a new constitution, the same could not be said of those in the West. There was no great enthusiasm for the Awami League's six points, but neither was there uniform opposition. In order to take advantage of this, Mujib carried his campaign to other political parties and political leaders in the West. In Sind, the Northwest Frontier Province, and Baluchistan, he found sympathy for the plight of East Pakistan. He attempted to cultivate support for the Awami League's program and for an immediate convocation of the National Assembly. The solid support for the Awami League in East Pakistan and the lack of cohesiveness in West Pakistan were factors behind the eventual decision to suppress the Awami League. Had East Pakistan been allowed to secede, provinces in the West wing might have been encouraged to seek greater autonomy.

The National Assembly was scheduled to meet in Dacca on March 3, 1971. Late in February, the Awami League was finalizing its draft of a proposed constitution which offended other political parties and which was cited as evidence of the League's intention to impose its will on the Assembly. Under these conditions,

the National Assembly would not be a true constitutional convention where various individuals and groups
collectively worked out an acceptable compromise, but
instead would merely be a formality ratifying a pre-
conceived document. West Pakistani political leaders
were unimpressed with Mujib's promise that he would
listen to and consider other points of view. Bhutto
went so far as to suggest that there be a kind of dual
political system with each wing having its own prime
minister. There was even some talk of two constitutions, held together by a higher constitution of some
kind under which Pakistan would remain a unified
country. But the Awami League's unwillingness to
discuss such proposals and their outright rejection of
most of them was taken as evidence that they intended
to have their way. On February 22, the cabinet of
President Yahya Khan was dissolved "due to the political situation obtaining in the country.[29]

And then on March 1 the President postponed the
National Assembly. He appears to have taken the action
rather precipitously without giving due consideration
to the likely consequences, perhaps hoping to pressure
the Awami League. Moreover, there is evidence suggesting that he acted without adequate consultation with
and preparation of all parties concerned, but instead
followed the hard line advice of Bhutto and Perzada, his
principal staff officer.[30] Yahya stated that he had
decided to postpone the summoning of the National
Assembly to a later date. He said when conditions
were "conducive to constitution-making, I will have no
hesitation in calling the session of the Assembly,
immediately."[31] The postponement was necessary, because
the parties of West Pakistan had been unable to reach a
compromise with the Awami League. Yahya noted that the
East Pakistanis had shown no inclination to bend in
their demands and apparently were holding out for a
constitution which would, in effect, partition the
country.

Meanwhile provincial governors were being replaced
with Martial Law officers. In the East wing, Vice
Admiral Ahsan was replaced with General Tikka Khan, a
hard liner who would soon earn the epithet "butcher of
Bengal." Ahsan was reported to have sympathy for
Bengali opinion and rapport with Mujib.[32]

It is possible the Awami League was contemplating
secession all along. Mujib admitted as much later, or
perhaps they were flexing their political muscles and
would have been willing to compromise, provided the
Awami League played a dominant role.

It is not clear the extent to which Yahya and
Bhutto cooperated and shared views during this critical
period. But they were closer than either was to Mujib.
Yahya's postponement of the National Assembly meeting
corresponded to a suggestion made earlier by Bhutto.

Bhutto had suggested to Mujib in early February that the convocation of the National Assembly be delayed, which, according to Bhutto, would allow more time for working out a compromise on the Awami League's demands. He also suggested as an alternative the removal of the 120-day limit imposed on the duration of the National Assembly in the Legal Framework Order. Delaying the meeting or extending the number of days allowed was unacceptable to the Awami League. Mujib made it clear that the National Assembly should meet on schedule. He pointed out that the scheduling of the Assembly for March 3 was in effect a delay from the point of view of East Pakistan and was already a considerable concession.[33] Rather than agree to extend the 120-day limit and thereby start a precedent that the LFO was negotiable, Yahya decided that postponing the convocation of the Assembly would allow the necessary time for negotiations.

Mujib's reaction to the postponement was immediate. The delay was interpreted as yet another attempt by West Pakistan to deny the East wing its rightful voice in the country's affairs. But he had become a victim of his and his party's own rhetoric. Moreover, the size of the Awami League's mandate on the six-point program made it difficult for Mujib to negotiate and compromise these fundamental points. To do so would have offended his constituents in East Pakistan and would have been risky given the extremely volatile nature of the situation. On March 2, Mujib escalated the political confrontation by calling for a general strike in Dacca to protest the postponement. The strike brought commercial activities, vehicular traffic and governmental operations to a standstill. While there was a general strike in East Pakistan to protest the postponement, the Pakistan People's Party called off their plans for a general strike for the same day, which was to have protested the Awami League's unyielding position.

In the midst of this intensifying confrontation, the United States was accused of meddling in Pakistan's affairs. Several political leaders became quite distraught over remarks made by President Nixon in his State of the World Message to Congress. Nixon observed that Pakistan faced a number of difficulties because of its two widely diverse wings, each having characteristic social patterns, traditions and political realities. These rather casual and certainly not erroneous statements brought on a most vigorous condemnation. The President of the Pakistan Justice Party branded Nixon's remarks as a "direct and mischievous attempt to interfere in Pakistan's internal affairs." He warned that "no self-respecting nation can tolerate such malicious meddling in such piously smug form." He was also disturbed, as were several others, by the visit of the

American Ambassador to Pakistan to Sheik Mujib. This was interpreted widely as a sign of American support for Mujib and the Awami League.[34] It would not seem inappropriate under normal circumstances to meet with the leader of the largest political party and putative head of the government. But these were not normal circumstances.

Yahya invited 12 elected representatives of various parties in the National Assembly to meet with him in Dacca on March 10. As an inducement to the Awami League, he said there should be "no reason why the National Assembly could not meet within a couple of weeks after the conference."[35] In East Pakistan the general strike quickly developed into violence. Non-Bengalis, particularly the Biharis, were intimidated and harassed. There were clashes between the army and East Pakistanis over the imposition of a curfew. Sheik Mujib and Nurul Amin, the only other leader with any following in East Pakistan, both turned down Yahya's invitation, saying that "we are being called upon to sit with certain elements whose devious machinations are responsible for the death of innocent, unarmed peasants, workers and students."[36] Yahya's efforts at furthering negotiations were floundering.

Mujib soon went even further, demanding an immediate end to martial law and a transfer of power to elected representatives. Such action by the federal government would have made the six points a fait accomplis. Suspension of martial law would have removed the legal basis under which Pakistan's political system was operating. The suspension of martial law would, therefore, have removed this legal framework. The resulting vacuum wuld presumably have been filled by the second dimension to Mujib's demand, that is, the immediate transfer of power to elected representatives. If Mujib's demand had been met, the Legal Framework Order would have been null and void. That portion of the LFO providing for the integrity of Pakistan would have not been applicable. As a result of their majority in the National Assembly, the Awami League could have enacted their six-point program without any legal or constitutional restriction. This is undoubtedly the reason Yahya refused Mujib's demands.

To increase the pressure, Mujib called on March 4 for the expansion of the strike in Dacca into a province-wide general strike. It was an ominous sign that he found it necessary to caution the people to avoid communal antagonisms and to resist arson and looting.[37] Despite Mujib's plea to avoid violence, there were reports of clashes between Bengalis and the army in Dacca, Chittagong, and other cities in East Pakistan.[38]

The government newspaper, The Pakistan Times, observed in an editorial on March 6 that Mujib and the

Awami League were attempting to achieve independence
for the East wing.[39] The _Times_ vigorously denounced
such a move, relying on the same argument as that used
to justify Pakistan's creation in 1947; that is, the
concept of the Muslim community. A Muslim state was
necessary to protect the Muslim community. By advocating independence, the East Pakistanis in effect were
denying the validity of the fundamental reason for the
existence of the state.

Apparently yielding to pressure, Yahya annnounced
on March 6 that the National Assembly would convene on
March 25, despite the fact that all efforts by himself
and others during the previous week to reach some
compromise on the constitutional deadlock had failed.
Indeed, the situation had grown worse. Yahya claimed
surprise at Mujib's reaction to his postponement of the
National Assembly and the call for a roundtable conference.

> In total disregard of my genuine and sincere
> effort to bridge the gap between the various
> points of view, the response to my call has been
> rather discouraging particularly from the leader
> of our majority party who, before the announce-
> ment over the radio, had given the impression that
> he would not be adverse to the idea of such a
> conference."[40]

Yahya Khan was known for his blunt and direct
manner. He served notice that he would not tolerate
secession. In his radio message announcing the date
for the convening of the National Assembly, he said,
"I will not allow a handful of people to destroy the
homeland of millions of innocent Pakistanis. It is the
duty of the Pakistan Armed Forces to insure the
integrity, solidarity and security of Pakistan--a duty
in which they have never failed."[41] As further
evidence that the government anticipated a showdown
with the Awami League, Bhutto announced within hours of
the President's message that he would attend the
National Assembly session. Since the position of the
Awami League had not changed, there is really no explanation as to why Bhutto suddenly decided to attend the
Assembly, unless he had a reasonably good idea that
there would not be any National Assembly.

In his announcement convening the Assembly for
March 25, Yahya devoted himself to criticizing the
Awami League. While the action taken later may be
difficult, if not impossible, to justify by any moral
or rational standard, it cannot be said that Yahya did
not make himself clear. He claimed that the sole
obstacle to drafting a new constitution was Mujib and
the Awami League. Any attempt to alter Pakistan and

create autonomous wings would not be tolerated. If the government was allowing a situation to develop where intervention in East Pakistan could be justified, then Mujib and the Awami League did nothing to prevent it from happening. Mujib's response to the announcement of the convocation of the National Assembly was even more recalcitrant, but actually he had little room to maneuver. On one hand, Yahya and Bhutto were placing the blame for the delays in convening the National Assembly squarely on him. On the other hand, he was being pressured by his own followers, particularly the militant students, to accept no compromise. In fact, the hawks in the Awami League were beginning to agitate for independence.

While calling for a continuation of the general strike, Mujib announced his intention to attend the National Assembly session, but only if four more conditions were met. The first requirement was the immediate suspension of martial law. Second, troops must return to their barracks, meaning those in East Pakistan which had been used to quell disturbances. Third, he demanded an inquiry into cases where the army had fired upon civilians. Finally, all political power must be transferred immediately to the elected representatives of the people. Apparently this last point meant that the Awami League should be given the reins of government immediately rather than after the drafting of a new constitution. He also demanded that a military build-up in East Pakistan cease immediately, and military personnel, who were primarily West Pakistanis, should not in any way interfere with government activities in East Pakistan, or Bangladesh, as it was now being called. The matter of law and order should be left entirely in the hands of the Bengalis. The army and the national government in Islamabad should not interfere, but rather Bengali police and the East Pakistan Rifles should be responsible for law and order, assisted wherever necessary by Awami League volunteers.

The stage was thus set for Yahya's contention that East Pakistan was disintegrating and that the only alternative was direct intervention. Mujib apparently thought that the general strike, and some violent clashes, would force the military government to lift martial law and hand power over to the Awami League. In reality, these disorders were interpreted as a demonstration of the political instability of East Pakistan and afforded an excuse for military action.[42]

The seriousness of the situation is shown by the fact that several foreign communities began to evacuate their nationals from East Pakistan. The British began the exodus on March 9, and ultimately almost all foreign residents left. Meanwhile, reports appeared in the Indian press of a continued troop build-up.[43]

On March 15 Yahya journeyed to Dacca for talks with Sheik Mujib, who on the same day announced that he was assuming control of East Pakistan. Mujib announced that the bureaucracy of Bangladesh would assume responsibility for all public affairs and there should be non-cooperation with national government agencies. After two days of talks between Mujib and Yahya, the martial law administrator for East Pakistan, Lt. General Tikka Khan, announced the formation of a commission of inquiry into the circumstances surrounding the firings on civilians between March 2 and 9. The commission, to be headed by a judge from the provincial High Court, included four other members, one each from the army, the police, the East Pakistan Rifles, and the civil services.[44] But on March 18, Mujib denounced this move as "a mere device to mislead the people."[45]

By rejecting the commission of inquiry, Mujib displayed his unwillingness to cooperate with the government in any way. The possibility of peaceful resolution of the crisis began to evaporate. Mujib subsequently established his own commission, but its representation was not as all-inclusive as that proposed by the government. All the members of Mujib's team were officials from the Awami League, who were to report directly to him.

While Yahya and Mujib continued their talks, Bhutto refused to join them, since to do so would "serve no useful purpose" until he had received "certain clarification."[46] On March 19 "experts" were reportedly working out details of a "common formula for the transfer of power to the people."[47] On March 21, having received "satisfactory clarifications," Bhutto joined the discussions in Dacca. The same day it was reported that an interim government to replace that of Yahya Khan would soon be announced.[48] But such was not to be the case, and the meeting of the National Assembly scheduled for March 23 was again postponed. Bhutto denied that he had been the cause of the breakdown.[49]

On the 26th Yahya announced in a nation-wide broadcast the suspension of all political activity and the banning of the Awami League as a political party.

> Mujib's obstinancy, obduracy, and absolute refusal to talk sense can lead to the conclusion--the man and his party are enemies of Pakistan and they want East Pakistan to break away completely from the country. This crime will not go unpunished, we will not allow some power-hungry and unpatriotic people to destroy this country and play with the destiny of 120 million people.[50]

While the army moved to gain control of East

Pakistan, Mujib was arrested and taken to West
Pakistan.

There is one obvious conclusion to be drawn from
this survey of political activity in the the weeks and
months before March 26, 1971. The government of Yahya
Khan and most politicians in the West wing were unwilling to move forward with the constitution-drafting
process unless the Awami League backed down and agreed
to compromise in its six points before the National
Assembly met. This meant that the new political order
would have to meet the specifications of Yahya, the
army, and the PPP despite the fact that the Awami
League had a clear mandate from a majority of the
people. These specifications did not encompass a dominant role for the East wing within a united Pakistan.
If this were not the case, then there was no reason
for the military to intervene until after the National
Assembly had met and the Awami League's intentions had
been put to the test.

NOTES

1. Pakistan Affairs, December 2, 1969.
2. Ibid.
3. Ibid.
4. Sheik Mujibur Rahman, Bangladesh, My Bangladesh;
Selected Speeches and Statements, October 28, 1970 to
March 26, 1971, edited by Ramendu Majumdar, New Delhi:
Orient Longman, 1972.
5. Ibid.
6. Morning News (Dacca), November 27, 1970.
7. For further information on Mujib and his political career see, for example, S.M. Ali, After the Dark
Night: Problems of Sheikh Mujibur Rahman, Delhi: Thom-
son Press (India) Ltd., 1973.
8. Amir Taheri, "An Interview with Mujibur Rahman,"
The Free Press Journal, February 20, 1971.
9. M. Rashiduzzaman, "The Awami League in the
Political Development of Pakistan," Asian Survey X
(July, 1970), 574-87.
10. On federalism see, for example, William Riker,
Federalism, Boston: Little, Brown, and Co., 19; K.C.
Wheare, Federal Government, New York: Oxford University
Press, 1964; B.M. Sharma and L.P. Choudry, Federal
Polity, Bombay: Asia Publishing House, 1967; and Khalid
B. Sayeed, "Federalism and Pakistan," Far Eastern Survey 23(September, 1954), 139-143.
11. Lawrence Ziring. Pakistan: The Enigma of Political Development, Boulder: Westview Press, Inc., 1980,
pp. 117-9.
12. It is interesting to note in view of the
party's subsequent history that the electoral symbol of

the Pakistan People's Party is the sword.

13. For a discussion of the political parties that contested the elections in 1970, see Craig Baxter, "Pakistan Votes--1970," Asian Survey XI (March, 1971), 197-218.

14. Ziring, Pakistan: The Empire of Political Development, p. 123.

15. Dawn (Karachi), November 29, 1970.

16. Ibid.

17. Ibid. Bhutto long felt that India contemplated the reunification of the subcontinent by force if necessary. Indian policy toward Kashmir he considered a part of this design. "Therefore, India's occupation of Jammu and Kashmir is only a stage, only a part of India's intentions, to subjugate and destroy Pakistan itself." Z.A. Bhutto, Indian Aggression and the Kashmir Dispute, Karachi: Government of Pakistan, 1965, p. 12.

18. Sherif al Mujahid, "Pakistan: First General Elections," Asian Survey XI (February, 1971) 164.

19. Baxter, "Pakistan Votes--1970," p. 202-9.

20. G. W. Choudhury, The Last Days of United Pakistan, Bloomington: Indiana University Press, 1974, p. 99.

21. For details on the election results see: Baxter, "Pakistan Votes--1970," pp. 210-17.

22. The Pakistan Times, January 3, 1971.

23. India News, February 19, 1971. Eventually a judicial inquiry in Pakistan determined that the hijackers were members of "Indian Intelligence." Hamid Yusuf, Pakistan in Search of Democracy; 1947-77, Lahore; Afrasia Publication, 1980, p. 106.

24. The Pakistan Times, February 4, 1971.

25. Although there were 250 overflights of Pakistani territory by Indian aircraft per week, the inconvenience to India was nowhere that confronting Pakistan. In addition to the extra cost of flying between the two wings via Ceylon, Pakistan lost its share of the lucrative Nepal tourist traffic and was forced to curtail Bangkok and Japan flights.

26. The government of Pakistan contended that the hijacking was part of a larger plot engineered by India to create a separate and independent state in East Bengal. Part of this plot was to block sea and air routes linking East and West Pakistan. "This plan was actually carried out by India in February 1971, when the hijacking of an Indian airlines aircraft to Lahore and its subsequent destruction by the hijackers, engineered by India's own agents, was seized upon by the Indian government to ban overflights of Pakistan's civil aircraft in order to increase difficulties and tensions between the two wings of Pakistan at a critical time in political and constitutional negotiations." Summary of White Paper on the Crisis in East Pakistan, September 4, 1971.

27. The Pakistan Times, January 4, 1971.
28. Ibid., February 16, 1971.
29. Ibid., February 22, 1971.
30. Choudhury, p. 156.
31. Daily News (Karachi), March 1, 1971.
32. David Loshak, Pakistan Crisis, London: Heinemann, 1971, p. 73.
33. The Pakistan Observer (Dacca), February 8, 1971.
34. The Evening Star (Karachi), March 4, 1971.
35. Dawn (Karachi), March 4, 1971.
36. Ibid.
37. The Pakistan Times, March 4, 1971.
38. See for instance, The Times of India, March 5, 1971.
39. The Pakistan Times, March 6, 1971. Keith Callard states: "The force behind its establishment was based very largely on a feeling of insecurity." Pakistan: A Political Study, New York: The Macmillan Co., 1957, p. 11.
40. The Khyber Mail (Peshawar), March 15, 1971.
41. Ibid.
42. The Karachi newspaper Evening Star reported a government estimate of 172 killed by the army the previous week.
43. The Times of India, March 15, 1971.
44. Dacca Betar Kendra (Dacca Radio), March 17, 1971, reported in The Times of India.
45. Rising Nepal, March 19, 1971.
46. The Pakistan Times, March 3, 1971.
47. Ibid., March 20, 1971.
48. Ibid., March 22, 1971.
49. Ibid., March 26, 1971.
50. Ibid., March 27, 1971.

7
The Politics
of Disintegration

The Collapse of United Pakistan

Yahya tried to bring about democratic, constitutional government, but instead he presided over the end of the state. Pakistan had emerged out of the British empire and carried with it the political baggage of the Raj. This included a very powerful bureaucratic elite that was strongly against sharing power with other political groups. This elite ruled in cooperation with and at the pleasure of the military. Now this arrangement was faced with serious challenge. Moreover, the secession of Bangladesh compromised the raison d'etat of Pakistan, i.e., the need for a separate state for Muslims. If there could be two Muslim states, why not more?

While the army moved, Yahya explained his decisions to the people. He said he agreed in principle the preceding week to Mujib's demands for the immediate end of martial law and the transfer of power to the National Assembly. For the period between the suspension of martial law and the beginning of the new constitution, Mujib had proposed that legality and legitimacy be covered by a proclamation by the President. Yahya's agreement was contingent on acceptance of the proclamation by all political leaders. Yahya claimed that apart from the Awami League, all political leaders were opposed to the suggestion on the grounds that such a proclamation had no legal or constitutional foundation. Moreover, it could be claimed that such presidential action would be in accordance with popular will. There was also opposition to Mujib's suggestion that the National Assembly be divided into two committees representing East and West Pakistan. A different suggestion called for the National Assembly to convene and enact an appropriate interim constitution bill. Yahya agreed to this and suggested that political leaders try and persuade Mujib to accept it. But according to Yahya, Mujib informed him that he was unwilling to make any

129

changes in his demands. Instead, the Awami League
intensified its non-cooperation efforts. Yahya branded
this an act of treason.[1] Clearly, the bond that held
the country together was dissolving. Z. A. Suleri
observed editorially: "The decline in the national
fortune is explained by one phrase--the erosion of the
spirit which created Pakistan. That spirit was the
only wherewithal on the basis of which the Pakistan
struggle was waged."[2]

One man who had come to power as a result of military intervention assumed the burden, with the support
of a small band of politicians, of arbitrating the
constitutional future of the country. The catastrophe
of the civil war was viewed as not too high a price to
pay for preserving the country in its original form,
even though the East wing, a majority of the population,
preferred it otherwise. Although Yahya admitted that
he did not possess the authority to declare an interim
government, he encountered no such limitations when he
found it necessary to ban all political activities.
The Awami League was banned as a political party; Mujib
was arrested to be tried for treason. Complete
censorship was imposed and a new set of martial law
regulations issued.

The army tried quickly to establish control and
eliminate resistance. This meant seizure of towns,
removal of the Bengali political elite and destruction
of all organized resistance. The Awami League,
students, police, and rebel troops were singled out as
targets. Students at Dacca University fiercely resisted
and were met with artillery, tanks, and other heavy
weapons, resulting in extensive loss of life and damage
to University buildings and grounds. Members of the
Awami League were rounded up together with others sus-
pected of sympathy with the party. The East Pakistan
Rifles went over to the rebels soon after the beginning
of hostilities. While there was considerable enthusiasm among the anti-government forces, they lacked
weapons and ammunition.

The dangers presented by the fighting and the
government's embarrassment over reports of brutality
led to the evacuation of foreigners. Foreign corre-
spondents were ordered out of the country, and in only
a few instances were there any independent reports on
the course of the war. Even the International Red
Cross was denied permission to undertake relief efforts.

After some initial success, the resistance forces
were driven from the major population centers. The
army's strategy was twofold. First, the border with
India had to be sealed off. Other than weapons and
supplies seized from the army, India was the only source
of aid for the rebels. Second, the army sought to gain
control of the cities and thereby dominate communications. The army had to achieve success quickly, as

the monsoon would arrive in two or three months, making large-scale troop movements impossible.

The military capabilities of the resistance--the Mukti Bahini--were limited. Very early in the fighting they were forced to adopt guerilla tactics. Few members of the Mukti Bahini were trained and properly equipped, although there was no shortage of untrained and unarmed volunteers. The proportion of Bengalis in the armed forces of Pakistan had always been small. The bulk of the trained military personnel in the Mukti Bahini came from the East Pakistan Rifles, the East Pakistan Regiment, and Bengali police units. Many enthusiastic recruits were students. But significantly, as with all successful guerilla efforts, the population as a whole was sympathetic to the resistance and provided them with food, shelter, and other necessities.

The army seemed to have taken as its mission not only the suppression of the rebellion itself, but the removal of all potential sources of resistance in the future. Intellectuals and politicians were rounded up and summarily executed. Those who escaped did so by fleeing to India.

The war also created hard conditions for religious minorities. There were reports of the army searching for and executing Hindus. One American official observed: "it is the most incredible, calculated thing since the days of the Nazis in Poland."[3] Another group which suffered were the Biharis. These people were Muslims who had fled India at partition but had not assimilated completely in the Bengali culture. Now they found themselves persecuted in their adopted country.

World opinion was strongly against Mujib's arrest and trial. The International Commission of Jurists, Secretary General U Thant of the United Nations, and political leaders of many countries protested the actions of the government. Mujib survived the war and his internment and was allowed to return to Bangladesh in January 1972. He was assassinated in a power struggle in 1975, which resulted in a military takeover.

On May 24 Yahya stated the ban on the Awami League that he had imposed on March 26 did not mean that all members of the League, and particularly those who had been elected to the National Assembly, were criminals. Only those whom he labeled anti-state elements and miscreants would be punished. The elected members of the League who had not participated in the rebellion retained their seats in the Assembly. The seats of those rebelling against the government would be vacated and bi-elections held to fill them.

The war brought the economy of East Pakistan to a standstill. The jute crop was ready for harvest, but because of the war one of the country's main earners of foreign exchange rotted on the ground. Also, costs of fighting the war brought the national government close to bankruptcy. To make matters worse, Pakistan was unable to obtain further foreign aid either from the nations which had been contributing the bulk of this assistance over the years or from the World Bank. By mid-1971, $35 million in interest on outstanding loans to the World Bank were scheduled for payment. Pakistan requested that either this payment be postponed or that payment be allowed in Pakistani currency. Neither the World Bank nor aid-giving countries favored this scheme for indirectly financing the war. Effective May 1, Pakistan suspended all foreign debt payments in foreign currencies for a period of six months. Rupee payments were continued.

Apart from the economic burden, the war brought only moderate inconvenience to West Pakistan. But in Bangladesh matters went from bad to worse. Even under normal circumstances East Pakistan had not produced sufficient food for its 78 million people. Approximately two million tons of foodstuffs had to be imported every year. During the war not only was the importation of goods through the principal port of Chittagong disrupted, but the distribution of supplies was virtually impossible because the government did not control communication and transportation links. The Mukti Bahini blew up bridges and disrupted road traffic, forcing the army to rely on airfields for supply, while the civilian population faced starvation. Relief supplies, including tons of grain provided by the United States, could not reach those in need. The government showed no great concern for relief and tried to use the situation to break the resistance.

The government faced mounting pressure from the international community. Yahya mixed candor with understatement in an attempt to minimize the consequences of the war and create the impression that the situation would soon be back to normal. He acknowledged most of the short-term problems and offered remedies for them. He recognized that it was necessary to establish and maintain order, to restore communications, and to deal with the refugee problem. Yahya claimed that there should be no difficulty in the refugees returning to their homes unless problems were created by the government of India. For its part, the government of Pakistan would provide opportunities for the refugees to return and to reestablish themselves. All the refugees had to do, apparently, was walk back home and resume their previous lives. No program for their reassimilation was considered necessary, although UN assistance in providing material help was welcomed. The existence of more serious problems such as famine, epidemics, and economic collapse were simply denied.

In his news conference of May 24, 1971, Yahya declared that he was prepared to grant amnesty to all those persons who had, in his words, been "misled" by the "anti-state elements and miscreants." But those who had rebelled or committed arson or rape would not be granted amnesty. Determination of the guilty was a matter of judgment, since most of the population of East Pakistan could be considered anti-state. Amnesty would be extended to members of the Awami League with only those guilty of rebellion or other crimes to face prosecution.[4] Very few persons were willing to take advantage of such a limited amnesty offer.

Economic imbalance had always been one of the issues dividing the two wings of the country, although efforts had been made during the later years of the Ayub regime to correct it. In a belated effort to win over the East wing, the National Economic Commission announced in June that a new $3.5 billion development program would give priority to East Pakistan.[5] Such a gesture had come too late.

On June 28 Yahya announced a program for reconstruction of the country once hostilities had ended. He contended that the short experience with democratic politics and constitution-making by means of the convention process had been unsuccessful. The alternative would be to bypass the constitutional convention and have a commission draw up a new constitution. The new plan abandoned the social-contract idea whereby the fundamental law of the land emanates from the people. The new document would be drafted under the direction of the President, who would himself interpret the needs and aspirations of the people. Yahya directed that most of the injunctions contained in the Legal Framework Order be included in the constitution. These included maximum provincial autonomy, but with a strong federal government able to maintain the integrity of a unified country.

In the same speech he imposed restrictions on political activity. He was most unhappy with political parties and felt that unrestricted party activity would again result in chaos. Accordingly, a ban was placed on parties limited to specific regions and those which were fragmented into several sub-units. Evidently legal parties would have to be truly national in scope, espousing the unified Pakistan idea, but not contain any factions or have regional variations. This suggests either Yahya did not understand the nature of political parties or he was creating conditions which would not allow parties to work. The measure affected both the Awami League and the PPP, since each was strong in only one wing. In November, seven right wing parties declared in Lahore that they would work together in the National Assembly under the leadership of Nurul Amin, President of the Pakistan Democratic Party.[6] Nurul Amin would become Vice President in the Bhutto government after the war.

Yahya seemed optimistic over the possiblity that there would be a return to normalcy after the war. After law and order had been restored and the machinery of government reestablished, he claimed, the transfer of power to civilian authority would not take more than a few months. "Appreciating the situation as it exists today and as it is likely to develop in the near future, it is my hope and belief that I would be able to achieve my goal in a matter of four months or so."[7] But this would be a civilian government in which political parties would play only a limited role because of the restrictions placed upon them.

In August the government completed screening elected officials to determine the extent to which each of them was involved in the attempt secession. Eighty-eight members of the National Assembly from the Awami League were cleared and allowed to participate in the Assembly, should it ever meet. Thirty were formally charged. Ninety-four League members of the Provincial Assembly of East Pakistan were also cleared.[8] By this action the government gave the impression that only a minority of East wing politicians were responsible for the civil war.

Effective September 3, a new civil government for the East wing was announced. The new governor, Dr. Abdul Motaleb Malik, a Bengali, and a new council of Ministers (appointed by the national government under martial law rules) were given the assignment of civil administration. The army was directed to turn over to the civil authorities the responsibility for law and order. However, it was made clear that the troops might be called upon again if the need arose.[9]

Yahya announced a new amnesty on September 5, which was broader than the one discussed in June. The new amnesty included "all those who have committed or are alleged to have committed offenses during the disturbances in East Pakistan beginning March 1, last and ending September 5."[10] Apparently the amnesty meant that except for those persons who by September 5 were being detained facing criminal proceedings, all others regardless of their offenses would be granted amnesty. Yahya also invited "all refugees to return to their homeland to rejoin their families and resume their normal vocations."[11]

The ban on political activity was lifted October 11, but the atmosphere was far from free and open. The new regulations on political activity prohibited "propagation of any opinion or act in a manner prejudicial to the ideology or integrity or security of Pakistan."[12] On October 13 Yahya announced that the new constitution would be published on December 20, followed by the opening of the National Assembly on December 27.[13]

The Government of Pakistan asked for the assistance

of the United Nations High Commissioner for Refugees to assist in the return of the East Pakistani refugees. Pakistan claimed that India was being uncooperative in the matter.[14] But India was being more than merely uncooperative; it was preparing an invasion. The activities of the government, and especially the statements by the President, were intended to minimize the significance of events in East Pakistan and give the impression that with relative ease the country's politics could be set on a normal path of development. But the situation in East Pakistan was beyond redemption by a few promises. After having experienced brutal suppression by the army at Yahya Khan's orders, the East Pakistanis were not willing to accept his authority or the legitimacy of his government.

India's Reaction

India has always regarded Pakistan as its main antagonist, and the fact that it consisted of two wings meant India faced its enemy on two sides. Hostility toward India has never been as great in Bengal as in the West wing, especially in the Punjab. Moreover, the policies of the government of Pakistan vis a vis India are more a reflection of the West wing than of the East. Most of the friction between India and Pakistan, including the fighting over Kashmir, has taken place in the western portion of the subcontinent. Disputes along the eastern frontier have not concerned territory as much as the equitable distribution of Ganges water. An independent state in East Bengal would weaken Pakistan, an agreeable development from India's point of view. India could also expect better relations with an independent Bangladesh than it had experienced with Pakistan. Both of these expectations have since proven correct.

The government and press of India made no secret of their enthusiasm for the independence movement in Bangladesh. The insurgents were consistently referred to as "liberation forces" or "freedom fighters." Despite denials, Indian involvement was more or less open from the start. Not only did India serve as a refuge for millions of persons displaced by the war, but it also served as a sanctuary for insurgent forces. The forces of Bangladesh moved freely back and forth across the border, receiving supplies, equipment, and training from the Indians. Soon Indian army personnel were directly involved in the fighting on the East Pakistan side of the border. Several members of the Indian Border Security Force were apprehended by the Pakistani army and displayed as proof of Indian interference. China protested to the Indian government for interferring in the internal affairs of Pakistan and for "conniving" at demonstrations in front of the

Chinese Embassy in Delhi.[15] Up to the actual invasion, Indian army units exchanged artillery and small arms fire with elements of the Pakistan army at various points on the border.[16] Pakistan appealed to the international community that Indian troops were creating "an explosive situation."[17] As events were to prove, these maneuvers were in preparation for invasion.

The Bangladesh independence movement and resulting civil war confronted India with a serious problem. While opinion in India was on the side of the Bengalis and the Government of India openly supported the insurrection, Mrs. Gandhi's government was unable to recognize the independence of Bangladesh formally as long as the government of Pakistan retained control. As a result, the question of recognition became a hotly debated issue in India. Indian involvement in the war was so open and direct it was becoming a serious provocation to Pakistan. Premature recognition of an insurgent government would have committed India to the success of Bangladesh at a time when such success was open to doubt. Accordingly, Mrs. Gandhi declared that Bangladesh would be recognized when and if the situation demanded.

The Samyukta Socialist Party called not only for immediate recognition, but also suggested that India take the initiative in calling for international volunteers to aid the Bengalis. The Hindu Mahasabha called for United Nation's intervention.[18] Indian Minister of External Affairs Sardar Swaran Singh called upon all Indians "for their whole hearted support of Bangladesh." He denied that the situation in East Pakistan was an internal matter of Pakistan.[19]

Throughout the summer and fall, pressure on the Government of India for intervention in Bangladesh mounted. Important political figures like Jayaprakash Narayan, Morarji Desai, and B. B. Vajpayee called for Indian military action. Narayan was the founder of the Gandhi Peace Foundation and an important political figure of years past. Desai was a leader of the opposition Congress party. Vajpayee was a leader of the Jana Sangh, a right wing Hindu communal party.[20]

A more serious force to be reckoned with by the Indian government was its own military. Many in the army saw in the unsettled situation in East Pakistan an opportunity to inflict a decisive defeat on Pakistan. In their view, victory had been denied them in 1965 when the politicians agreed to a ceasefire. Now, with the Pakistan army engaged in a civil war and new support for India in the form of an alliance with the Soviet Union, the Indian advantage was seen as decisive.

Another factor influencing the Indian government was the presence of 10 million refugees by November 1971. East Bengal had to be stabilized in order that the refugees could be returned home. Minister of

137

External Affairs Swaran Singh in the upper house of the Indian parliament stated:

> The basic question in Bangladesh is a matter between the military regime and the people of Bangladesh.... We are determined and we have also made it clear that the basic question is the res- toration of conditions in Bangladesh which might result in creating confidence in the minds of these refugees so that they can return to Bangladesh with honor and safety.[21]

But India was not interested in simply alleviating the refugee problem. A permanent solution was needed. Accordingly, a suggestion, accepted by Pakistan, that United Nations observers be posted along the border was rejected. The reason given was:

> Mere posting of observers in Bangladesh, par- ticularly on the border, is not likely to create the necessary feeling of confidence among the refugees who are now in India. What is needed is immediate stoppage of military atrocities so that further influx of refugees may cease and a political solution acceptable to the people of Bangladesh through their already elected repre- sentatives is brought about.[22]

On October 26, Yahya accepted UN Secretary General U Thant's offer of good offices for mediating the dispute. He invited the Secretary General to visit the subcontinent immediately "to discuss ways and means of withdrawal of forces from the explosive India-Pakistan borders."[23]

The Refugee Problem

> They came by the millions, most of them with nothing but a few rags and a small bundle of per- sonal possessions. They flowed toward the towns where temporary relief camps were established where some kind of free accommodation and sustenance was available. And there many of them stayed, hundreds of thousands of them huddled into squalid overcrowded huts without adequate water and with almost no sanitation.[24]

Keith Callard wrote the above words describing the refugees in 1947, but the description also fits the situation of 1971. In 1947 the refugee problem was greatest along the western border, while in 1971 it was limited to the eastern border. By the end of 1971, the number of persons crossing the border had reached 10 million. These refugees presented a serious problem to the Government of India, which already faced serious population problems of its own. By and large the refugees brought little or no possessions with them. They were forced to find accommodations wherever they could, and these often were most unsuitable. Some people took shelter in large drainage pipes at construction sites, for example. While the Indian government made efforts to deal with the flood of refugees, there were only limited resources available. Accommodations, food, and medical attention were inadequate, given the large numbers of people requiring help.

The World Bank calculated that the refugees would cost India approximately $700 million for the period April 1971 to March 1972. This figures out to be about $70 per refugee to maintain them for a period of one year. While $70 is not much to sustain a person for a year, the total burden on the economy was considerable. India's desire for the early return of the refugees is therefore understandable.[25]

The refugees' plight was compounded by the fact that they came during the monsoon season, which created, among other things, a serious health problem. Cholera epidemics soon broke out in the camps, resulting in thousands of deaths. An uncontrollable disaster was averted by massive innoculations. Still, the immediate problem of feeding and caring for the refugees was a matter of great concern. Prime Minister Gandhi made it clear that the refugees were not welcome to stay indefinitely. "Conditions must be created to stop any further influx of refugees and to ensure their early return under credible guarantees for their future safety and well-being."[26] India could not, of course, be expected to serve as a sanctuary for all Bengalis who chose to leave East Pakistan.

India asked other countries for help in caring for the refugees. Agencies of the United Nations contributed. Many countries provided foodstuffs, medical supplies and money. The Russians and Americans, in addition to refugee relief, provided airplanes to move the refugees from West Bengal to other parts of India where they could be accommodated more effectively. In July, President Yahya agreed to a proposal offered by UN Secretary General U Thant that "an international body of United Nations observers in East Pakistan be allowed to supervise the return of the refugees."[27] The object of such international observers was to provide assurances that the refugees could return to their homes safely. Although such assurances had been demanded by the Indian government, India did not regard UN observers as conducive to resolution of the refuge problem. Accordingly, India turned down the idea.

For the Government of Pakistan, the existence of the refugees compromised its claims that it was in political control of East Pakistan and that the

situation there would shortly return to normal. Moreover, the issue of the effectiveness of political
control over East Pakistan was vital for Pakistan's
economy. Foreign aid and international commercial
dealings were, for all practical purposes, suspended
during the civil war. Foreign governments and the World
Bank were either hesitant or simply refused to deal with
the government until the situation in East Pakistan had
been resolved. Presumably the Government of Pakistan
hoped that UN observers would provide the reassurance
necessary to allow the resumption of foreign assistance
and commercial transactions.

Yahya Khan also expressed a willingness to meet
with Mrs. Gandhi to discuss the refugee question.
According to Mrs. Gandhi, such a meeting would be to no
avail because of the belligerent attitude on the part
of Yahya Khan. Yahya, on the other hand, suggested
that India's refusal to station UN observers and to
entertain the idea of a summit conference was proof of
India's uncooperative attitude toward the refugee
situation and the civil war.

The refugees were not only a serious financial and
administrative problem for the Indian government, but
they also proved to be a cause of the outbreak of
general war. The refugees would be unlikely to return
home as long as the civil war continued. Nor would
they be encouraged to do so, out of fear of reprisals,
if the Government of Pakistan reestablished political
control. Thus it was in India's interest that an independent Bangladesh be established. Support of the
Mukti Bahini might have achieved this goal, but the
process would likely be a lengthy one. There was also
the possibility that the Government of Pakistan might
win the war. Thus the optimum solution for India was
its own military intervention.

The United States and Arms Aid

Ever since Pakistan joined the American alliance
system in 1956 and received large amounts of military
equipment, India has expressed concern over the potential uses of this equipment. Despite frequent reassur-
ances from the United States that aid was intended exclusively for protection from communist aggression, the
Indians remained skeptical. These doubts ultimately
proved well founded. In 1965, American military equipment was used in the war against India. One result of
the 1965 war was the temporary suspension of this aid.

From 1965 to 1970 the United States maintained an
embargo on military aid. However, some additional
equipment and much-needed replacement parts were obtained from other countries. In particular, tanks sent
to Italy as part of the NATO agreement eventually found
their way into Pakistan. In October 1970 the Nixon

administration decided to resume military assistance on a "one time only basis." The reason for this was never made clear. Administration spokesmen stressed frequently, however, that this was to be the only instance of arms aid. According to the Washington Post, the arms deal was to include 300 armored personnel carriers, 18 F-104A Starfighters, and seven B-57 bombers.[28]

Much of the military equipment supplied under Mutual Security agreements is, in the context of modern weapons systems, obsolete. For example, F-86 aircraft of Korean War vintage which were given to Pakistan many years ago were used against the Mukti Bahini. In dealing with situations like the East Pakistan insurrection, highly sophisticated equipment is not really necessary. Under American security doctrine, more sophisticated military aid was intended for use against communist aggression, meaning The Soviet Union or China. In practice, however, Pakistan used these weapons against India. American doctrine also included provisions for internal security problems, meaning rebellion fomented by indigenous communist groups. For this, light weapons, communication and transportation gear, and other counter-insurgency equipment were given. As it turned out, this aid was appropriate for use against the Bengalis. Neither in 1965 nor in 1971 was there a threat of internal or external communist aggression.

One probable explanation of the decision to resume military aid was to preserve American links with the Government of Pakistan. This may have been considered especially important in view of the steady decline of American influence in South Asia since 1965. American popularity in India has been eroding for a long time, while the stock of the Soviet Union has increased. Failure to support Pakistan in 1965 undermined American popularity in that country. There is considerable anti-Americanism to be found, especially in the vernacular press throughout South Asia. Juxtaposed against the declining role of the United States has been the rise of Soviet and Chinese involvement. The Indo-Soviet Friendship Treaty signed in October 1971 marked an increase in the role the Soviet Union played in South Asia. China had been linked for some time with Pakistan and was the only strong supporter of its actions in East Bengal.

The combination of these factors created difficulties for American policy. Officially the United States condemned the actions of the Pakistan government. There was great indignation in the American Congress, however, and there were demands that all aid to Pakistan be suspended.[29] Compared to the unequivocal and enthusiastic Chinese support, the United States policy was a low-key, wait-and-see approach. The Nixon administration attempted with little success to play down the matter of arms aid and to draw attention to the non-military aspects of American aid programs. The United States moved quickly to become one of the first and largest contributors to the Indian effort to aid the refugees.

The United States was particularly concerned that the East Pakistan situation might endanger world peace. The prospect of great power involvement, especially with the Soviet Union and China showing such willingness to take sides, was particularly disturbing. The possibility that India might defeat both wings of Pakistan encouraged the quest for a rapid solution to the Bangladesh problem. As a result, the United States increased pressure on Pakistan to end the fighting and back down from its belligerent posture toward India.

One of the most effective tools open to the United States and other countries was economic. The civil war brought Pakistan to the verge of bankruptcy; foreign exchange reserves dwindled, exports dried up, agricultural production almost ceased, and the problem of repayment of foreign debts became an immediate crisis. Large payments on loans from the United States and the World Bank fell due by the end of June. Pakistan requested deferment of the repayment due and that the loaning countries accept rupees, which were overvalued, as payment. Moreover, Pakistan's request for standby credits from the international Monetary Fund met with opposition.[30] All in all, this economic pressure probably contributed to Yahya Khan's decision to attempt a quick restoration of "normalcy" in East Pakistan. These efforts, however, were confounded not only by the action of the Bengalis, but by the deteriorating relationship with India.

Pakistan complained to the United States about Indian actions. UN Ambassador Mahmud Ali pleaded with Secretary of State William Rogers "that India was not only supporting the 'Bangladesh' guerillas but was moving its own troops to the East Pakistan border." Earlier the Secretary of State had urged Indian Foreign Minister Swaran Singh "in the strongest possible terms" to get a dialogue started with the government of Pakistan.[31]

On November 8, 1971, it was announced that the United States would cease arms deliveries to Pakistan. The announcement coincided with a visit to the United States by the Indian Prime Minister and came at a time when conflict along the East Pakistan border with India was escalating. This left Pakistan with only one supporter--China--to take up the slack left by the unwillingness of the U.S. and other countries to continue assistance.

Soviet and Chinese Involvement

Both the Soviet Union and China took bold positions in the struggle between India and Pakistan. Unlike the

United States, neither communist country attempted an "even-handed" approach. China regarded the war as an internal domestic matter, which meant support for the Government of Pakistan. Moreover, China vigorously denounced both the United States and the Soviet Union for interferring in Pakistan's internal affairs. Throughout the war, China proved to be Pakistan's only forthright supporter pledging both military and economic aid.

China's attitude toward Bangladesh seems most inappropriate given its ideological enthusiasm for "wars of national liberation," a doctrine which rests on the idea that peoples of the world who are exploited by colonialism should seize the opportunity to liberate themselves from this oppression. Such wars would occur in the underdeveloped countries and would most likely follow the experience of China itself. One of China's favorite slogans had been the condemnation of various countries as "running dogs of imperialism." This refers to some governments' cooperation with imperialist and colonialist countries, particularly the United States. India was the recipient of this epithet for many years despite that country's pronounced independence of Western foreign policies and consistent support of China. In the Bangladesh context, then, the Chinese appeared to be violating their own teachings on at least two counts. In the first place, Pakistan had been one of the most notorious "running dogs" to the extent that it participated in two American alliances--CENTO and SEATO. India, on the other hand, had been a strong critic of American foreign policy and champion of non-alignment. Secondly, the Bangladesh independence movement seemed to be a perfect example of a war of national liberation. But somehow the Bengalis did not qualify. Instead, the secessionist movement was seen as the result of a plot engineered by India.

China's credibility as a revolutionary spokesman also suffered as a result of its position on the war. Its failure to endorse and support the liberation movement in Bengal was especially disillusioning for the Maoist revolutionaries in India, such as the Naxalites in West Bengal.

Despite its victory over India in 1962, China had been neither willing nor able to play a significant role in the strategic developments in South Asia. Since 1962, China consistently condemned India and offered support for Pakistan, mostly of a verbal sort. Military and economic aid was extended, which became more important as the United States reduced its commitment. In the long run, however, this was not adequate, as Pakistan's forces, even with Chinese aid, were no match for India. For its part, China chose to stay out of the conflict except for offering moral support to Pakistan.

Last minute efforts to gain international support

for Pakistan's position found Z. A. Bhutto on a mission to Peking. At the same time Mrs. Gandhi was giving her version of developments to President Nixon in Washington. Acting Foreign Minister Chi Peng-fei assured the Pakistani delegation that should Pakistan be attacked, the people of China would "resolutely support them in their just struggle to defend their sovereignty and national independence."[32] President Yahya Kahn asserted in an interview with CBS News that the Chinese would "help in whatever way they can" should India attack.[33] India did not take any of these threats too seriously.

The war gave the Soviet Union a chance to expand its ties with India. The Soviets decided against trying to retain any significant measure of influence with Pakistan. But this was more or less consistent with Soviet policy since 1947. The Soviet Union has never been particularly warm toward Pakistan; in fact, Stalin regarded it as an absurdity.[34] It is true that Nehru was at first regarded as a capitalist stooge, resulting in poor Soviet relations with the entire subcontinent. But after Stalin's death and the resulting thaw in Russian foreign policy, it proved easier to develop cordial relations with India, given its opposition to American foreign policy.

On August 9, 1971, a 20-year treaty of peace, friendship, and cooperation between the Soviet Union and India was signed. The Russians, in effect, pledged to support India's security.[35] This agreement complemented extensive ties between India and the Soviet Union. The Russians had been active in aiding Indian economic development, and an expanded trade agreement was signed in December 1970. The Treaty of Peace, Friendship, and Cooperation added security to the list of Soviet commitments to India.

For a brief period of time during 1968-69, Soviet policy toward Pakistan changed. Perhaps in an attempt to undercut the United States and to offset growing Chinese influence, Russia extended military aid to Pakistan. After Yahya Khan's takeover there were Soviet overtures for closer economic ties. But in 1969 Russian aid ceased because of Moscow's inability to determine in what direction Yahya was going to take Pakistan's foreign policy. Pakistan was not making any move toward the settlement of the Kashmir issue. The Russians had been instrumental in bringing about an end to the 1965 Kashmir war, but no progress had been made beyond the declaration of Tashkent. The August agreement with India ended the brief rapproachement between Moscow and Islamabad.

The war over Bangladesh brought a distinct polarization in Asian relations, marking a culmination of trends which began in the early 1960's. The Soviets and the Indians lined up against the Chinese and the

Pakistanis. The United States found itself more or less caught in the middle.

On November 12 Mrs. Gandhi stated in Bonn, West Germany, that she would be willing to "accept the good offices of neutral mediators provided they are willing to see the question in its entirety." She also claimed to be willing to meet with Yahya to consider all the questions between the two countries.[36]

Invasion

On November 22 India launched an all-out attack on East Pakistan. Pakistan acknowledged that small gains were made but "at great cost to the invader." Mrs. Gandhi asked Yahya to withdraw his troops from East Pakistan "in the interest of peace."[37] Meanwhile, Pakistan claimed it had launched a counter offensive.

On December 4 India opened a second front in the west. Amritsar, Srinagar, Pathankot, Avantipour and Agra were bombed by Pakistani planes but with little effect. Pakistan claimed all planes returned while India claimed all were shot down. Ground attacks were launched by India at 3:30 in the morning in Sialkot, Chhamb, Jassar, Lahore, Rajasthan, and Rahimyar Khan sectors. The situation was bad enough in the East, where Pakistan's forces could only be supplied via Ceylon. But in the West there was the real possibility that Pakistan's army might be overrun. This brought an immediate "tilt" by the United States which was of the view that India would not be satisfied with anything less than the complete destruction of Pakistan.[38] Urgent messages were sent to India and its ally the Soviet Union discouraging any widening of the war.[39] The United States also sent a naval task force, including a nuclear-power aircraft carrier, into the Bay of Bengal in a show of force. These actions were probably intended to reassure Pakistan and China, with which the United States was attempting to develop better relations, as much as they were to show displeasure with Indian and Soviet actions.[40] On December 17 Mrs. Gandhi called for a ceasefire, since all her objectives had been reached. This was accepted by local commanders in the East and then, accepting the inevitable, by Yayha Khan "in the interest of peace." Yahya said: "this is not the end of the war...we may lose a battle but victory is ours."[41]

On December 19 Yahya announced his resignation. He requested Zulfiqar Ali Bhutto to return to Pakistan from New York, and upon his arrival "power would be transferred to a representative government."[42] Bhutto immediately assumed the duties of President and Chief Martial Law Administrator. In his first speech as leader of the country he pledged "never to abandon East Pakistan."[43] Nurul Amin was sworn in as Vice President.

That Bhutto's accession to power would bring in its wake considerable change in Pakistan's politics was soon evident when, on December 22, the government impounded the passports of the 22 richest families in the country. This was an effort to gain the return of assets held abroad.[44] The government would continue to try to reduce the economic and political power of the country's leading families.

On January 3 Bhutto announced that Sheikh Mujib would be released unconditionally and returned to Bangladesh. Bhutto acknowledged that his action had been requested by "the three superpowers" the ambasadors of which had recently informed him of their wishes.[45] At three in the morning, Mujib was flown from Rawalpindi to London on a plane provided by the government of Pakistan. At the same time it was announced that General Agha Mohammed Yahya Khan had been placed under house arrest.[46] Yahya subsequently became almost a non-person and his death on August 8, 1980, received only a small notice in the back pages of the newspapers.

The Bhutto government placed the blame for Pakistan's debacle upon Yahya's ruling "junta," which desired to retain its political dominance after a new constitution had been introduced. This involved a scheme whereby a weak party government headed by Sheikh Mujib would give the appearance of democracy but would be dominated by a strong president. Yahya's efforts to achieve this goal were frustrated by the size of the Awami League victory and Bhutto's political strength.[47]

Bhutto's offer to establish a link with Bangladesh was rejected by Mujib who declared the ties between East and West Pakistan had "been snapped for all time to come."[48] Mujib also suggested that "war criminals" would be tried. This became a matter of considerable anxiety for Pakistan, as India held over 90,000 prisoners of war. Bhutto continued to display a spirit of accommodation and a willingness to negotiate.[49] On January 17 he offered to renounce his office and step aside if Mujib were prepared to become President or Prime Minister "or whatever he wished, to preserve Pakistan's oneness," but Mujib showed no interest in the offer.[50]

In late January, preparations were under way for convening of the national and provincial assemblies. The Legal Framework Order would be amended to make the National Assembley "fully sovereign." But it would be necessary to retain martial law for some time and to postpone elections which were scheduled for local government offices.[51] Elections were held to fill women's seats in the Provincial Assemblies. the PPP won eight, six in the Punjab, and two in Sind. The Nap won the two seats in NWFP, and the NAP-JUI coalition took the only seat in Baluchistan.[52] On March 3,

146

changes in the military leadership were announced. General Tikka Khan was made head of the army, and Air Force Marshal Zafar Chaudhry took over control of the air force.[53]

NOTES

1. The Pakistan Times, March 26, 1971.
2. Ibid., August 1, 1971.
3. Quoted in Time, August 2, 1971.
4. The Pakistan Times, September 1, 1971.
5. Ibid., June 18, 1971.
6. Ibid., November 16, 1971.
7. Federal Intervention in Pakistan: Background Report IV, 1971, Washington: Embassy of Pakistan, p. 11.
8. The Pakistan Times, October 10, 1971.
9. Ibid., September 1, 1971.
10. Dawn (Karachi), September 5, 1971.
11. Ibid.
12. The Pakistan Times, October 10, 1971.
13. Ibid., October 13, 1971.
14. Ibid., August 30, 1971.
15. Ibid., April 8, 1971.
16. Ibid., October 30, 1971.
17. Ibid., October 22, 1971.
18. The Times of India, April 6, 1971.
19. Ibid., August 13, 1971.
20. Narayan: "The country, the government, and the people are unworthy if they are not prepared for war." The Hindustan Times, July 7, 1971. "The time for action has come. We must give the Liberation Army heavy artillery, guns, anti-tank weapons machine-guns and explosives." The Times (London), July 5, 1971.
21. India News (Washington: Embassy of India), August 6, 1971.
22. Ibid., August 13, 1971.
23. The Pakistan Times, October 26, 1971.
24. Callard, Pakistan: A Political Study, p. 19.
25. India News (Washington: Embassy of India), November 5, 1971. The Indian government levied new taxes to meet the costs of refugee relief.
26. Ibid., June 4, 1971.
27. The Financial Times (London), July 19, 1971.
28. Washington Post, October 8, 1971.
29. See, for example, The Congressional Record for June, 1971.
30. The Financial Times (London), June 18, 1971, The Times of India, April 11, 1971.
31. The Pakistan Times, October 9, 1971.
32. Ibid., November 8, 1971.
33. Ibid., November 9, 1971.
34. The Times of India, April 7, 1971.

35. The relevant article of the treaty states: "Each High Contracting Party undertakes to abstain from providing assistance to any third party that engages in armed conflict with the other Party. In the event of either Party being subjected to an attack or a threat thereof, the High Contracting Parties shall immediately enter into mutual consultations in order to remove such a threat and to rake appropriate effective measures to ensure peace and security of their countries." India News (Washington: Embassy of India), August 13, 1971. Also see J.A. Naik, Soviet Policy Toward India: From Stalin to Brezhnev, New Delhi: Vikas Publications, 1970.

36. The Pakistan Times, November 11, 1971.

37. Ibid., December 1, 1971.

38. Henry A. Kissinger, The White House Years, London: Weidenfeld and Nicolson and Michael Joseph, 1979, p. 901.

39. Kissinger says of the Soviet Union: "Moscow was acting like a pyromaniac who wants credit for having called the fire department to the fire he has set." Ibid., p. 874.

40. Anwar H. Syed, "Pakistan's Security Problem: A Bill of Constraints," Orbis, XVI (Winter, 1973) 967.

41. The Pakistan Times, December 17, 1971.

42. Ibid., December 20, 1971.

43. Ibid., December 21, 1971.

44. Ibid., December 23, 1971.

45. Ibid., January 4, 1972.

46. Ibid., January 9, 1972.

47. Ibid., January 10, 1972.

48. Ibid., January 11, 1972.

49. Ibid., January 13, 1972.

50. Ibid., January 18, 1972.

51. Ibid., February 18, 1972.

52. Ibid., February 21, 1972.

53. Ibid., March 4, 1972.

8
The Frustrations
of Foreign Policy

Pakistan in World Affairs

No country, especially small and underdeveloped ones, can hope to escape the influence of their neighbors. One unfortunate tendency in the way states relate to one another is the extent to which they exaggerate differences, ignore common interests, and cling to fantasies about themselves and one another. This tendency has been particularly evident in the modern history of South Asia.

Pakistan comes out of a historical-cultural tradition shared with other countries of the subcontinent, especially India. By asserting their Islamic distinctiveness, which is one part of this tradition, the Pakistanis emphasized differences rather than commonalities vis a vis their neighbors. The people of the two wings actually had more in common with Indian Pubjab and Indian Bengal than they had with each other. But it has not been common interests that have been the basis of foreign relations. Rather, it has been the differences that have proved decisive.

This chapter will not review foreign relations as such but will attempt to show how these relations and the consequences of them influenced the course of Pakistan's politics. Pakistan's foreign relations, both friendly and otherwise, have not been a positive factor in the country's political development.

Until 1971, Pakistan's relations with other countries were largely a function of the Kashmir issue. Friendly relations with China and the United States were intended to strengthen Pakistan's bargaining position vis a vis India. But China and Pakistan have shared relatively few substantive interests apart from their common antagonism toward India. Hostility between China and India continued long after the 1962 border war and the Chinese takeover of Tibet because of India's ties to the Soviet Union. Since the early 1960's, Sino-Soviet relations have been especially hostile. China

thus sees Pakistan as "an enemy of mine enemy."
The connection with the United States has been the most important influence on Pakistan's internal and external behavior. Unfortunately the international perspectives and policies of the United States were fundamentally different from those of Pakistan. Although there was a formal alliance between the two countries, both wrongly interpreted the goals and intentions of the other.

The United States saw Pakistan's participation in the anti-communist alliance system as an indication of acceptance of the American strategic point of view. Pakistan, however, saw the alliance as an opportunity to bolster its own strategic interests, which were concerned more with India than with possible Soviet or Chinese aggression. In this regard, American foreign policy was an important contributing factor in the confrontation with India over Kashmir, which in turn undermined Pakistan's ability to develop politically.

The alliance and the program of arms aid made it difficult for the United States to deal with the secessionist government in Bangladesh and to develop a working relationship with the Bengali nationalists. American dissatisfaction with Pakistan's actions came about slowly, and pressure to seek a solution to the problem was applied in small increments. It should have been clear that efforts to suppress the independence movement would ultimately end in failure. The logistics of the matter alone would suggest that. At the risk of offending India and driving it closer to the Soviet Union, the United States maintained modest support for Pakistan. American efforts at a diplomatic solution were unrewarded. Bangladesh and India with its Soviet ally would settle for nothing short of complete independence and, for the matter, why should they.

Soviet global ambitions seem to have sharply expanded in the last few years. The measure of this is its willingness and even enthusiasm for close attachment to the fortunes of other countries. Cuba, Egypt, and India, among others, have received Russian diplomatic support and material assistance. This is perhaps surprising, given the often unhappy experiences of the United States with such policies. That the Soviet Union has ambitions in the Mediterranean and the Indian Ocean should come as no surprise, however. The Russians are pursuing an ambition which dates back to Peter the Great--access to the world's principal waterways and with such access a greater share of trade, influence, and prestige. To achieve this goal, they are willing to accept the dangers of deep involvement in highly unstable situations and, as in the case of Egypt, considerable frustration.

It is a commentary on the shifting sands of history that the United States and China should find

themselves more or less on the same side of the South
Asian crisis. In the past, the foreign policies of
both countries drew criticism from India and the Soviet
Union. With India's intervention in Bangladesh, the
roles were reversed. While millions of refugees provided compelling reasons for intervention, the fact
remains that India's actions amounted to direct intervention in the internal affairs of a foreign country.
The Mukti Bahini had not established control over the
East wing, although the effectiveness of the national
government was far from complete.

The emergence of an independent Bangladesh altered
the relationship among the countries of South Asia.
The Indo-Pakistan relationship assumed altogether different characteristics. While both sides may continue
to press their differences and there may be more
fighting, India is now strategically dominant. Independent Bangladesh immediately became a client state of
India. But given the nature of politics in Bengal,
both East and West, this relationship has not been cordial. Nor for that matter does the destruction of the
East wing of Pakistan eliminate all of India's security
problems. Pakistan remains although it poses much less
of a threat to Indian security. But the Soviet invasion of Afghanistan in 1979 created a completely new
set of worries for both Pakistan and India. Moreover,
the problems of antagonism between the Hindu and Muslim
communities has not gone away. Communal difficulties
continue to be a problem, especially for India. The
economic system of Bangladesh was virtually destroyed
by the war. The war did little damage to industry,
since there was little to begin with. But the absence
of banking and currency systems, investment capital and
administrative machinery made economic life difficult.
The problems of refugees, famine, disease, housing,
sanitation, and all public services were not resolved
with peace and independence. The Indian government had
to continue to bear a responsibility for the people of
Bangladesh. The problems that had divided East
Pakistan and India, such as control over Ganges water,
remained. For Bangladesh it was, for the most part, a
matter of starting at the beginning.

Pakistan and the United States

Soon after World War II, the United States adopted
the position that international peace and order were
threatened by the spread of communism, which was being
controlled directly by the Kremlin. The containment of
communism became the goal of American policy, rendering
other matters of secondary importance. But this overly
simplistic approach to world affairs failed for several
reasons. First, it did not accept the fact that communism could take many forms. It was taken as an

article of faith that communism is the same in the Soviet Union, in Yugoslavia, in China or anywhere else. Because of this view, the United States was unable to develop a constructive relationship with China.

Second, containment did not recognize the possibility that the use of force to prevent communist takeovers may ultimately result in even worse disasters, as the Vietnam debacle was to prove. Instead of an essentially nationalistic regime in Vietnam and perhaps independent regimes in Laos and Cambodia, in a pluralistic Southeast Asian power matrix with China as the key but not overwhelmingly dominant power, the Soviet Union now holds sway over most of the area acting through its Vietnamese client. By deeply involving itself in Southeast Asia and then failing in the effort, the United States lost its ability to influence the course of events in the entire region.

Third, the United States assumed that each of its allies must share its world view, since they were, after all, allies. But many of these allies were more concerned with relations with one another than with American global designs.

Fourth, it was assumed that communism would expand outward from the Soviet Union and be imposed by force, since no country would willingly choose that form of government. But it soon became apparent that countries could succumb to communism from within. Hence, allies and others had to be provided economic and military aid to promote internal security. The tactic of supplying military aid to regimes facing leftist revolutionary movements is still popular today, although it enjoys no more success now than it ever did.

In 1947 the United States government considered the subcontinent the responsibility and interest of the British. Even though they had given up their Indian empire, as far as international politics were concerned, the British were still the dominant power in the area. Moreover, the United States was preoccupied with Europe, where it was heavily involved in helping repair the damage resulting from the war. The threat of Soviet communism was also thought to be mainly directed toward Europe. It was only after 1949 and the advent of communist China that the United States took greater interest in Asia. In the immediate postwar years, the United States viewed communism as by nature expansionist, which, if left unopposed, would conquer or take over by internal subversion any country in its path. Accordingly, the United States, as the strongest non-communist power to emerge from the war, reluctantly assumed the responsibility of preventing communist expansion.[1] The centerpiece of this strategy was the creation of a system of multilateral and bilateral alliances.

The Korean war produced two significant shifts in American policy. The first was the perception that communist expansion might most likely occur outside Europe. This brought about an expansion of interest and concern for the underdeveloped countries of the Middle East and Asia. Initially the United States expected other Western countries to preserve the integrity of their former colonies. But it soon became apparent that neither Britain nor France were willing or able to deal effectively with the unconventional tactics of the communists. The second change was in the character of the American foreign assistance program. Foreign aid introduced first as temporary aid to Greece and Turkey and then implemented on a semi-permanent basis in the Marshall Plan was intended primarily to provide the ecomonic wherewithal to rebuild wartorn Europe. However, the Korean war brought a major de-emphasis in the economic aspects of foreign assistance in favor of military aid. From 1951 to 1956 more than half of American foreign assistance was of the military variety. Although most of the aid went to NATO countries, throughout the 1950's the proportion going to non-Western countries increased significantly.

The problems facing India and Pakistan were brought home to the United States in the early 1950's when both countries experienced serious famines. In early 1952 India asked for food assistance, to which the Congress responded by authorizing a gift shipment. In June 1953 the United States gave one million tons of wheat to Pakistan. Later in the same year work began on a long-range program for the dispensation of surplus agricultural products. This program came as a recognition of the long term shortages that would be facing many underdeveloped countries. Since the United States had an existing problem of storing agricultural surpluses, the two circumstances went hand in hand to produce the Food for Peace Program, otherwise known as PL 480.

In the early 1950's, South Asia was considered part of a larger area particularly vulnerable to aggression. In 1953, Secretary of State John Foster Dulles encouraged Arab countries to carry a larger share of the burden for their own defense. He had in mind a Middle Eastern defense system patterned after NATO. Recognizing the need for enthusiasm and cooperation for such an alliance, Dulles offered a promise of American assistance as an inducement. He reported that many of the countries were receptive to his suggestion.[2]

As British influence in the Middle East declined, the United States considered it increasingly imperative that some kind of defense arrangement be encouraged. Accordingly, in early 1954 the United States conferred with Iraq, Saudi Arabia, and Iran on the subject of mutual defense. These discussions led to a series of bilateral assistance pacts between the United States and various Middle Eastern countries. Two of the earliest participants in this program were Turkey--already a member of NATO--and Pakistan. Other Arab countries were not enthusiastic about the program. Egypt and Syria in particular were extremely critical of American military alliance policies. The Arab countries most receptive to an alliance scheme were those closest to the Soviet Union. These countries, known as the northern tier states, entered into a defensive agreement in November 1955 when Britain, Pakistan, Iraq, Turkey, and later Iran formed the Baghdad Pact.

Americans were encouraged by these developments, seeing in the Baghdad Pact a way to reduce the dangers of small wars like Korea. Also, it was hoped that the Pact would set an example for other countries to follow.[3] The United States was not a member of the alliance but actively supported it through sizeable economic and military assistance. Iraq withdrew from the Pact in 1958 following a coup which overthrew the government. Subsequently, the alliance was known as the Central Treaty Organization, or CENTO.

However, the United States failed to consider the impact of security alliances uppon regional disputes, in particular that between Pakistan and India over Kashmir. In order to insure that limited military efforts would not succeed in taking over Pakistan, the defensive capabilities of that country would be strengthened. Potential aggressors would need to mount a massive attack in order to overcome local defenses. Such an attack by its very nature would trigger an American response. The thinking was that such a strategy would deter brush fire wars and, should they occur, American involvement would be less likely. On February 23, 1954, the United States announced that military assistance would be given to Pakistan as part of the overall effort to strengthen the defensive capabilities of the Middle East. Rumors of the possibility of such aid were circulating as early as November 1953, contributing to the disruption of relations between India and Pakistan. Prime Minister Nehru informed Pakistan that acceptance of American assistance would affect relations over Kashmir.[4]

Nehru raised three main objections. First, by receiving military aid, Pakistan brought great power involvement to the subcontinent, threatening the international stability that all countries needed so they could concentrate on internal affairs. Second, military aid to Pakistan upset the local balance of power, forcing India to take some sort of remedial action. Third, the United States had established a foothold in South Asia, raising the possibility of some new kind of Western dominance.[5] Thus, rather than promoting international stability as intended, American support for

Pakistan contributed to the instability of South Asia, at least in the view of India.

Pakistan replied that India's concern for the balance of power in South Asia disguised its real intentions. Ayub Khan later rejected India's plea for assurances that American military equipment would not be used against India, which, in Pakistan's view, was interpreted to mean that the United States should promise not to support Pakistan in the event of Indian aggression. Since India had always contemplated reuniting the subcontinent, it wanted guarantees that the United States would not interfere when the time came to take over Pakistan by force.[6]

Pakistan was critical of India's acceptance of military assistance when it was attacked by China in 1962. This was also interpreted as an attempt by India to mask its intentions of conquering Pakistan. President Ayub argued that there was really no need for India to improve its military position vis a vis China, because the Sino-Indian border problem could be resolved peacefully. According to Ayub, the Chinese were willing to seek pacific settlement; it was the Indians who were standing in the way of such an agreement.[7] Outside support, military and otherwise, served to stoke the fires of hostility in Indo-Pakistan relations.

President Eisenhower reaffirmed American policies and intentions in a special message to Congress in January 1957. This statement subsequently came to be known as the Eisenhower Doctrine. Congress supported this Doctrine via a joint resolution which was passed March 9, 1957. Essentially the Eisenhower Doctrine stipulated that the United States was willing to support any country in the Middle East requesting such assistance in "resisting aggression from any country controlled by international communism."[8]

Pakistan was linked with the United States through a second alliance, the Southeast Asia Treaty Organization.[9] Established in September 1954, SEATO included--in addition to Pakistan and the United States--Great Britain, New Zealand, France, Thailand, and the Phillipines. As with the Middle East and South Asia, in Southeast Asia the United States became entangled in local quarrels. The conflict here, however, differed from the others in that the United States became itself directly and massively involved in the actual fighting.

Several SEATO members, including France, Britain, and Pakistan, did not participate in the Vietnam war. France, whose colony Vietnam originally was, withdrew in 1954; others were never involved. Pakistan did not even support American policy. This resulted in part from cooperation and understanding that developed between Pakistan and China during the 1960's. Suffice it to say that Pakistan received American assistance and support through the medium of SEATO but did not support the activities or policies of the organization. Nevertheless, Pakistan argued that it could not fulfill its role in the alliance system without greater American assistance.[10]

Foreign assistance, especially from the United States, has been very important for Pakistan. From 1946 to 1964, total American economic aid was in excess of 2.5 billion dollars. During the first five-year plan, almost one-half of the budget came from external sources. The second five-year plan included about the same percentage of foreign assistance but twice the amount of the first plan. Although India had received a higher dollar amount than had Pakistan, the amount of aid to the latter was more in per capita terms and in percentage of the total budget.[11]

President Eisenhower attempted to allay Indian suspicions by emphasizing the desirability of strengthening Pakistan's defensive capability and by reassuring India that the United States would not allow American military equipment to be used against them. In a letter to Prime Minister Nehru, Eisenhower even held open the possibility that simliar arrangements could be forthcoming involving India.

> What we are proposing to do, and what Pakistan is agreeing to, is not directed in any way against India. And I am confirming publicly that if our aid to any country, including Pakistan, is misused and directed against another in aggression I will undertake immediately, in accordance with my constitutional authority, appropriate action both within and without the United Nations to thwart such aggression. I believe that the Pakistan-Turkey collaboration agreement which is being discussed is sound evidence of the defensive purposes which both countries have in mind....We also believe it in the interest of the free world that India have a strong military defense capability and have admired the effective way your government has administered your military establishment. If your Government would conclude that circumstances require military aid of a type contemplated by our mutual security legislation, please be assured that your request would receive my most sympathetic consideration.[13]

Despite these assurances, military assistance was not always used in the fashion for which it was intended. Pakistan was supposed to strengthen its positions along the northern frontier, i.e., the frontier closest to the Soviet Union and China. It chose instead to place its strength along its southern frontier, i.e., its frontier with India. A study by the Foreign Affairs Committee of the House of Representatives of March 1961 expressed concern for this tendency, even though Department of Defense specifications stated that the location of military installations should be "in relation to the most likely direction of Soviet-led or inspired attack."[13]

Pakistan demonstrated little enthusiasm for the broader goals of American foreign policy. In 1962 the United States began a troop buildup in Thailand. Other SEATO members followed suit, but not Pakistan. It declined on the grounds that it could not spare the troops because of the continued Indian threat, although the extent of such a threat at the time is doubtful. During this period, India had military contingents in two United Nations peace-keeping forces: a brigade participated in the Congo operations, and Indians constituted the largest contingent in the Gaza Strip force. Although Pakistan did not contribute forces to Thailand because of a fear of India, it was able, in the space of a few months, to send 1500 troops to West Guinea to constitute a UN force in that area. The inconsistency is explained perhaps by Pakistan's desire to avoid being placed in a position which might help frustrate Chinese aims. Since the situation in West Guinea was not of immediate interest to China, Pakistan could participate in this activity without fear of interfering with Chinese ambitions.

In March 1963 the Pakistanis announced they had reached agreement with China over their common boundary, which included sizeable portions of Pakistan-held Kashmir.[14] By this action, China recognized Pakistan's claim. In addition, the two countries agreed to establish regular air service. In February 1971 a highway through Karakoram linking China and Pakistan formally opened. On this occasion both countries expressed mutual friendship and support.[15]

Foreign Relations During The Bhutto Period

After the 1971 war, Pakistan's foreign policy underwent significant changes. The Bhutto government attempted to broaden its connections with Middle Eastern and Soviet bloc countries while reducing its reliance on the West. One of his earliest actions was to withdraw from the Commonwealth of Nations, a decision which he said was "final and irrevocable." The decision resulted from the recognition of Bangladesh by Great Britain and the Commonwealth, an action which "puts the seal of approval on an act of blatant aggression.[16] Relations with Commonwealth countries continued on a bilateral basis.

Attempts to improve relations with the Soviet Union met with only limited success, especially due to its alliance with India. Bhutto visited Moscow in

March and announced that Pakistan was not interested in the Kremlin-sponsored Asian Security Pact,[17] an arrangement which would have in effect placed the entire region under the dictates of Soviet strategic doctrine.

1972 marked the formal recognition by many nations of altered strategic relationships in Asia and the need to change policies accordingly. President Nixon visited China and opened relations between that country and the United States. American involvement in Vietnam ended, and the importance of the United States as a military factor in Asia was reduced. Soviet involvement grew with its new ties to India and Vietnam, and, of course, Pakistan had been partitioned. In light of this, Pakistan served formal notice of its intention to withdraw from SEATO. At the same time it was decided that diplomatic relations would be established with North Korea. While SEATO was considered irrelevant to Pakistan's needs, CENTO was still important, considering the Indo-Soviet treaty and the fact that CENTO included Iran and Turkey, Islamic countries close to and important for Pakistan.[18] On November 15 Pakistan announced its decision to recognize East Germany.[19]

Relations with China continued on a cordial basis. Bhutto visited Peking and was able to get the Chinese to write off part of Pakistan's debt and to extend new credits. China also renewed its pledge to aid Pakistan in the event of aggression.[20]

In the United States, the Vietnam war had ended the public consensus supporting an assertive-interventionist foreign policy and ushered in a period of self-doubt. As a result "U.S. policy was not only unfocused, it was disspirited."[21] American policy toward South Asia became increasingly ambiguous. While support for Pakistan continued, efforts were also made to woo India away from the Soviets. The United States pressured Pakistan to abandon plans for a nuclear capability, while at the same time it supplied nuclear fuel to India. Pakistan also contributed to the ambiguity of the relationship by its efforts to broaden its international connections. Later developments in Iran and Afghanistan would add to the confusion. But in the final analysis, the United states was Pakistan's principal ally. In March 1973 the United States eased its arms embargo, thus opening the way for shipment of armored personnel carriers, spare parts, parachutes, and aircraft engines. Bhutto had claimed Pakistan was entitled to American arms under bilateral agreements of 1954 and 1959.[22]

The main foreign policy issue was the resolution of the Bangladesh problem. Bhutto moved to accept the fact of East Pakistan's independence, something that was not universally welcome in West Pakistan. His new constitution left open the possibility of the Bengalis rejoining the union, however. The recognition of Bangladesh was a precondition imposed by India before several outstanding issues would be addressed. There were millions of refugees to be repatriated. There were people in each wing who wanted to be in the other. There was the longstanding question of refugee property, a matter that had never been resolved since the partition of 1947. There were 90,000 Pakistani prisoners of war in the hands of the Indian army. India wanted to return the refugees and POW's in the hands of the Indian army. India wanted to return the refugees and POW's as soon as possible, as their maintenance imposed considerable expense. But by holding them, India was able to pressure Pakistan to accept its terms. Even with that obstacle overcome, another arose when Bangladesh insisted on trying 195 of the POW's as war criminals under the Genocide Convention. Pakistan protested and took its case to the International Court of Justice, which ruled in its favor. The ICJ petitioned India not to transfer the POW's to Bangladesh for trial.

On August 29, agreement was reached on the repatriation of the POW's and civilian internees. The issue of the 195 accused of war crimes was held in abeyance for the time being. They would eventually be released. Pakistan wanted the POW's back and an end to the crisis, as it was distracting attention away from the process of political reconstruction. The desire for revenge for the atrocities committed by the Pakistan army during the war was satisfied by Pakistan's recognition of Bangladesh and the acknowledgement that atrocities had been committed.[23] Bhutto and Mujib were able to come to terms at the 1972 Islamic Summit Conference which was hosted by Pakistan.

The Impact of the Soviet Invasion of Afghanistan

For years the Soviet Union considered Pakistan an American puppet and had little respect for India's nonalignment. All this had changed by 1971 when the Soviets signed a treaty of Peace and Friendship with India. This arrangement, in conjunction with Pakistan's loss of East Pakistan the same year, altered the power relationships in South and Central Asia. Another unsettling development was the fall of the Shah in Iran. With the Soviet invasion of Afghanistan, the area assumed greater strategic significance than at any time since World War II. Pakistan's security position became delicate, if not precarious. Relations with the Soviet Union over the years were never cordial, and now Pakistan faces the Soviet Union directly across the Afghan border.

Pakistan is serving as an unenthusiastic sanctuary for Afghan rebels as well as a refuge for about three million uprooted victims of the war. The Soviets and

ghan clients, apart from occasional raids along
er, have not put great pressure on Pakistan to
wn on the movement of people and equipment into
tan. Nothing like the Israeli raids on Pales-
positions in Lebanon has yet occurred. Yet its
opp‸‸‸‸ion to the Soviet presence across the border
cannot lead Pakistan to provide more support for the
Afghan resistance without running the risk of provoking
a vigorous Soviet response.

Historically, the United States has not viewed
Pakistan as a particularly useful ally, and Pakistan
sees the United States as unreliable. Soviet actions
in Afghanistan prompted a reassessment on both sides.
The Reagan administration, which is much more anti-
Soviet than its recent predecessors, has called for a
1.6 trillion dollar defense budget over a five-year
period. While alliances and foreign bases are either
passe or politically impractical, American planning for
contingencies includes the temporary use of facilities
during emergencies. Egypt, Somalia, Israel, Oman, and
Kenya, among others, may allow American use of their
territory under certain circumstances. The base on
Diego Garcia in the Indian Ocean is being expanded.
Other measures include a larger naval presence and a
rapid deployment force. Should it desire to do so,
Pakistan could play an important part in these plans.[24]

Pakistan's new strategic importance encouraged the
United States to offer military and economic assistance.
President Carter offered 400 million dollars after the
invasion of Afghanistan, but General Zia dismissed the
offer as "peanuts." The Reagan administration's offer
of 3.2 billion dollars, which includes among other
military hardware the high performance F-16 aircraft,
was more to Zia's liking.

Negotiations in 1981 went well, and both sides
expressed satisfaction. Congress approved the package,
although there was some concern about sending sophisticated weapons.[25] A compromise suggestion to send
F-5's, a much less sophisticated aircraft, and a few
F-16's was rejected by Pakistan. The major worry of
opponents to a renewal of arms aid to Pakistan has been
the potential development of an "Islamic bomb." American laws prohibited aid to any country acquiring ura-
nium enrichment materials or technology. This provision
affected Pakistan, and President Carter did, indeed,
suspend all except food aid. This problem was overcome
when Congress amended the law to cover only the actual
testing of nuclear weapons.

How appropriate is this arms package, and particularly the F-16, to Pakistan's security requirements?
India claims that it upsets the military ratio in the
subcontinent and encourages an arms race. The problem
with this argument is that Pakistan, even with F-16's,
would be in no position to attack anyone. Moreover,

Pakistan could never be capable of stopping a determined Soviet or Indian attack. While there are few military obstacles to keep them from doing so, the Soviets are not likely to attempt an armed takeover of Pakistan. Such an action would result in a substantial interruption of trade and financial dealings with the West. The Soviets are heavily dependent on Western technology, finance, and agricultural products. They cannot afford to throw it all away for territorial gains of dubious value. They would also lose favor among non-aligned countries, something that has already occurred as a result of Afghanistan. Arms reduction talks, which are not now going well, would probably cease altogether.

While the new weapons cannot stop the Soviets, they do reduce Pakistan's vulnerability to Soviet intimidation. The Soviets now face greater risks of defeat for limited military operations. To overcome these risks, they would have to undertake higher levels of military involvement, something they are probably not willing to do. Pakistan has thus gained an increased measure of security.

Soviet opportunities are not confined to military operations, however. Separatist movements are features of the politics of both frontier provinces--NWFP and Baluchistan. The Soviets do not appear to be encouraging such movements at the moment, but once Afghanistan is secure, they may regard tribal areas as targets of opportunity. Some Pakistani Baluch have advocated independence and may welcome Soviet assistance.[26]

Given these considerations, accommodation with the Soviet Union might appear as the more attractive alternative for Pakistan. But this would involve greater sacrifices than gains. The Soviets can do little to relieve the refugee burden short of leaving Afghanistan, a slim prospect at best. Pakistan cannot close its borders to the refugees simply as a practical matter. China, one of Pakistan's new consistent friends, would not favor closer ties between Pakistan and the Soviet Union because, in their view, this would contribute to Soviet "hegemonism." The Soviets would be unlikely to downgrade their relations with India for Pakistan's friendship. The Soviets could conceivably use its withdrawal from Afghanistan as a quid pro quo for closer relations with both India and Pakistan, but this is an unlikely prospect.[27]

Soviet actions and continuing Indian hostility put great pressure on Pakistan to acquire a nuclear capability. General Zia and other leaders have repeatedly given assurances that nuclear weapons are not being developed, although they express interest in expanding nuclear science and technology.[28] Given its pronounced military inferiority vis a vis India, nuclearization has definite attractions for Pakistan. Atomic weapons would virtually erase India's conventional advantages and would likely deter any Indian initiatives. Pakistan cannot defend itself by conventional means, so an Indian attack would necessarily trigger a Pakistani nuclear response. Since Pakistan cannot expect to win a war, its security planning must be geared either to deterrence or accommodation. The former could be achieved with even a modest nuclear weapon system.

But there are also compelling arguments against nuclearization. A nuclear Pakistan would encourage India to enhance its own capabilities, both conventional and nuclear. The United States is committed to suspend aid, should Pakistan conduct a nuclear test. The developing prospects for rapprochement between India and Pakistan would be sabotaged if the latter went nuclear. There is also the possibility of an Indian preemptive strike.[29] Such a precedent was set by the Israelis, who destroyed the Iraqi nuclear facility in June 1982. Should India be convinced that Pakistan is indeed acquiring nuclear weapons, concern for its own security could weigh heavily in favor of preemptive action.

In late 1981 President Zia proposed a no-war pact with India and a freeze on arms along their common border. The suggestion was not new, since its call for the renunciation of force was already a part of the Simla agreement of 1972. Zia's initiative attracted considerable international interest and support and made India appear to be the obstacle to rapprochment. Mrs. Gandhi dismissed the idea, labelling it propaganda.[30] While circumstances forced her to at least discuss the matter, she quickly found an excuse for delay. When Pakistan's representative to the Human Rights Commission in Geneva mentioned his country's concern about Kashmir, India denounced the act as a violation of the Simla accords and suspended further discussions. Mrs. Gandhi also suggested that Pakistan wanted the insurgency in Afghanistan to continue because of the benefits derived from it. Considerable aid is received to help the refugees, and revived American interest would likely be much less absent the Afghanistan crisis.

As the above discussion shows, Pakistan's foreign relations have played a key role in shaping its internal politics. Several factors, especially the Kashmir dispute, resulted in a state of perpetual hostility with India. While Pakistan's claim to Kashmir has considerable merit, the fact is, India controls most of it. Efforts to end this control culminated in the 1965 war, which led to the fall of the Ayub Khan government and the abrogation of the 1962 constitution.

American policy initiatives found favor in Pakistan not because of the confluence of strategic views, but because a close association with the United States afforded Pakistan an opportunity to gain military strength. Had the military capability to press its quarrel with India not been available, Pakistan's political leaders could conceivably have focused greater attention and effort on resolving internal political and economic problems. These unresolved problems eventually resulted in the secession of the East wing.

The Soviet presence in Afghanistan poses a very real threat to Pakistan's security. American and Pakistani strategic perceptions are now, as a result, more in harmony than they have ever been. But critics of the martial law regime of General Zia argue that current American military aid to Pakistan bolsters an unpopular authoritarian government and reduces the chances that progressive political development can occur. In their view, Zia uses the Soviet presence in Afghanistan to postpone political liberalization. While the dimensions of foreign relations have changed over the years, they continue to have an important impact on Pakistan's political development.

NOTES

1. See, for example, Department of State Bulletin, XXVIII, No. 707, January 12, 1953, pp. 43-46 and No. 714, March 2, 1953, 331-333.

2. Department of State Bulletin, XXX, No. 766, March 1, 1954, p. 327.

3. Ibid., XXX, No. 773, April 19, 1954, 581.

4. "Letter of the Prime Minister of India Addressed to the Prime Minister of Pakistan 9 December 1953," in K. Sarwar Hasan (ed.), Documents on the Foreign Relations Relations of Pakistan: The Kashmir Question, Karachi: Pakistan Institute of International Affairs, 1966), pp. 344-47, also see Jyoti Bhusan Das Gupta, Indo-Pakistan Relations, 1947-1955 (Amsterdam: Djambatan, Djambatan, 1958) p. 146.

5. Ibid.

6. Mohammed Ayub Khan, Pakistan Perspective, (Washington: Embassy of Pakistan, 1965) pp. 18-28.

7. Mohammed Ayub Khan, "The Pakistan American Alliance: Stresses and Strains," Foreign Affairs 9 January, 1964), 196 and 204.

8. Alexander De Conde, A History of American Foreign Policy (New York: Charles M. Scribner's Sons, 1963), pp. 755-56.

9. The alliance system placed the United States in an awkward position in 1961 when India seized Goa. India had considered itself more than patient in waiting for Portugal to relinquish voluntarily the small enclave on the west coast of India. Finally unable to resist the nationalist pressures any longer, Nehru agreed to evict the Portuguese by force. Since Portugal

was a member of NATO, the United States felt obliged to side with its ally and criticized Indian "aggression." American prestige in India was not enhanced by identifying itself with this vestige of colonialism.

10. See, for example, The New York Times, November 17, 1955, p. 14.

11. Norman D. Palmer, South Asia and United States Policy (New York: Houghton Mifflin Co., 1966), pp. 139-43.

12. Department of State Bulletin, Vol. 768, March 15, 1954, p. 400.

13. U.S. Congress, House of Representatives, Committee on Foreign Affairs, Report of U.S.-Financed Military Construction at Kharian and Multan in West Pakistan, 87th Congress, 1st Session, 1961, p. 4.

14. "Boundary Agreement Between the Governments of the People's Republic of China and Pakistan, 2 March 1963," in Hasan, pp. 384-97.

15. The Pakistan Times, February 17, 1971.

16. Ibid., January 31, 1972.

17. Ibid., March 29, 1972.

18. Ibid., November 10, 1972.

19. Ibid., November 16, 1972.

20. Ibid., February 3, 1972.

21. Wilcox, Wayne, The Emergence of Bangladesh: Problems and Opportunities for a Redefined American Policy in South Asia, Washington: American Enterprise Institute for Public Opinion, 1973, p. 11.

22. The Pakistan Times, September 27, 1972.

23. Ibid., August 30, 1972.

24. For further information see Rasul B. Rais, "An Appraisal of U.S. Strategy in the Indian Ocean," Asian Survey, XXIII (September, 1983), 1043-51.

25. U.S. Congress, House, Committee on Foreign Affairs, Hearings, Security and Economic Assistance to Pakistan, 97th Cong., 1st Sess., 1982.

26. Selig Harrison, In Afghanistan's Shadow: Baluch Nationalism and Soviet Temptations (New York: Carnegie Endowment for International Peace, 1981), pp. 42-52; Pervaiz Iqbal Cheema, "The Afghanistan Crisis and Pakistan's Security Dilemma," Asian Survey, XXIII (March, 1983), pp. 238-9.

27. Mehrunnisa Ali, "Soviet-Pakistan Ties Since the Afghanistan Crisis," Asian Survey, XXIII (September, 1983), 1025.

28. The Economist, April 25, 1981, p. 3. Also see Ashok Kapur, "A Nuclearizing Pakistan: Some Hypotheses," Asian Survey, XX(May, 1980), 504-5.

29. The CIA reported just such a possibility which was vigorously denied by India. India News, December 27, 1982.

30. The Economist, September 26, 1981, p. 16.

9
Bhutto and Bonapartism

Political Developments

In his book _Politics in Pakistan,_ Khalid B. Sayeed makes the observation

> Ever since Ayub seized power in 1958, Pakistan has been governed by a Bonapartist regime. By this is meant not just the rule of an arbitrary dictator but the rule of a leader who derived his power and authority from a well-established institution like the army, in the case of Ayub, or from a political movement, in the case of Bhutto.[1]

Thus Bhutto continued the practice, although in different form, of personalized rule at the expense of institutional development.

Politically, Pakistan was worse off following the debacle in East Pakistan than it was at the time of its founding. In 1947, repeated failures and frustrations had not been experienced, and the future could be anticipated with hope. But in 1972, the economy was in jeopardy. The prestige of the most powerful national institution, the military, had been compromised, and the ruling elite had demonstrated its inability to hold the country together and govern effectively. Not only was the military humiliated by the surrender, but many officers, especially among the junior ranks, felt they had been sold out by senior commanders. The rapid Indian thrust to Dacca had demoralized the high command but had not actually resulted in the defeat of many units of the army. Thus the military was embittered against itself and would take some time to recover its confidence.[2]

After the defeat, Yahya Khan turned power over to Bhutto, although it is not clear what authority he possessed to do so. Yet Bhutto was the most popular politician with the largest following in the country, and he was certainly the man of the hour. At the time of the surrender, he was in New York presenting Pakistan's case to the United Nations. Apparently surprised with the news of surrender, he tore up a copy of the UN ceasefire resolution and left the chamber. With this melodramatic gesture, he seemed to dissociate himself from any responsibility for the capitulation.[3]

First, Bhutto had to gain control of the country's political affairs before policy initiatives could be undertaken. Now that East Pakistan was gone, there arose the delicate task of defining or redefining the nature of the country. The independence of Bangladesh was a fact, and there was nothing to be gained by pretending otherwise. Nevertheless, some of Bhutto's supporters opposed recognition of Bangladesh or acceptance of the secession. Yahya served as a convenient scapegoat. He was arrested, and the Supreme court later determined that his seizure of power from Ayub Khan had been illegal. Mujib was released, which paved the way for return of the POW's held by India and for the Simla agreement between Bhutto and Mrs. Gandhi.

The two traditional power centers of Pakistan--the military and the bureaucracy--had to be neutralized if Bhutto's political plans were to succeed. The military, although temporarily stunned by its defeat, was not inclined to forego political influence. But Bhutto had other plans. In March 1972 he purged real and potential opponents. The acting Commander-in-Chief, Lt. General Tikka Khan, who by reputation was more willing than other military leaders to accept civilian authority, was made army chief of staff.[4] Another "reliable" general promoted by Bhutto was Zia ul-Haq.

The bureaucracy and especially the elite corps--the Civil Service of Pakistan--had not neen tarnished by the civil war and subsequent loss of the East wing and had, therefore, suffered no diminuation of its influence. While there were about one million people in the bureaucracy in 1971, there were only 320 in the CSP. Of the top 300 administrative posts in the government, 225 were held by the members of the CSP.[5] Moreover, many top positions were reserved exclusively for the CSP, and once in office the rules governing job security made it very difficult to remove them. Membership in this privileged elite was much coveted but hard to come by.

In order to reduce the political influence of the CSP, Bhutto announced in late March a series of administrative reforms. He wanted the CSP dissolved as a separate structure and its members integrated into a unified civil service.[6] Bhutto also created employment opportunities in the public service for his followers. He planned to curtail the importance of the bureaucracy in policy-making. In the past the bureaucracy always had a key role in policy alternatives, leaving the actual decisions to the new governing elite.[7] Despite these efforts, the power of the bureaucracy was not curtailed. Although the military's influence was initially reduced, it was ultimately reasserted. The political influence of these groups was so deeply entrenched that to permanently alter their role in the political process would have required more extensive organizational restructuring.

Bhutto's government faced yet another problem. Support from followers of left wing philosophies soon began to erode. In the first place, support for the government's policies declined. Second, left-wing politicians became disenchanted with the government's failure to promote even more dramatic change and to include more leftists in key posts. In their view, the government had not succeeded in taking power away from the upper classes.[8] Bhutto's new coalition was further weakened by the tendency toward factionalism. Many of the new people brought into the system developed their own loyalties and became less responsive to Bhutto's leadership. The government thus rested on a shallow base of support. The traditional centers of power, the bureaucracy and the military, were not integrated into the new order, nor was their ability to challenge it neutralized.

Two main opposition parties--the National Awami Party and the Jamiat-ul-Ulema-e-Islam--were enlisted in the national cause through a Tripartite Agreement with the PPP on March 6, 1972. The Agreement involved an apparent trade-off where the NAP-JUI would consent to the constitution-making process, while the PPP would accept NAP-JUI governments in NWFP and Baluchistan. However, the spirit of cooperation and compromise did not last long. Bhutto delayed appointing governors to the two provinces acceptable to the parties. Sensing a lack of faith on Bhutto's part, the coalition announced that the agreement was not binding. Bhutto's foot-dragging may have been caused by pressure from the army and by large landowners who found the NAP-JUI too radical.[9]

The constitution had barely been introduced when Butto tried to blunt all opposition. He removed an issue that could have been exploited by his antagonists by announcing that the end of martial law would be April 21 rather than August 14 as originally declared. He also included Khan Abdul Qayyum Khan, leader of an opposition Muslim League faction, in the cabinet, thus stilling another critical voice. But Bhutto was increasingly inclined to deal with opposition another way. He established a special police--the Federal Security Force--which physically intimidated government opponents. The activities of the FSF would ultimately be cited by Bhutto's opponents as an example of his abuse of power, an issue that would be used to overthrow his goverment.

Bhutto moved quickly to normalize relations with India. He met with Mrs. Gandhi in India, and after an initial deadlock they reached agreement and signed the Simla Accord on July 2, 1972. The prisoner-of-war issue would be dealt with after Bhutto had met with Mujib. After the "modalities of peace" had been worked out, the Indian and Pakistani armies in the West were to withdraw to pre-December positions, i.e., the line of control which, although disputed, has served as the international boundary since 1965. The two leaders declared their intention to work toward normalization of relations and resolution of outstanding problems, including Kashmir. The accord stated that the two heads of government would meet at a future date. Lower level discussions seeking, among other things, "a final settlement of Jammu and Kashmir," were to precede this meeting.[10]

Kashmir presented Bhutto with a political dilemma. He seemed inclined to accept military disengagement with India; political disengagement with his own people was to prove more difficult. He recognized that in the minds of many Pakistanis, accommodation with India meant surrender of Kashmir. In order to avoid jeopardizing popular support for his government, he had to at least nominally support Pakistan's traditional claim to Kashmir. But these actions were taken as a provocation by India, which insisted as a condition of improved relations that no mention of Kashmir should be made outside formal bilateral discussions. Bhutto also felt India exaggerated the importance of the little assistance Pakistan received from the United States and other countries. His belief that India and Pakistan should be able to negotiate a method by which both countries could feel secure was thus frustrated. On July 18, 1972, he stated in a speech to the National Assembly that Kashmir would not be solved by negotiations through the UN. The people of Kashmir must fight for their right of self-determination.[11] Later, in a trip through Azad Kashmir, he called upon the people of "occupied Kashmir," that portion of Kashmir controlled by India, to observe a hartal, or strike, to be called by himself to demonstrate their feelings and to protest the unwillingness of the Indian government to allow a plebiscite. He did, however, discourage any action at that time, instead preferring to allow the negotiation process to run its course. Should it fail, he said, "then we will see what to do."[12]

Policy Initiatives

Pakistan's political difficulties can be attributed in part to the failure of economic programs and policies. The disequilibrium in economic development between the two wings has already been noted. Ayub's economic programs brought significant growth, but the benefits were enjoyed by relatively few. The political collapse of 1971 ended the Ayub system and demonstrated the inadequacy of the coalition of power groups upon which it rested. The Bhutto regime sought to build a broader coalition by promoting major changes in public policy. As Burki has pointed out, "the initiation of economic reforms is to a considerable extent a function of the perceived need of the elite for political legitimacy."[13]

Part of the problem was considered to be the extraordinary influence enjoyed by a very small elite. In the view of the Bhutto government, this situation resulted from antiquated and inadequate laws governing economic activity. These laws, created to serve British imperial interests mainly in jute, tea, textiles and coal, were too limited for modern requirements. The PPP's solution to the problem was suggested by its ideology. During the 1970 campaign, the party had espoused the principles of Islam, Socialism and Democracy and the populist slogan roti, kapra, and makan (bread, clothing, and shelter). Its election manifesto declared, "the ultimate objective of the Party's policy is the attainment of a classless society, which is only possible through socialism in our time. . . ."[14] A host of reforms introduced in 1972 reflected this ideology. In January the Planning Commission began work on a document which would define short, medium and long-range goals guided by the commitment to a socialist order.

The economic constituencies of the PPP consisted of those groups which had benefited from economic growth in the 1960's and were, as a result, upward-mobile and highly politicized. The PPP also mobilized those attracted to the ideological left. These included peasants and sharecroppers of the Northwest and the proletariat in the industrial centers of the Punjab.[15] Also in this category were students who were highly susceptible to political mobilization. The third constituency consisted of the large-landed aristocracy in Sind and adjacent areas of the Punjab. A less compatible gathering of followers is hard to imagine.

Bhutto chose to take a less active part in the determination of economic policy. His own time and energies were devoted to an effort to shore-up Pakistan's international stature. He felt Pakistan had not been well-served by its ties with the West, and he sought to replace them with strong links with Muslim countries with which Pakistan shared not only a common religion but similar concerns for Indian Ocean and Persian Gulf security. Pakistan also stood to benefit financially from oil rich countries like Saudi Arabia.

Since the oil crisis of 1973, the petroleum exporting
countries, and especially those in the Middle East,
experienced a rapid growth in their economic influence.
This was particularly welcomed by poor Islamic countries
like Pakistan. Before 1973, Pakistan received no economic assistance from Islamic countries. But one-third
of the total amount of financial assistance from all
foreign sources over the next three years came from
Muslim countries.[16]

Economic initiatives were left to those members of
the new coalition who had policies and programs to put
forward. The left wing of the party exercised considerable influence over economic and other areas of
policy until 1974, when public opposition to its
programs increased.[17] But by then the general policy
framework had been established, and much of it would
endure long after Bhutto had departed the scene.

The first step in the strategy designed to break
the power of the economic elite was to take management
control out of their hands and place it with the
government. This was not nationalization, the government claimed, as ownership remained with the
shareholders.[18] Although Bhutto gave assurances that
he was not anti-capitalism, on January 3 he issued the
Economic Reform Order by which 10 categories of
industries were put under state control. This action,
he claimed, was "for the benefit of the people."
Industries involved included iron and steel, basic
metals, heavy engineering, heavy electrical, motor
vehicles, tractor plants, heavy and basic chemicals,
petro-chemicals, cement, electricity, gas, and oil
refineries. Bhutto recognized the continuing need for
foreign investment in the economy and promised that his
economic programs would not affect foreign holdings.[19]

By taking over major industries and banks, the
government planned to reduce the advantages the top
economic groups had enjoyed under the previous regime.
"The power of capitalists or big business which had
figured so prominently during the Ayub-Yahya periods
was with one stroke virtually obliterated," noted one
observer.[20] Exercising management control over
industry put the government in a position to implement
policies that favored industrial workers by increasing
wages and controlling prices.

Control of the price of vegetable oil in particular had considerable popular appeal, especially
among the poorer sectors of society. By late 1974 the
real wages of unskilled workers in government-
controlled industries were six percent higher than they
had been in 1969.[21]

The government was not always able to keep prices
from rising because of increasing costs of production.
This put a squeeze on industrial profits, which in turn
reduced government revenues. The squeeze on profits

also reduced the amount of investment funds available from private sources. Resulting shortages in various categories of consumer goods created increased pressures on prices, which the government was forced to raise in 1975, causing violent public protests.[22]

In a move against wealthy interests, the government asked for an accounting of their foreign exchange holdings. Such declarations were supposed to be voluntary, but only Rs. 120 million were reported, prompting stronger action. Finance Minister Mubashar Hasan told a press conference in January 18, 1972, that the maximum penalty for foreign exchange defaulters might be increased from life in prison to death.[23]

For the benefit of industrial workers, a variety of actions were taken, increasing wages and benefits. Workers' share of profits was increased from four percent to five percent. Twenty percent of factory level management was to consist of workers. Improved fringe benefits included education for workers' families and health care at no cost to the employee. The labor movement was strengthened, and the frequency of strikes increased.[24]

A second main area of economic policy concerned the terms of trade between the agricultural and non-agricultural sectors. This had been one of the disputes before 1971 between the West wing with its greater industrial development and the East wing which was mainly agricultural. By setting the valuation of the rupee at 4.76 to the U.S. dollar, the Pakistani currency was grossly overvalued, a condition which, together with the bonus voucher scheme, tended to favor industry. On May 11, 1972, the rupee was devalued to a rate of 11 to the U.S. dollar. This was only the second time in the country's history that the currency had been adjusted. The first time the rupee was devalued was in 1955 when it was changed from 3.31 to the dollar to 4.76, where it remained for 17 years. The bonus voucher scheme, which had been proposed 13 years previously by a German economic advisor as a "temporary" approach to foreign exchange problems, was also abolished at the time of the devaluation.[25]

The platform of the PPP blamed the poverty of the rural population on "a feudal system of land tenure" and called for land reform to break up the large estates. The platform also envisaged the establishment of "social cooperative farms." The purpose and organization of these farms sounded somewhat like the Chinese communes, but participation in them was to be voluntary.[26] In March 1972 the government expanded on the land reform scheme first introduced by Ayub Khan. The new land reform law, contained in Martial Law Regulation #115, defined limits of landholding and established an administrative procedure for redistribution. Landholding per person was limited to 150 acres of irrigated land, 300 acres of unirrigated land, or an amount of land determined by soil classification. The landowner decided which land he would surrender if he held an excess. Disputes would be decided by the Land Commissioner. The Land Commissioner was chosen by the Land Commission which consisted of the provincial governor and three others appointed by him. While the regulations assigned responsibility for production costs, including taxes to the landowners, there was no limit on the amount of the crop that could be charged to the tenant in the form of rent.[27] While there was supposed to be 4.8 million acres of surplus land, the amount actually made available was much less because the ceilings applied to individuals. Large estates could be divided among members of a family, thus conforming to the letter, but not to the spirit, of the law.[28]

While the government made many organizational and policy changes which benefited the peasants and the urban working population, these actions were not matched by public expenditures. For example, in 1972-73 over half the budget was allocated to defense. Twenty million dollars was allocated to low-cost housing and environmental improvement and 23 million to a public works program. Over three million dollars went for a new house for the President.[29]

In March, the government unveiled a plan for a broad-range program of national health service. The scheme would provide general health coverage for the population to be financed by a "special, but small tax distributed equitably on the community."[30]

In education, Bhutto was confronted with two problems. In order to break the institutional privileges and "old-boy" networks, education had to be broadened and made more accessible to the masses. Education was supposed to serve as a vehicle of attainment and reward for the new support groups Bhutto was cultivating. The education system had traditionally been the spawning ground for anti-government movements. There was student political activity during the British period as far back as the founding of the Congress. Students were involved in the opposition to Ayub Khan and in the secession of East Pakistan. Violent student political activities occurred in 1963 with protests against the University Ordinance (the law regulating the operation of higher education.) The anti-Tashkent demonstrations after the 1965 war increased student political involvement and, more importantly, rallied left-wing students who would later join with the PPP.

Despite the popularity of the PPP, the Jamiat-i-Islami party, which espouses fundamentalist Islamic Ideas, has been the most active and successful among students. The student arm of the party, the Islami Jamiat-i-Tulaba, has traditionally been and remains today the only organized and disciplined group on the campuses.

As with economic policy, the PPP left-wing was very influential in education. The thrust of educational reforms was to make educational opportunities widely available to the masses both in terms of access and variety of programs offered. The elimination of illiteracy was given the highest priority. This was an ambitious goal, given the fact that illiteracy was around 85 percent. Primary education, under reforms announced by Bhutto on March 16, 1972, would become free and universal from October 1. This would extend to secondary education on October 1, 1974. Under Martial Law Regulation #118 promulgated March 29, privately-owned schools and colleges were nationalized, although exceptions allowed for any school or college run on a "genuinely benevolent, philanthropic and non-commercial basis." Private institutions that had served the well-to-do were opened to all "gifted children" without preference to financial or social background. Ultimately only foreign-managed institutions escaped takeover, and not even all of them did. The nationalization of private institutions did not entail compensation.[31] By September, 175 private colleges had been taken over. Private schools, below the college level, were nationalized over a two-year period. The status of teachers was improved through increased salaries and rent-free housing. Expenditures for education doubled in the first year and were to increase 15 percent in future years.[32]

It was anticipated that the reforms would more than double the enrollment of students in primary and secondary education by 1980. All boys were to be enrolled by 1979 and all girls by 1984.[33] These goals proved unrealistic because sufficient resources were not available. The goals were later revised with the target of full enrollment for boys moved to 1983 and for girls to 1987.[34] To combat illiteracy and provide teachers for the rapid influx of students, unemployed and retired civil servants, retired military personnel and college students were recruited. Because 80 percent of university enrollment was in the arts, enrollment increases in these fields was limited to five percent per year, while that of the sciences was allowed to increase by 10 percent per year.[35]

In an important action designed to remove a source of student agitation, the government changed the University Ordinances under which institutions of higher education operated. These Ordinances were very unpopular with students, faculty and administrators. They were replaced on October 1 with new "enlightened and progressive legislation." The reform gave students and faculty greater voice in the governing of the institutions. An important feature was the recognition of Student Unions and the inclusion of student representatives in university senates.

Although the reforms emanated from the central government, the actual authority under which the universities operated was the province. Later, in 1978, the central government assumed responsibity for funding the university system, leaving administration in the hands of the provinces. Typically University Ordinances established a governing authority including the chancellor (the provincial governor), the pro-chancellor (a new post to be filled by the provincial education minister), the vice-chancellor (equivalent to an American university president), senate, syndicate, and academic council. While the syndicate was the executive authority of the university, the senate could make rules and take action wih the consent of the chancellor. The senate consisted of administrators, faculty and student representatives plus some others. Student representatives were chosen from the student unions of the university and the colleges affiliated with it. The syndicate consisted mainly of government officials, members of the provincial assembly, a judge of the high court, the education secretary, and the president of the public service commission. The syndicate also included one student and some faculty and university administrators.[36] The academic council consisted mainly of faculty and some university and provincial bureaucrats and advised the syndicate on academic matters such as curriculum and exams.[37]

Several new universities were planned, and three engineering colleges were elevated to university status. Youths 17 to 23 were affected by a planned national service corps, to be used in a literacy campaign and military training for one year.[38]

In another area of public policy, the government took action which limited the significance of the restoration of fundamental rights as provided by the constitution. In the first place, the emergency of 1971, which caused their suspension in the first place, remained in force. Moreover, in October 1974, the Suppression of Terrorist Activities (Special Courts) Ordinance was issued.[39] The Terrorist Activities measure was intended to deal with growing opposition to the government. In Baluchistan in particular, extensive military force was used against the opposition. A special police called the Federal Security Force was set up in 1973. Bhutto considered such a force necessary, because the regular security forces, especially the police, were not reliable.[40] The activities of the FSF during the 1977 election campaign produced complaints that Bhutto was abusing his power.

Federal Issues

The politics of the Northwest Frontier have always been stormy. This area constituted the outer reaches of their empire which the British attempted to secure against real and imagined threats from Russia. Throughout much of the 19th century, the British tried to enlist Afghan cooperation in preventing Russian penetration of West and Central Asia. It took two wars before the British were able to get their way. Under the Treaty of Gandamak of 1878 the terms of which were sustained by the Second Anglo-Afghan War, the British assumed control of Afghanistan's foreign policy.
Afghanistan assumed full sovereignty only after the Third Anglo-Afghan War in 1919. The British, with Russian cooperation, established Afghanistan's northern border at the Amu Darya in 1895. The southern border, again drawn by the British, was the Durand Line, which now serves as the international boundary between Pakistan and Afghanistan. Under the "forward policy," the British maintained an uneasy state of semi-belligerency with the tribes of the hill areas. These people have never willingly participated in any political system outside their own tribal groups. This was the situation inherited by Pakistan in 1947. Afghanistan considered the Durand Line illegal, having been imposed by an imperial power without the consent of the peoples involved. The line divides an extremely independent people--the Pashtuns or Pathans--into two groups. The logic of the line was based on a "market watershed." Those people who marketed north would be in Afghanistan and those who marketed south would be on the British, or the Pakistan side. Unfortunately, people move about for reasons other than marketing. This is especially true for the seasonal nomads, for whom the border is completely artificial. Afghanistan has called for a Pakhtunistan, an ambiguous idea involving a province of all Pathans within the political fabric of Afghanistan which is already dominated by Pathans. For Pakistan, the Northwest Frontier has posed persistent difficulties of integration into the overall political system.

For their part, the Pathans are divided between desires for greater independence from Pakistan and a lack of enthusiam for the Kabul government. Now with the Soviets in Afghanistan, the Pathans are in no mood for closer ties with the Afghan government. They are, moreover, divided on the subject of the suitability of Marxism as a solution to their problems. Some local leaders, such as Abdul Ghaffar Khan and his son Wali Khan, have long been suspicious of the Soviets. Others, like Ajmal Khattak, would welcome Soviet aid in pursuit of an independent Pathan state.[41]

The origins of the Pakhtunistan issue lie with the empire of Ahmad Shah Durrani, a Pathan, who gained control over the entire area from Persia to the Indian Ocean to Delhi by the late 18th century. This empire did not last long and was soon replaced by Sikh, British, and local Afghan authority. But it is the memory of this empire that provides the legacy for those advocating Pakhtunistan. Another issue is the boundary which Pakhtunistan advocates claim was the result of imperialism and should give way to "self-determination." This argument is weakened by the fact that Abdur Rahman, the Amir of Afghanistan, agreed to the mission and requested Durand to head it, probably recognizing the need to have a border somewhere rather than allowing the British to continue nibbling away at his territory.

The promotion of the Pakhtunistan issue by Afghanistan soured relations with Pakistan. In the Northwest Frontier Province the idea gives expression to provincial politics, and the National Awami Party claims Pakhtunistan is a better name for the Province. Upon coming to power, Bhutto tried to improve relations with Afghanistan and went to Kabul for this purpose.[42] There was some movement toward reconciliation between the two governments, with encouragement coming from the Shah of Iran. In 1976, Bhutto and Mohammed Daud, President of Afghanistan, exchanged visits. General Zia and Daud exchanged visits in 1978. But the overthrow of the Daud government in 1978 and the downfall of the Shah less than a year later altered the picture. Now there are Soviet troops in Afghanistan and a regime dominated by fundamentalist cleric in Teheran. These developments raise serious questions about Soviet intentions and the prospects for leftists in the frontier provinces of Pakistan and Iran.

In Baluchistan, the Baluch themselves make up less than half of the population of the province. More Baluch live in Karachi, which is in western Sind, than in Baluchistan. But here they are the lower class labor force and find leftist ideologies attractive. Bhutto attempted to mobilize the workers by socialist programs. The Baluch in Baluchistan are divided into several tribes and clans organized into the semi-feudal Sardari system. The Sardar is the headman symbolizing the tribe vis a vis other tribes. The Sardari system precluded any cohesiveness among the tribes. Bhutto played the Sardars against one another, and finally in 1976 he declared the system abolished, although this was easier said than done.[43]

Sind, of all provinces of Pakistan, has had the most population change. Many refugees who came at the time of partition were better educated than the indigenous population and soon held the better jobs in government and industry. Many Punjabis and former military and government officers received land in Sind opened up by government irrigation projects. The result has been an upsurge of Sindhi self-consciousness and a call for a Sindhi homeland. The disputes over Urdu must be viewed in this light. Bhutto also tried to exploit this provincialism in his efforts to politically isolate Sind landlords and Karachi industrialists.[44]

One of the great problems dividing the two wings of Pakistan was different languages. The government initiated an effort to have Urdu made the official language of the entire country, which provoked the Bengalis to resist an essentially alien language. After the East wing seceded, the language issue did not disappear. The four provinces of West Pakistan themselves had and continue to have language disputes. The dominant Punjab population favors Urdu, while the Sindhis, Pathans, and Baluch desire to retain their own local languages. Without agreement on a national language, English has served as a common language. But nationalist sentiment favors its abolition, especially from the educational system where most instruction has been in English. However, the availability of textbooks and technical material in English gives considerable weight to arguments opposing its elimination. One practical suggestion would be to use Roman script in Urdu, which is better adapted for printing than Arabic or Persian.[45] Under Zia, "Islamization" has led to a suggestion that students learn Arabic--the language of the Quran.

The language issue caused riots in Karachi in July 1972 leaving several persons dead. Advocates of Urdu were provoked by a bill enacted by the Provincial Assembly making the official language of the province Sindhi. Urdu speakers, amounting to 50 percent of the population, feared this would put them at a disadvantage. Initially Sindhi and Urdu would both be recognized, but as finally passed, only Sindhi was included. On July 15 Bhutto announced an agreement ending the crisis. For a period of 12 years, there would be no discrimination in hiring, promotion, or continuation of service in Sind on the grounds that one did not know Sindhi or Urdu.[46]

Although it was the majority party in the country, the PPP did not control the two frontier provinces. In Baluchistan, Bhutto's party held none of the 20 seats in the Provincial Assembly and only three out of 40 in NWFP. Both provinces were dominated by NAP-JUI coalitions, with which Bhutto initially seemed willing to cooperate. On March 6, 1972, in the interest of national unity, an accord was reached among the PPP and NAP and the JUI which was intended to facilitate the adoption of a new constitution. Within a matter of days, however, the agreement fell apart when Khan Abdul Wali Khan of the NAP disputed a section concerning a vote of confidence in the government and the extension of martial law. The passage states: "it was settled that there would be a vote of confidence in the Government and approval of the continuation of Martial Law until August 14, 1972." Wali Khan did not agree with PPP interpretation that the accord bound the parties to vote confidence in the government and in favor of extending Martial Law. He stated that "the Agreement was on what you would call the agenda, and it could never convey that we were bound to vote in favor of Martial Law."[47]

Bhutto responded in February 1973 by dismissing the two governments and moved to install his own people. In Baluchistan this produced active resistance which was met by the military, the imprisonment of local leaders, and the installation of a puppet government loyal to Bhutto. He moved against the NWFP government following the assassination of his closest aide in that province--Hyat Mohammed Khan Sherpao. NAP leaders were arrested, the party dissolved, and its assets confiscated.[48]

Opposition was restricted in other ways. In November 1973 an ordinance was issued imposing a maximum seven-year prison sentence and possible fine for "anti-national activity prejudicial to the country's sovereignty, territorial integrity, and internal peace."[49] Participation in any group or association declared anti-national would also result in a jail sentence. To determine whether a group was anti-national, a special tribunal was established under a judge of the High Court. Further steps were taken in February 1975. The Constitution (Third Amendment) Bill allowed for the continuation of a state of emergency beyond six months. By other legislation, members of the National Assembly and members of the provincial assemblies could be detained for security reasons when legislatures were in session. The Political Parties Act of 1962 was amended to declare "foreign-aided" political parties unlawful.[50]

This episode illustrates the frustration not only of the central government but of the provincial parties and politicians as well. Bhutto and the PPP wanted an alliance to promote national integrity and generate a consensus in support of the new constitution, certainly a legitimate concern. But on the other hand, by subordinating their individual and parochial interests in the name of national unity, the NAP, JUI, and other opposition parties ran the risk of being consumed or at least obscured by the dominant party, the PPP.

The Punjab has consistently dominated Pakistan's politics, a fact that has been resented by the other provinces. The lion's share of government jobs and positions in the military have consistently gone to Punjabis. This has been due in part to recruitment patterns established by the British. The Punjab is also the agricultural heartland of the country and has experienced much industrial development. The new federal capital--Islamabad--was built outside the Punjabi city of Rawalpindi. The strength of the PPP is in Punjab and especially in the city of Lahore which has been a center of political activity throughout Pakistan's history and before that was an important center of Islamic culture, a capital of the Moghul empire, and the center of Sikh influence. Given the almost overwhelming preponderance of the Punjab economically and politically, it is little wonder that the other provinces, especially those on the frontier, would find their lives frustrating. As with all federal systems, an arrangement which gives weight to states irrespective of population discriminates against the more populous parts of the country. A scheme which counts only population eclipses the smaller units. A solution to this problem has not yet been invented. There are only proximate solutions, which are accepted as the best available.

Pakistan's federal problems did not end with the fall of Bhutto. Upon assuming power, General Zia tried a more flexible approach in dealing with the provinces, although he has shown no tolerance for autonomy or self-determination. The altered circumstances of Afghanistan are changing the politics of Pakistan's frontier provinces in ways yet to be determined.

The Fall of Bhutto

Bhutto's rise to power was the result of a combination of factors. The collapse of the Ayub regime in 1969 left a constitutional vacuum which the elections of 1970 did not correct. In fact, the elections led to an even worse disaster, the secession of the East wing. Pakistan's political fortunes had reached their lowest point since the founding of the country. Conditions were favorable for the appeal of a charismatic figure. Bhutto fashioned an effective political vehicle in the PPP. The party was the largest and the most effective in the entire country although, unfortunately, this strength was concentrated in the Punjab. Along the frontier where tribal loyalties and family ties were more important, the PPP was unable to generate much of a following. Bhutto may perhaps have been the most skillful and popular politician in Pakistan's history. But he was unable, as were his predecessors, to translate personal popularity into popular support for political institutions. He succumbed to the temptation to promote and protect his own power rather than use his personal popularity to promote the integrity of the regime.

In addition to his skills as a politician, Bhutto was knowledgable and worldly. He was able to bring considerable imagination and creativity to the task of building a new political order and addressing the vast array of problems he had inherited. While recognizing the importance of Islam, he was not doctrinaire in that or any other system of values. He was often adroit in seeming to have it both ways as, for example, in his advocacy of "Islamic socialism."

Bhutto lacked a single distinguishing characteristic. He was not a man of the army as Ayub had been. He could not claim the mantle of "father of the country" like Jinnah. He could not wrap himself in a cloak of religion as Zia has done since. Instead he drew his political strength from his charismatic appeal to the people. While the crowds would turn out in the thousands to see him, he did not possess great oratorical skills. In fact, he did not speak Urdu particularly well and was more comfortable in English. He did, however, possess great acting ability and a sense of the spectacular. For instance, on one occasion when he was being heckled, he took off his jacket and threw it into the crowd. In the ensuing melee, the jacket was torn to shreds. Drawing an object lesson form the incident, Bhutto observed to the crowd that although he had given his coat away, no one had been able to benefit from it. Therefore, for him to give up his land (the issue for which he was being heckled) would serve no purpose.[51]

Bhutto's personal life brought him some opposition and criticism. His cosmopolitan outlook created suspicion among those members of society who held traditional values. Moreover, he had an eye for the ladies and was known to consume alcohol. As a response to the latter criticism, he introduced prohibition in 1977. He was also a Shia in a largely Sunni population and was regarded as a poor one at that, as he did not spend a great deal of his time in religious observances. These issues were used by his fundamentalist opponents to mobilize public opinion against him personally.

On January 7, 1977, Bhutto announced that elections to the national and provincial assemblies would be held on March 7 and 10 respectively. Whereas the elections and associated events eventually led to his political downfall, at the time he called for elections he seemed to be fully in control. Although there were occasional outbursts of discontent, the organized opposition had been neutralized. Bhutto wanted a popular vote to legitimize his rule thus far and to gain a mandate to continue the political course he had set the country upon. Unfortunately, serious problems lay beneath the surface, some of his own creation. Economic reforms were causing difficulties, and the sweeping educational reforms had resulted in deterioration of the educational system. His earlier supporters--the working classes, intellectuals, and students--were losing their enthusiasm.[52]

Although in disarray, the opposition pulled itself together and formed the Pakistan National Alliance. The Alliance consisted of the Tehriq-e-Isteqlal, Jama'at-i-Islami, Pakistan National Democratic Party, Jamiat-ul-Ulema-e-Islam, Jamiat-ul-Ulema-e-Pakistan, All Jammu and Kashmir Muslim Conference, and the Khaksars.[53] The issues of the campaign were essentially pro-Bhutto and anti-Bhutto; substantive issues played little part. Although the PNA drew large crowds and there was evidence of a groundswell of support for the anti-Bhutto forces, the PPP scored overwhelming victories at both national and provincial levels. In fact, the scope of the victory was just too good to be true, and the opposition immediately charged the results were fraudulent. The PPP won 155 seats of the 200 total. The PNA captured only 36, the Qayyum Muslim League took one seat in NWFP, and there were eight independents. Claiming the PPP rigged the election, the PNA boycotted the National Assembly elections in Baluchistan and the provincial elections in all four provinces. As a result, the PPP got 232 out of the 240 seats in Punjab, all of the 100 seats in Sind, 68 out of 80 in NWFP, and 35 out of 40 in Baluchistan. While claims of vote-rigging were probably exaggerated, the suggestion of them seemed credible in the face of such a landslide. Agitation grew, which resulted in widespread violence.

At first, the government was more concerned with its own security than with removing or ameliorating the causes of opposition. But in the face of growing hostility, Bhutto attempted to compromise. To mollify the traditional Islamic groups, he closed all bars and nightclubs and ordered prohibition. To allay the clamor against the election results, he promised to hold new elections in October to be supervised by the army. The PNA was at first inclined to go along with this arrangement in order to get the country out of the impasse. But the opposition was unwilling to accept this solution. On July 3, Ret. Air Marshal Asghar Khan announced that the PNA Central Committee had rejected the agreement. Violence and disorder continued, resulting in military intervention. On the night of July 4, General Zia ul-Haq, whom Bhutto had installed as Chief of Staff because he was considered "safe," took control of the government.

Bhutto was taken into "protective custody," the national and provincial assemblies were dissolved, and martial law was imposed. Zia announced new elections would be held on October 18, 1977, but they were postponed, and in late 1983 he concluded that the country would not be ready until 1985. Bhutto was later charged with complicity in a political murder, convicted, and hanged in the Rawalpindi jail on April 4, 1979.

NOTES

1. Khalid B. Sayeed, Politics in Pakistan: The Nature and Direction of Change, p. 89.
2. Shahid Javed Burki, Pakistan Under Bhutto, New York: St. Martin's Press, 1980, p. 60.
3. Ibid., p. 61.
4. Ibid., p. 71.
5. Shahid Javed Burki, The State and Society in Pakistan: 1971-77, London: The Macmillan Press Ltd., 1980, p. 99.
6. Lawrence Ziring, "The Phases of Pakistan's Political History," in Naim, Iqbal, Jinnah and Pakistan: The Vision and the Reality, pp. 167-8.
7. Laporte, "Succession in Pakistan: Continuity and Change in a Garrison State," Asian Survey, IX (August, 1969) 1098.
8. Sayeed, Politics in Pakistan: The Nature and Direction of Change, p. 46.
9. Satish Kumar, The New Pakistan, New Delhi: Vikas Publishing House Pvt. Ltd., 1978, p. 13.
10. The Pakistan Times, July 3, 1972.
11. Ibid., July 19, 1972.
12. Ibid., November 3, 1973.
13. Shahid Javed Burki, "Politics of Economic Decision-making During the Bhutto Period," Asian Survey, XIV (December, 1974) 1126.
14. The Pakistan Times, January 5, 1972.
15. Burki, "Politics of Economic Decision-making During the Bhutto Period," p. 1134.
16. M. G. Weinbaum and Gautam Sen, "Pakistan Enters the Middle East," Orbis, 22 (Fall, 1978) 602.
17. Burki, Pakistan Under Bhutto, p. 108.
18. The Pakistan Times, January 4, 1972.
19. Laporte, "Succession in Pakistan: Continuity and Change in a Garrison State," p. 194; The Pakistan Times, January 3, 1972.
20. Yusuf, Pakistan in Search of Democracy, 1947-77, p. 130.
21. Burki, "Politics of Economic Decision-making During the Bhutto Period," p. 1135.
22. Ibid.
23. The Pakistan Times, January 19, 1972.
24. Ibid., February 22, 1972; Kumar, The New Pakistan, pp. 122-3.
25. The Pakistan Times, May 12, 1972.
26. Bruce J. Esposito, "The Politics of Agrarian

Reform in Pakistan," Asian Survey, XIV (May, 1974)
p. 430.
27. Ibid., pp. 431-2.
28. Sayeed, The Politics of Pakistan; The Nature and Direction of Change, p. 55.
29. Esposito, "The Politics of Agrarian Reform in Pakistan," p. 436.
30. The Pakistan Times, March 27, 1972.
31. Government of Pakistan, Ministry of Education, Islamabad, The Education Policy, 1972-80, p. 19.
32. The Pakistan Times, March 16, 1972.
33. The Education Policy, p. 3.
34. Development of Education in Pakistan, Unesco, 1977, p. 6.
35. The Education Policy, pp. 6, 13.
36. Gazette of Pakistan, February 9, 1973, pp. 75-98.
37. The Pakistan Times, October 6, 1972.
38. The Education Policy, pp. 35-6; Hasan Askari Rizvi, The Military and Politics in Pakistan, Lahore: Progressive Publishers, 1974, p. 257.
39. Herbert Feldman, "Pakistan in 1974," Asian Survey, XV (February, 1975) 115.
40. Yusuf, Pakistan in Search of Democracy, 1947-77, p. 146.
41. Lawrence Ziring (ed), The Subcontinent in World Affairs: India, Its Neighbors and the Great Powers, New York: Frederick A. Praeger and Co., 1978, p. 106.
42. The Pakistan Times, May 15, 1972.
43. Ziring, The Subcontinent in World Affairs, p. 108.
44. Ibid., pp. 110-11.
45. The Pakistan Times, November 20, 1972.
46. Ibid., July 16, 1972.
47. Ibid., April 11, 1972.
48. Ziring, Pakistan: The Enigma of Political Devel valley to create large outwash plains.
49. The Pakistan Times, November 11, 1973.
50. Kumar, The New Pakistan, pp. 100-1.
51. Khalid B. Sayeed, "How Radical is the Pakistan People's Party?" Pacific Affairs, 48(Spring, 1975), 52.
52. Burki, Pakistan Under Bhutto, pp. 172, 187.
53. Kumar, The New Pakistan, p. 338.

10
Conclusions

At the outset of this study, it was suggested that Pakistan's political development has been shaped by five factors. The first factor concerns the philosophical or theoretical foundation of the political system. Competing concepts regarding the nature and location of authority have not been fused and synthesized in such a way as to provide for an effective and durable political regime. These concepts can be divided into three categories. First are those that are contained in classical Islamic political thought, which can, for convenience sake, be labeled traditional. Second are those which take classical Islamic thought as a point of departure but modify it to fit contemporary circumstances. This category can be called modern. Third are those concepts which are essentially a product of Western political thought and experience.

While there are certain inconsistencies and incompatibilities among these concepts, the basic problem has been the failure to develop a process of fusion and growth leading toward philosophical consensus. This has been particularly evident in the three constitutions which should have provided a context for expressing basic political values and a process for their synthesis. But each of the three constitutions was aborted with the abrogation of the first two and the corruption of the third.

The constitutional point of departure has been and remains Islam. There is a strong philosophical and historical legacy to draw upon. The emphasis upon community and consensus in Islam provides one avenue for the development of representative institutions. There is no basic conflict between Islam and constitutionalism. The fact that democratic institutions have not flourished in Islamic countries seems to be less a philosophical problem than a failure of leadership. In Pakistan, as elsewhere, the growth process has been interrupted by the insistence that institutions and policies conform to the tenets of Islam. This has proved unworkable, because there are no accepted procedures to determine what is Islamic. Thus constitutions, as the highest political law of the land, are compromised by the insistence that secular law conform to Islam. It is not that the sovereignty of Allah and constitutional supremacy are incompatible. The problem is the relationship is essentially irrelevant. Since the concept of the sovereignty of Allah has no instrumental value, Allah does not rule, authority to govern must be located somewhere. But the traditional school is reluctant to take that step, insisting there is no authority outside Islam. Theirs is a failure to recognize the difference between the source of authority and the location of authority.

The modernists are confronted with two problems in fitting traditional Islamic thought to contemporary conditions. One is the relationship of the "Islamic way of life" to institutional legitimacy. Historically there has been a tendency to equate the two. Indeed, the latter has been measured by the extent of the former. This is especially true with the current regime's stress on Islamization. But the extent to which political life is Islamic is a policy question. There is no necessary institutional connection. A parliamentary system is neither more nor less Islamic than any other arrangement.

Another problem for the modernists is the institutional barrenness of Islamic political history. The historical record going back to Mohammed provides little precedent as to which institutions, in the context of Islam, are appropriate or legitimate. Thus the modernist must invent institutions which are consistent with Islam, which facilitate the realization of an Islamic way of life, and which are generally effective and durable. But in this effort the modernist is provided with few if any helpful precedents.

The experience with British political institutions and practices provides another source of ideas regarding authority. These concepts are viewed by many as alien and inappropriate for non-Western societies. The current Islamic revivals in Pakistan and elsewhere view with suspicion most everything of Western origin. Given this negative bias, many Pakistanis consider political development an attempt to impose Western ideas and practices. Since these ideas and practices are not derived from the Islamic experience, they cannot be Islamic and are, therefore, unIslamic.

A second factor shaping the course of Pakistan's political development has been the adequacy and effectiveness of public policy. This basically involves a failure to fulfill the demands of the modern state. In the last half of the 20th century, tremendous burdens are placed on the state to meet all manner of needs and demands of society. There was a time when the state did little more than collect taxes and wage an occasional war. States could flourish under an able and wise leader but did not necessarily suffer under a poor one. But today this is not the case. The state must be effective or society suffers. Three main power blocs have dominated Pakistan politically and economically since independence: the bureaucracy, the military, and the economic elite. These blocs are mutually reinforcing and supportive. They have not been effective in promoting and integrating the broad interests of society but have instead used the instruments of political power to serve their own interests. During the Bhutto period there were attempts to weaken the power of these groups and to include other social sectors in the regime's support base. These efforts failed because Bhutto "deliberately discouraged political mobilization within the population as a whole."[1] This ultimately led to the loss of legitimacy among the very groups Bhutto relied on for support.

The third factor is the persistence of regional and social imbalances within the political process. Those who have controlled political and economic power have determined the nature of public policy and set the priorities of development. There were often serious disparities and inequities in public policy programs and development efforts. The most pronounced of these was that between the two wings of the country. But the frontier provinces of Baluchistan and Northwest Frontier and to some extent Sind have not benefitted to the extent they should from government activity. Economic policies have worked to the advantage of specific groups, especially West Pakistan industrialists, and have not significantly altered the condition of the great mass of the population. Politically, emergent groups such as the urban proletariat and professionals have not been integrated into the system.

A fourth factor has been the failure of political actors to support the integrity of political institutions. Two aspects of political behavior have worked against the development of durable and effective institutions. One, and probably the most important, is a tendency to elevate personal political power and fortune above coalition and institution-building. From 1947 until Ayub Khan's takeover, the wrangling and squabbling among politicians delayed the enactment of the first constitution until 1956, and even then there was little commitment to work constructively together. This led to the first coup d'etat and a permanent political role for the military. Ayub's 1962 constitution showed both imagination and promise. But the regime did not grow and develop with changing conditions in the country. Ayub's regime was grounded on the politics of personality. When he was driven from power, the entire regime went with him.

Yahya Khan attempted to promote a broader-based
constitutional arrangement. But his own limitations as
a leader plus the intransigence of Mujib and Bhutto led
to the civil war and the independence of East Pakistan.
Bhutto's new order fashioned in the 1973 constitution,
like Ayub's before it, showed an awareness of the
requirements of an effective constitutional arrangement. But Bhutto also fell victim to the tradition of
personal or Bonapartist power politics.

Under Zia ul-Haq, politics have taken a somewhat
different direction. The constitution of 1973 was not
abrogated but has been retained in qualified form as
the basis of the regime. However, Zia has introduced
significant changes in it under his authority as Chief
Martial Law Administrator. He has also declared himself President and promised to hold elections.
However, these have been consistently postponed on the
grounds that the country is not "ready." Thus, while a
constitution exists in theory, it has little practical
significance. Zia's rule, like that of his predecessors, is the rule of personal power.

Political shortcomings cannot be all laid at the
door of failed leadership. A second aspect of political behavior is the tendency to oppose governments by
rejecting institutions. This is due in part to popular
frustrations over the inadequacy and ineffectiveness of
government. But the problem goes deeper than that.
There has never been a strong commitment to political
institutions and a desire to make them work. Instead,
when governments become unpopular, the entire constitutional framework is rejected. Both Ayub and Bhutto,
when faced with mounting opposition, offered solutions
that could have allowed for reform and survival of the
system. Ayub promised he would not run again for
President. But public opposition was not satisfied
with only his removal; the system he had created had to
go as well. Similarly, Bhutto offered to hold new elections supervised by the army. But this was not enough.
Bhutto had to go, and the price paid by the country was
the compromising of the consitution and a military
government committed to "Islamization." An Islamic
state is to be created by government decree, even though
the questions concerning what that is have not been
resolved. As one author has observed: "Despite the
secession of East Bengal in 1971, the Pakistani social
mosaic--Punjabis, Sindhis, Pathans, Baluchis--is held
together precariously by Islam and the Army."[2]

The final factor is international relations.
Throughout most of its history, international relations
have not contributed positively to Pakistan's political
development. But this situation began to change in the
late 1970's. / Pakistan has been catapulted into an
important international position as a result of developments in the Persian Gulf area, especially the

Iranian revolution and the Soviet invasion of Afghanistan. The United States has once again asserted the strategic importance of Pakistan and, in keeping with that, has offered to modernize Pakistan's military system. A more active role is also being played in the Islamic world, a policy initiated by Bhutto. Pakistan's affiliation with Saudi Arabia, especially, together with its renewed ties with the United States make it an important player in the strategic relationships revolving around the Middle East. President Zia's intiatives to improve relations with India were timely and may very well introduce a new era in South Asian regional relations. International relations, therefore, may cease to be a force confounding Pakistan's political endeavors and become one which tends to promote favorable internal development.

One of the most striking things about Pakistan's political history has been the persistent absence of a political consensus. Not only has there been a lack of durable public support for political institutions, but there has been little agreement about present realities or future prospects. Among Pakistanis today there seem to be three general points of view concerning the country's past and future. A large and seemingly growing number of people are pessimistic and regard the past as a failure and the future as essentially hopeless. This view stresses the repeated failures of the past and regards this record as indicative of a basic inability to develop a political system capable of meeting the needs of society and at the same time achieving the goals of democracy and social progress. Since there seems to be no way out and the future is grim, many people of this persuasion are seeking to emigrate to another country or, by acquiring a safe haven somewhere else through investments or purchases of property, have a place to escape to in an emergency.

A second group are equally pessimistic about the past but are rather more optimistic about the future. The situation is not regarded as completely hopeless. Even though the probabilities of major successful developments are not considered very good, there is at least the possibility. Here there seems to be a willingness to wait, a feeling that the present repressive military regime will not last forever, that something better will eventually come to pass.

In the third group are found those who think that Pakistan simply has not tried hard enough. They do not regard any of the failed regimes as better than the others. Nor do they consider political development to have been sabotaged by some powerful interest like the military. The general view is that various institutional approaches failed because they were inadequate. For this group, all history is prologue. What is needed is a more vigorous approach, a more radical solution.

One such approach moves under the banner of Islamization. Past failures are seen as an abandonment of the requirements for Islam. Past leaders have attempted to create institutions which were foreign rather than drawing upon the true strength of the country, which is clearly manifested in the teachings of Islam. Such, of course, is the strategy currently being employed by the government of President Zia.

Another viewpoint sees the current political strategy as oppression, cloaking itself in the mantle of Islam. Since the leaders of Islam do not represent the true spirit of religion, and since the liberal democratic approaches employed in the past have failed, the only alternative is a radical strategy coming from the left. In this view, what Pakistan needs is a revolution. This point of view has become much more widely discussed, if not necessarily more widely followed, since the Soviet invasion of Afghanistan in 1978.

The central question facing Pakistan today is the same one that has faced the country since its inception almost 40 years ago. The nature and dimensions of authority are still not clearly defined. The incongruity among different points of view on the subject of authority are, if anything, worse today than they were in the past. Internal and external forces promote the concept of an Islamic state to an even more vigorous extent than has been experienced.

With a martial law regime and the expanded role for religious elites, the problems of political participation and institutional response are worse now than during the periods of Bhutto and Ayub Khan. The difficulties that eventually made these regimes unworkable have not gone away or been solved. There are now fewer outlets for satisfying political demands, and the prospects for making the regime more flexible and responsive seem to be limited. While the strength of conservative, religion-oriented politics is considerable today, this does not mean that other ideologies and philosophies are permanently excised from the political process. Moreover, the separatist tendencies in Baluchistan and Sind have not been overcome by effective processes of integration, but rather have been masked by the more pressing issue created by the Soviet presence in Afghanistan.

One of the fundamental reasons for the secession of Bangladesh in 1971 was the distortion and imbalance in the economy, especially between the two wings. These economic distortions are less since the departure of the East wing, but the problems remain. Pakistan still is an underdeveloped economy with only modest prospects for achieving significant economic growth. Problems of inequitable distribution of social wealth among classes has, if anything, worsened in recent years. That these underlying problems have not created

greater political problems than they have is due less
to the effectiveness or correct strategy of the current
regime and more to the infusion of money coming from
Pakistanis working abroad. The oil boom in the Persian
Gulf area brought considerable benefits to Pakistan
because many Pakistanis have for several years been
working in that area and remitting part of their in-
comes back home. But this is at best a temporary
arrangement and serves to disguise the fundamental
weaknesses in the economy. With rapid population
growth and inadequate economic development, the political problems associated with this pattern are merely
being postponed.

NOTES

1. Gerald A. Heeger, "Politics in a Post-Military
State: Some Relections on The Pakistan's Experience,"
World Politics 29 (January, 1977) 254.
2. R. Hrair Dehmajian, "The Anatomy of Islamic
Revival: Legitimacy Crisis, Ethnic Conflict and The
Search for Islamic Alternatives," The Middle East
Journal 34 (Winter, 1980) 11.

Bibliography

PRIMARY SOURCES

Abbott, F. Islam and Pakistan, Cornell University
    Press, Ithaca, New York, 1968.
_____. "The Jama' at-i-Islami of Pakistan," The
    Middle East Journal, 11(Winter 1957), 37-51.
Ahmad, A. "Cultural and Intellectual Trends in
    Pakistan," The Middle East Journal, (Winter 1965),
    35-44.
_____. Islamic Modernism in India and
    Pakistan: 1857-1964, London: Royal Institute of
    International Affairs, 1967.
_____. "Return of the Islama in Pakistan"
    Scholars, Saints, and Sufis: Religious Institu-
    tions in the Middle East Since 1500 Nikki R.
    Kiddie (ed.), Berkeley: University of California
    Press, 1972, 257-272.
Ahmed, A. S. Religion and Politics in Muslim Society
    Order and Conflict in Pakistan, Cambridge
    University Press, 1983.
Ali, T. Pakistan: Military Rule or People's Power,
    New York: Morrow, 1970.
Al Mujahid, S. "The Assembly Elections in Pakistan"
    Asian Survey, V(November 1965), 538-51.
_____. "Pakistan: First General Elections" Asian
    Survey, XI(February 1971), 159-171.
Andrus, J. R. The Economy of Pakistan, Stanford
    California Stanford University Press, 1958.
_____. Trade, Finance and Development in Pakistan,
    Stanford, Stanford University Press, 1966.
Asad, M. The Principles of State and Government--Islam,
    Berkeley: University of California Press, 1961.
Ayub, M. (ed.). The Politics of Islamic Reassertion,
    New York: St. Martin's Press, 1981.
Ayub Khan, M. "The Pakistan-American Alliance:
    Stresses and Strains," Foreign Affairs, (January
    1964), 195-209.
_____. Pakistan Perspective; A Collection of

Important Articles and Excerpts from Major
Addresses, Washington,D.C., Embassy of Pakistan,
1965.

Bains, J. S. "Some Thoughts on Pakistan's New
Constitution," Indian Journal of Political Science
23(July and September 1962) 209-224.

Baxter, C. "Constitution Making: The Development of
Federalism in Pakistan" Asian Survey, XIV(December
1974), 1074-1085.

_____. "The People's Party Vs. The Punjab Federa-
lists," Journal of Asian and African Studies,
VIII(July and October 1973), 166-189.

Bean, L. L. and A. D. Bhatti. "Pakistan's Population in
the 1970's: Problems and Prospects," Journal of
Asian and African Studies, VIII(July and October
1973), 259-278.

Bhutto, Z. A. Foreign Policy of Pakistan, Karachi:
Pakistan Institute of International Affairs, 1964.

_____. The Myth of Independence, Karachi: Oxford
University Press, 1969.

Binder, L. "Pakistan and Modern Islamic-Nationalist
Theory" Middle East Journal, 11(Fall 1957),
382-396.

_____. "Pakistan and Modern Islamic-Nationalist
Theory" The Middle East Journal, 12(Winter 1958),
45-56.

_____. "Problems of Islamic Political Thought in
the Light of Recent Developments in Pakistan,"
Journal of Politics, 20(November 1958), 655-75.

_____. Religion and Politics in Pakistan,
Berkeley: University of California Press, 1961.

Birkhead, G. S. (ed.). Administrative Problems in
Pakistan, Syracuse: Syracuse University Press,
1966.

Bolitho, H. Jinnah: Creator of Pakistan, New York: The
Macmillan Co., 1955.

Braibanti, R. "Pakistan: Constitutional Issues in
1964," Asian Survey, V(February 1965), 79-87.

_____. Research on the Bureaucracy of Pakistan,
Durham: Duke University Press, 1966.

Brown, W. N. The United States and India and Pakistan,
2nd ed. Cambridge: Harvard University Press, 1963.

Burki, S. J. "Politics of Economic Decision-Making the
Bhutto Period," Asian Studies, XIV(December 1974),
1126-40.

_____. "Twenty Years of the Civil Service of
Pakistan: A Reevaluation," Asian Studies,
IX(April 1969), 239-254.

Burks, A. W. "Constitution Making in Pakistan"
Political Science Quarterly, 69(December 1954),
541-564.

Callard, K. Pakistan: A Political Study, New York:
The Macmillen Co., 1957.

_____. Pakistan's Foreign Policy: An Interpreta-

195

tion, New York: Institute of Pacific Relations,
1957.
_____. Political Forces in Pakistan, 1947-1959,
New York: Institute of Pacific Relations, 1959.
_____. "Political Stability of Pakistan," Pacific
Affairs, 29(March 1956) 5-20.
Campbell-Johnson, A. Mission with Mountbatten, London:
Robert Hale Ltd., 1952.
Caroe, O. The Pathans, New York: St. Martin's Press,
1958.
Chaudri, M. A. Pakistan and the Great Powers, Karachi:
Council for Pakistan Studies, 1970.
Choudhury, G. W. "Constitution of Pakistan," Pacific
Affairs, 29(September 1956), 243-52.
_____. "Constitution-Making Dilemmas in Pakistan,"
Western Political Quarterly, 8(December 1955),
589-600.
_____. "The East Pakistan Political Scene,"
Pacific Affairs, XXX(December 1957), 312-320.
Davis, K. The Population of India and Pakistan,
Princeton: Princeton University Press, 1951.
Donohue, J. and J. Esposito. Islam in Transition,
Oxford University Press, 1982.
Goodnow, H. F. The Civil Service of Pakistan, New
Haven: Yale University Press, 1964.
Gorvine, A. "The Civil Service Under the Revolutionary
Government in Pakistan," The Middle East Journal,
19(Summer 1965) 321-36.
Gustafson, W. E. "Economic Problems of Pakistan Under
Bhutto" Asian Survey, XVI(April 1976), 364-380.
_____. "Economic Reforms Under the Bhutto Regime,"
Journal of Asian and African Studies, 241-258.
Handy, P. The Muslims of British India, London:
Cambridge University Press, 1972.
Hassan, F. The Concept of State and Law in Islam,
Washington, D.C.: University Press of American,
1981.
Heeger, G. A. "Politics in the Post-Military State:
Some Reflections on the Pakistani Experience,"
World Politics, 29(January 1977), 242-262.
Hussain, A. Pakistan: Its Ideology and Foreign Policy,
London: Frank Cass and Co., Ltd., 1966.
Jahan, R. Pakistan: Failure in National Integration,
New York: Columbia University Press, 1972.
Khalilzad, Z. "Pakistan: The Making of a Nuclear
Power," Asian Studies, XVI(June 1976), 580-92.
Korson, J.H. "Bhutto's Educational Reform," Journal of
Asian and African Studies, VIII(July and October
1973), 279-306.
La Porte, R. Jr. "Succession in Pakistan: Continuity
and Change in a Garrison State," Asian Studies,
IX(August 1969), 842-861.
Lerski, G. J. "The Pakistan-American Alliance: A
Reevaluation of the Past Decade," Asian Studies,

196

VIII(May 1968), 400-415.
Levi, W. "Pakistan, the Soviet Union and China,"
    Pacific Affairs, 35(Fall 1962) 211-222.
Lewis, S. R. Economic Policy and Industrial Growth in
    Pakistan, London: Allen and Unwin, 1969.
_____. "Effects of Trade Policy on Domestic
    Relative Prices: Pakistan, 1951-64," American
    Economic Review, 58(March 1968), 60-78.
_____ and S.E. Guisinger. "Measuring Protection in
    a Developing Country; the Case of Pakistan,"
    Journal of Political Economy, 76(November 1968),
    1170-1198.
Loshak, D. Pakistan Crisis, London: Heinemann, 1971.
Malik, H. "The Emergency of the Federal Pattern in
    Pakistan," Journal of Asian and African Studies,
    205-215.
_____. Iqbal: Poet-Philosopher of Pakiston, New
    York: Columbia University Press, 1971.
_____. Sir Sayyid Ahmad Khan and Muslim Moderni-
    zation in India and Pakistan, New York: Columbia
    University Press, 1980.
Maniruzzaman, T. "Bangladesh: An Unfinished Revolu-
    tion?" Journal of Asian Studies, XXXIV(August
    1975), 891-911.
_____. "Group Interests in Pakistan Politics,"
    Pacific Affairs, 39(Spring/Summer 1966), 83-98.
_____. "National Integration and Political
    Development in Pakistan," Asian Survey, VII(Dec-
    ember 1967), 876-885.
Mannan, M. A. Economic Problems and Planning in
    Pakistan, 4th Ed., Karachi: Ferozsons, 1970.
Maududi, S. A. A. The Islamic Law and Constitution,
    2nd Ed. Trans. and Ed. by Khurshid Admad.
    Lahore: Islamic Publications, 1960.
May, L. S. Iqbal: His Life and Times, Lahore: Sh.
    Mohammad Ashraf, 1974.
Metcalf, B. D. Islamic Revival in British India:
    Deoband 1860-1900, Princeton: Princeton
    University Press, 1982.
Moon, P. Divide and Quit, Berkeley: University of
    California Press, 1962.
Mosley, L. The Last Days of the British Raj, London:
    Weidenfeld and Nicolson, 1961.
Naqvi, S. N. H. "On optimizing Gains from Pakistan's
    Export Bonus Scheme" Journal of Political Economy,
    79(January 1971), 114-27.
Naim, C. M. (ed.). Iqbal ,Jinnah, and Pakistan: The
    Vision and the Reality, Foreign and Comp. Studies,
    S. Asia Series II s; Maxwell School of Citizenship
    and Public Affairs, Spokane University, 1979.
Newman, K.J. "The Constitutional Evolution of Pakis-
    tan," International Affairs, 38(July 1962),
    353-64.
Palmer, N. D. "New Directions for Pakistan," Current

History, 46(February 1964), 71-77.
_____. "Pakistan's Mood: The New Realism,"
Current History, 43(November 1962), 263-71.
_____. South Asia and United States Policy,
Boston: Houghton Mifflin Co., 1966.
Papanek, G. F. Pakistan's Development: Social Goals
and Private Incentives, Cambridge: Harvard
University Press, 1967.
Qureshi, S. M. M. "Pakistani Nationalism Reconsidered,"
Pacific Affairs, (Winter 1972-1973), 556-72.
_____. "Party Politics in the Second Republic of
Pakistan," The Middle East Journal, (Autumn 1966),
456-472.
Rahman, F. "Islam and the New Constitution of
Pakistan," Journal of Asian and African Studies,
VIII(July and October 1973), 190-204.

Rahman, S. M. B. Bangladesh, My Bangladesh, New
Delhi: Orient Longman Ltd., 1972.
Rajan, M. S. "The Tashkent Declaration: Retrospect and
Prospect," International Studies, 8(July 1966-
April 1967), 1-28.
Rashiduzzaman, M. "Election Politics in Pakistan
Villages," Journal of Commonwealth Studies,
IV(November 1966), 191-200.
_____. "National Assembly of Pakistan
under the 1962 Constitution," Pacific Affairs,
42(Winter 1969-1970), 481-93.
_____. "The National Awami Party of Pakistan,"
Pacific Affairs, XLIII(Fall 1970), 394-409.
_____. Pakistan: A Study of Government and
Politics, Davis: Ideal Library, 1967.
Rizvi, H. A. The Military and Politics in Pakistan,
Lahore: Progressive Publishers, 1974.
Rosenthal, E. I. J. Islam in the Modern National
State, Cambridge: Cambridge University Press,
1965.
_____. Political Thought in Medieval Islam,
Cambridge: Cambridge University Press, 1962.
Roth, I. J. "Government and the Development of Industry
in Pakistan--1947-67," Asian Survey, (June 1971),
570-81.
Sayeed, K. B. "The Capabilities of Pakistan's Political
System," Asian Survey VII(February 1967), 102-110.
_____. "Collapse of Parliamentary Democracy in
Pakistan," Middle East Journal, 13(Fall 1959),
389-406.
Sayeed, K. B. "Federalism and Pakistan," Far East
Survey, 23(September 1954), 139-143.
_____. "How Radical is the Pakistan People's
Party," Pacific Affairs, 48(Spring 1975), 42-59.
_____. "The Jama'at-i-Islam Movement in Pakistan,"
Pacific Affairs, XXX(March 1957), 59-68.
_____. "Pakistan: New Challenges to the Political

198

System," Asian Survey, VIII (February 1968), 97-104.

_____. Pakistan: The Formative Phase, 1857-1948, (2nd ed.), London: Oxford University Press, 1968.

_____. "Pakistan's Constitutional Autocracy," Pacific Affairs 36(Winters 1963-1964), 365-77.

_____. "Pakistan's Foreign Policy: An Analysis of Pakistani Fears and Interests," Asian Survey, IV(March 1964) 746-756.

_____. "Political Role of Pakistan's Civil Service," Pacific Affairs, 31(June 1958), 131-146.

_____. The Political System of Pakistan, Boston: Houghton Mifflin Co., 1967.

_____. Politics in Pakistan, The Nature and Direction of Change, New York: Praeger Special Studies, 1980.

_____. "Religion and Nation Building in Pakistan," Middle East Journal, 17(Summer 1963), 279-91.

Seth, S. P. "Russia's Role in Indo-Pak Politics," Asian Studies, IX(August 1969), 614-624.

Smith, D. E.(ed.). South Asian Politics and Religion, Princeton: Princeton University Press, 1966.

Spain, J. W. "Military Assistance for Pakistan," American Political Science Review, 48(September 1954), 738-751.

_____. People of the Khyber: The Pathans of Pakistan, New York: Frederick A. Praeger, Publisher, 1963.

Syed, A. "Pakistan's Security Problems: A Bill of Constraints," Orbis, XVI(Winter 1973), 952-74.

_____. "Politics of Sino-Pakistan Agreements," Orbis, 11(Fall 1967), 798-825.

Trager, F. N. "The United States and Pakistan, A Failure of Diplomacy," Orbis, IX(Fall 1965), 613-29.

Vorys, K.V. Political Development in Pakistan, Princeton: Princeton University Press, 1965.

Weinbaum, M. G. and Gautam Sen. "Pakistan Enters the Middle East," Orbis, 22(Fall 1978), 595-612.

Wheeler, R. "Pakistan: New Constitution Old Issues," Asian Survey, 3(February 1963), 107-115.

_____. The Politics of Pakistan: A Constitutional Quest, Ithaca: Cornell University Press, 1970.

White, L. J. Industrial Concentration and Economic Power in Pakistan, Princeton: Princeton University Press, 1974.

Wilcox, W. A. "Pakistan: A Decade of Ayub," Asian Survey, IX(February 1969), 87-93.

_____. "Pakistan Coup d'etat of 1958," Pacific Affairs, 38(Summer 1965), 142-63.

_____. Pakistan: The Consolidation of a Nation New York: Columbia University Press, 1963.

_____. "Political Change in Pakistan: Structures, Functions Constraints, and Goals," Pacific Affairs, VI(Fall 1968), 341-54.

Zia, A. Q. "Some Radical Changes in Pakistan's Foreign Policy," Asian Profile, 2(August 1974), 421-33.

Ziring. L. The Ayub Khan Era; Politics In Pakistan 1958-69, Syracuse: Syracuse University Press, 1971.

_____ and R. La Porte. "The Pakistan Bureaucracy: Two Views," Asian Survey, XI(December 1974), 1086-1103.

_____. "Pakistan: A Political Perspective," Asian Survey, 629-644.

_____. "Bhutto's Foreign Policy, 1972-3," Journal of Asian and African Studies, VIII(July and October 1973), 216-240.

Index